2.50

golf in Hardy country

Author's acknowledgements

This book of record is the product of many diverse inputs including research among newspaper and Council archives, reference libraries and Club records, contributions from local historians, and discussions with people with the precious gift of a good memory.

I particularly wish to acknowledge the help given to me by the reference libraries at Bournemouth, Poole and Weymouth, by the County Record Office and the Planning Department at County Hall.

John Morton of the Yeovil Golf Club was particularly helpful at a time when he was heavily involved with his duties as Captain. Thanks to his enthusiasm and perseverance we succeeded in producing a reasonable review of the history of his Club from what at first appeared to be barren ground. Similarly Wareham's Major John Holloway uncovered a great deal of 'lost' evidence about the struggle to create a golf course out of quite unsuitable terrain, and Harry Austin came to my rescue with details of the Lyme Regis Golf Club when time was fast running out.

Peter Fry is a tireless researcher, and I am grateful for his contributions on Crichel Park and the Naples Bay golf course. Peter Ward supplied the invaluable cuttings book kept by Walter Little, the Secretary at Came Down during the early years of the County Union's formation. This contained vital information about early matches which were not recorded in the County Union Minute Books.

I am particularly grateful to Mrs Blakely for giving me access to her father's journal and scrapbook which provided such a fascinating insight into the life and times of a golf professional in the 1930s.

Finally, a word of thanks to Malcolm Sutherland and his team at Roman Press for their help during the production of this book.

I hope that the publication of this book will persuade Clubs to preserve their records and perhaps follow the example of the Parkstone Golf Club who keep a scrapbook of newsworthy items in the lounge for anyone to browse through. A number of Clubs have lost their early records due to clubhouse fires, so it is advisable to ensure that records are kept in a safe place, preferably in the Bank vault.

November 1993   LCJ

golf in Hardy country

L C Jenkins

Dorset County Golf Union

To the thousands of golfers of all abilities in Dorset. May you derive pleasure from and be inspired by this tribute to the individuals, clubs and county teams, many of whom will be familiar or even related to you. May their successes encourage you to improve your own playing ability and enjoyment of the game, to contribute towards the stature of your Club, to your County Union and to a place in any future archival record

© Published by the
  Dorset County Golf Union 1993

British Library Cataloguing in Publication Data
Jenkins, L C
  golf in Hardy country
  A catalogue record of this book is
  available from the British Library

ISBN 0 9522319 0 5

All rights reserved

The moral rights of L C Jenkins to be identified as the author of this work have been asserted by him in accordance with the Copyright, Designs and Patents Act 1988

This book may not be reproduced in whole or in part, in any form (except by reviewers for the public press), without acknowledging the source

Printed in England by Roman Press Limited, Bournemouth, and bound by Butler and Tanner Limited, Frome, Somerset

Contents

	page
Foreword by Peter Alliss	(viii)
Preface	(x)
1 The 'County' Scene	1
2 Directory of Clubs and Courses	73
3 The County Union 1923-1992	137
4 The Honours Boards	
Dorset County Golf Union	206
Bournemouth & District Professional & Amateur Golfers' Alliance	222
South Western Counties Golf Association	224
Appendix	
Members of the Dorset County Golfers' Association	254

Publisher's acknowledgements

The Dorset County Golf Union is grateful to the following sponsors, without whose support this book could not have been produced:

Bulbury Woods and Lytchett Matravers Golf Clubs
Bray and Sears Limited Bournemouth
Brian Crutcher Parkstone   Keith Durbin Broadstone
East Dorset Golf Club   Eldridge Pope & Co plc Dorchester
Ellis, Fowler, Belcher Bournemouth   Frank Foster Ferndown
Hall & Woodhouse Limited Blandford   Hawtree Woodstock Oxon
W Hayward & Sons (Bournemouth) Limited   Henkel Germany
Dr Donald Holmes Ringwood   George Houghton OBE Bridport
Lansdowne Private Hospital Bournemouth
Leval Lingerie Canford Cliffs   J T Lowe Limited Christchurch
Merlo UK Limited Ringwood
Brian D Pierson (Contractors) Limited Wimborne
I A Pritchard Stockbrokers Limited Bournemouth
Rhys Francis & Partners Lilliput   Salterns Hotel Lilliput
Donald Steel Chichester   the Patrick Tallack Organisation
the Willis Group London

Foreword

My first glimpse of the Dorset countryside was in 1938. I was seven years of age and father was about to take up the position of Head Professional at the Ferndown Golf Club. Prior to that he had been at the Temple Newsam Golf Club on the outskirts of Leeds. The position there had not worked out, so father, yet again, took a bold step (he had been a bit of a traveller in his time) and decided that life in the South was the thing for him.

He was in the throes of sorting out somewhere to live, also the building of a new clubhouse and pro shop had not been completed... the old wooden clubhouse having burned to the ground. We were lucky in being able to stay with a friend of my father's, Harry Sales, the professional at the Isle of Purbeck. I remember distinctly that the people spoke with very different accents to the ones my young ears had been attuned to in Yorkshire, but it did not take me long to realise that this was a very beautiful place. Even today when you look out across Poole harbour from the Isle of Purbeck clubhouse the view is staggering. Blocks of flats break the skyline, but it has not been totally ravaged by so-called progress.

After a few weeks we moved into 263 New Road Ferndown, 350 yards from the Club and my new life was about to begin. Ferndown was where I learned to play my golf. Many people assume that my father taught me night and day... but not so... he was a great one for making you use your own intelligence. 'Watch other people; see how they do it; try to understand why they do it; and if you don't understand, then come and ask me and I will do my best to tell you'. That was the way it was.

Many of the people you will read about in this book were my friends and mentors. I can't count the number of times I played with Joe Close, Roy Jenkins, Pat Crow, Maureen Garrett, George Newton and the rest; and was not my greatest friend at that time Ernie Millward, the ex-Commando who won the English Championship in 1952 at Burnham and Berrow... was it really more than forty years ago!

There is such a rich mixture of golf courses in Dorset: the colourful heather, the pine and silver birch belt around Bournemouth and Poole; the downland courses towards Dorchester and Weymouth; and the numerous little inland treasures where, even if the courses were not masterpieces, the friendliness of the welcomes certainly were.

Eventually, after a few practice shots and two years of National Service, my brother Alec and I were appointed joint professionals at the Parkstone Club. The date was April the first 1957... well, it was as good a day as any to start. Thirteen very happy years went whizzing by, and once more the friendships grew: Dick Peach, a Scot and a stalwart of Dorset golf, Ken Longmore, and Jack Santall.

Then there was Graham Butler, who for a time was an Assistant to my father, but realised early on that professional golf was not for him, and he went back into his father's business and took up the cudgels as an amateur, and how well he played. If he had been in a more fashionable county his career might have blossomed even more.

I have already mentioned Pat Crow, what a superb striker of the ball she was. Another stalwart of Dorset ladies' golf was Esme Stuart-Smith. Then there was Jean Bisgood and Maureen Garrett, members of Ferndown and Parkstone respectively, but Jean played for Surrey and Maureen for Middlesex, so were not available to bolster the resources of our tiny county.

I think one of my most joyous memories was seeing Barbara Mackintosh (nee Dickson) setting sail to play in the English Ladies Championship. If memory serves me right her handicap was about 4 (it may even have been 6), but off she went with our blessings. We followed her progress through telephone calls from the few supporters that went along to give her cheer. Lo and behold, round after round she won and at the end of the day came out victorious. The year was 1969, the venue Burnham and Berrow, what a happy hunting ground that was for Dorset players. She beat Miss M Wenyon in the final 6 and 4...I wonder where Miss Wenyon is today?

Happy memories indeed...I think Barbara's victory was akin to Dorset winning the County Championship in 1992. Against the might of all those other counties they sailed through. A team mixture of young, and perhaps not-so-young, but when it came to the crunch there certainly were oldish heads on youngish shoulders.

I shall be eternally grateful for the time I spent in Dorset. The friendships I made; the joy of playing with Charles and Ernest Whitcombe; seeing Charles hit a ball sweet as a nut, even though he was then into his 70s. The tricks I learned in the art of golf club repair from my father's Assistant Charlie Trickett. Conversations with J C Beard, the crusty Secretary at Ferndown who guided me in my pre-National Service days. The sight of the greenkeeping force cycling alongside the eighteenth on their way to the sheds by the side of the second green. Ah...riding on the tractor with Jim Bracher, totally taboo these days of course, but how wonderful for a ten year old. The smell of new mown grass mingled with paraffin...amazing how romantic that seemed at the time.

I am very glad that the County Union has decided to chronicle the growth of golf in Dorset. It might not have the same cachet as the Home Counties or of some of the more populated counties of England, but your successes are proof of the value of early recognition and the judicious coaching of young talent, of which the County Union can be justly proud...Good Luck to all your efforts in the future...I only wish that I could find the magic potion that would take me back to those wonderful, learning, lovable days of yore.

Dorset I love you.

Peter Alliss

Preface

Most golfers will be aware that the true origins of the game are a matter of pure conjecture, but golf historians now accept that the game has been played in some form or other in Europe since the Middle Ages. It was known to be popular in Scotland in 1437 because of the James the Second edict banning the game *(that golfe and futeball be utterly cryed downe)*.

Another, more dubious pointer is the fourteenth century stained glass window in Gloucester Cathedral which includes a figure swinging what appears to be a golf club. This was erected by Sir Thomas Bradstone in memory of those who died at the Battle of Crecy, but although the figure is popularly known as The Gloucester Golfer, there are many who believe it to depict a man playing a club-and-ball game of Roman origin called *Cambuca*.

A more simplistic explanation is offered by Sir W G Simpson in his classic book *The Art of Golf* in which he suggested that it all might have started with a shepherd, tending his flock on the links at St Andrews, knocking a pebble into a rabbit hole with his crook. He was challenged by a companion to do it again, and the game of golf was born !

Following the peace treaty between England and Scotland in 1503 the Scots were allowed to resume their golfing activities and when James VI succeeded to the English throne in 1603 to become James I of England, he brought the game south of the border and is reputed to have been responsible for golf being played on the Blackheath Common. As explained later, private golf clubs did not begin to be formed until about the middle of the eighteenth century, and although golf was being played on the heath from 1608, the Royal Blackheath Golf Club was probably formed in 1787.

'No written evidence of any Society of Blackheath Golfers of earlier date than 1787 have come down to us.' *(Chronicles of Blackheath Golfers* by W E Hughes).

So, although the game had been played in Scotland for a great many years, it had been on publicly owned land and was not organised in any way. The first official golf society was that of the Honourable Company of Edinburgh Golfers who in 1744 were presented with a silver club by the Edinburgh Council for annual competition among 'Noblemen and Gentlemen from any part of Great Britain and Ireland', and at the same time the first Rules of Golf - thirteen in all, were drawn up for the inaugural tournament. Ten years later, in 1754, the Honourable Company of St Andrews Golfers was formed, and when in 1834 King William IV became its patron, the title was changed to the Royal and Ancient Golf Club of St Andrews.

Obviously then, the game already had a long history before it reached the south-western counties of England: Royal Blackheath was the first official golf club outside Scotland, with the Old Manchester Club on Kersal Moor (1818) the second oldest; but it took nearly fifty years before a seaside golf links, comparable to the Scottish links courses, opened in England, and this was marked out by "Old Tom" Morris for the Royal North Devon Golf Club at Westward Ho! in 1864.

At this stage in the evolution of the golf course it is important to avoid the use of the term *build*, because golf course designers in those early years were primarily 'First Class Golfers', and they did little or nothing to alter what nature had sculpted out of the sandy, windswept areas skirting the seashore, they merely indicated where the holes should be cut and where surfaces should be levelled to make putting areas and even this refinement did not appear until the early 1700s when the habit of teeing one's ball a club's length from the hole just completed, was abandoned in favour of teeing areas.

All modern golf courses evolved from the playing fields in the sandy links lands of Scotland, and it is perhaps fitting that a short summary of the evolution of the golf course as we know it should preface the history of the game in this small county of Dorset, where the first course, a nine-hole "green" as they were then called, was laid out by a small group of enthusiasts on the cliffs above West Bay in 1891.

The game of golf in England was essentially one for the rich and leisured classes, but because links lands were largely publicly owned, and the Northerly latitude extended the hours of daylight from 3am to 11pm, it was possible for the working man to use them, thus establishing an early democratic tradition for the game in Scotland.

It has been a widely held belief that the term "links" referred to Scottish courses located on the sandy deposits left centuries ago along the sea coasts by the receding oceans, but this is only partly true. The North Sea may well have deposited rolling dunes of sand, but the true links land consisted of rich alluvial deposits laid upon the sand by a river flowing into the sea. True links would then be golf courses formed by nature on or near river estuaries. In fact, the first games of golf to be played in Scotland were on just such land along the estuaries of the rivers Eden, Tay and Forth.

These links were designed entirely by nature; they consisted of high, windswept sand dunes and hollows, in which, if there was sufficient soil to support it, stiff, erect bentgrass would grow. The terrain alone dictated the route the players would follow, aiming their "featheries" for the nearest playable sward, and doing their best to avoid the dunes with their covering of gorse. There were few, if any trees or water, but there would have been plenty of other natural hazards, which in the course of time became bunkers. These would be formed by the combined effects of the weather and by the sheep and other livestock grazing bare the scant grassed areas. In time this allowed the wind and rain to erode the light covering of soil, to reveal the underlying sand, which would eventually become hollows where the animals could shelter, and so further deepen the hollow. The nests and holes of small game would collapse into small pits, which the wind and rain would transform into potholes. The early golfers would hope to avoid them, but the unfortunates who did get in to the holes would further advance the erosion process by their vigorous efforts to hack out again.

There would have been no "fairways" or putting greens. The putting areas would be the same bristly grass that grew elsewhere and as it was customary to tee-up one's ball within a club's length of the cup, a well-manicured putting surface was not known or required.

Obviously there would have been no course maintenance of any kind; bird and animal droppings and the rainfall kept the turf reasonably healthy, grazing animals kept it short, and the sandy base ensured that drainage was not a problem.

It is possible that the earliest links consisted of single holes, played out and back to a starting point, but as the popularity of the game increased, and because the common links lands were not restricted by boundaries, the golfers would have wandered as far as they could find playable ground before turning back. So there would have been no standard number of holes for a round of golf. For example, the early links at Leith and Musselburgh had five holes, North Berwick seven, Gullane thirteen and Montrose twenty-five. Royal Aberdeen, as late as 1875, had only fifteen holes, and when the first open championship was played at Prestwick in 1860, the course consisted of twelve holes and was played three times round.

In England The Royal Blackheath had five holes, and was played three times round. Then in 1844 it was increased to seven holes, again played three times, but because the heath was common land, criss-crossed by cart tracks and public footpaths, the holes had to be cut each time the club played.

The premier course then... as it is today, was the old links at St Andrews and there are records of its existence in a primitive form dating back to as early as 1414. Purists may claim that the course is no longer a true links, because of the rapid recession of the sea during the last century or so, but it *began* as a totally natural links. The playable areas of grass were bordered by patches of thick heather, and the majority of the natural sand bunkers were hidden from the player's view until he went in search of his ball.

In plan form the course resembled a shepherds crook, but this was a simple fact of nature and not design. It had twelve putting areas, ten of which served both the outward and homeward trek... the arrangement which led to the terms *out* and *in,* to designate which of the common holes the golfer

St Andrews

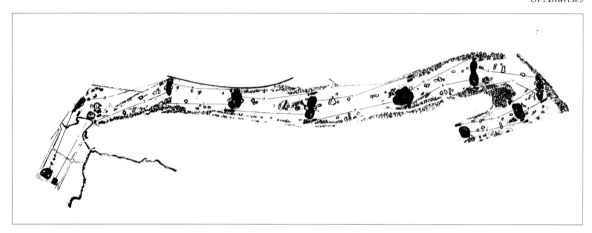

was playing. The remaining two holes were used only once, as the eleventh, and the home holes. A round at St Andrews therefore consisted of twenty-two holes, eleven out to the furthest point, and eleven coming back home.

Around the middle of the eighteenth century two innovations to the existing game were introduced: one was the creation of private clubs, but whose members continued to play on the public links land; and the other, which first occurred at St Andrews, was that man began to change some of nature's handiwork, firstly by the introduction, some time in the 1700s, of turfed areas to serve as putting greens, which must soon have been followed by the introduction of separate teeing areas.

In 1764 the Society of St Andrews Golfers decided that the first four holes were not sufficiently challenging, and they consolidated them into two long holes. This eliminated two greens and four holes, so reducing the round to eighteen holes.

A much more romantic explanation for the change to eighteen holes is provided by an old Scottish legend. A bottle of Scotch whisky contained eighteen jiggers, and with a consumption rate of a jigger per hole, the St Andrews golfers felt that the round should end when the bottle was empty!

In 1832 the practice began of cutting two holes in each of the common greens, so creating eight double greens, on which two matches, one heading out and the other coming home, could play.

The Honourable Company of Edinburgh Golfers disbanded at Leith in 1831 and re-established itself at Musselburgh in 1836, and again at Muirfield in 1891. In the meantime the links at Leith, deprived of its main supporter, soon deteriorated, so that it was in no position to dispute St Andrews' claim in 1834 to be the "home of golf" and the Society the foremost authority on the game.

Eighteen holes became the standard for all new golf courses, and because purists objected to the use of the term 'links' to refer to any terrain unlike that at St Andrews, new terms were invented to describe inland... and by implication, inferior golfing grounds.

The first term "greens", led to the derivatives greenkeeper, green fee, and green committee. Later, golfing grounds became golfing course, and finally golf course.

When the revolutionary gutta-percha ball arrived on the scene in 1848 it signalled the beginning of the end of the exclusive nature of golf. Featheries were very expensive (about four shillings) whereas the new gutty, at about a quarter of the cost, was affordable to a much wider range of potential players, and because it offered greater resistance to the 'less than perfect' blow, they lasted longer. The tougher ball also marked the virtual end of the hand made wooden club. "Cleeks' ', or metal headed clubs made their appearance, and these in their turn had the unintentional effect of widening the fairways as they beat down the heather, so allowing the coarse grass to grow in its place! Many of these early iron clubs were made by blacksmiths, to designs dictated by the exclusive band of 'First Class Golfers'. The clubs were distinguished by the name of the golfer, but the blacksmith also scratched on his own initials and one of these rare clubs, made some time between 1688 and 1720, was sold at a recent Sotheby's sale for £92,400.

Royal North Devon & West of England Golf Links
Plan supplied by the Curator of the Royal Blackheath G.C. museum

The gutty survived for over fifty years until it was ousted by the invention of the rubber cored ball by American dentist Dr Coburn Haskell, but since that date a new "best" ball has appeared on the market at least once every decade!

Willie Park claimed to have anticipated the possibility of a rubber cored ball when he was a very young boy, 'when I was about eleven years of age I was of an inventive turn of mind, and I remember that I applied myself to the production of a ball that would go farther than the gutties, and indeed I may claim to have been the maker of the first rubber ball. I made a mixture of ground cork, ground rubber and gutta percha and forced it down a funnel into an iron mould. The ball that resulted after the mixture had set seemed alright, but after playing a few shots, it expanded enormously and I had to give the idea up'. Park began his experiments in 1875/6 and Haskell introduced his (successful) ball in 1898.

Blackheath Golf Course
Reproduced by kind permission of the Royal Blackheath Golf Club

Handicapping

Golf has always been a highly competitive sport, so it is natural that betting should have been associated with the game since its inception. If evidence was needed this has been provided by the Historian of the R & A who found references to a form of handicapping in a Bet Book dated 1789 belonging to the Honourable Company of Edinburgh Golfers.

The term originated from horse racing when the jockey was handed his odds for the race in a cap (hand-in-cap). But in golf the concept preceded the word; the act of allowing strokes was called 'assigning the odds' and was done by the forerunner of the modern handicap committee, who was called the 'Adjuster of the Odds'.

According to the records of the R & A, towards the end of the nineteenth century, clubs, societies and associations devised their own methods of allowing strokes. This was usually achieved by monitoring the scores of their best player, known as the 'Backmarker' and taking the average for each hole, which became the 'ground score'. This method, although quite practical within a club, was unsatisfactory for away games and in open competitions, not only when judged against the differing quality of the courses, but more importantly, because of the wide variations in the degrees of skill between the clubs' Backmarkers.

In about 1890 a variation between matchplay and strokeplay was introduced in the form of a competition against 'Bogey'; a term invented at the Great Yarmouth Club, but the military title is attributed to the United Services Club, playing at Alverstoke, where all the members were either army or navy officers. The mythical "Colonel" was the personification of the demon golfer who played every hole in the standard score.

According to *Nisbet's Golf Year Book* for 1891 'the bogey of a hole or round is the number of strokes in which they can be taken without serious mistakes and may be said to represent good steady play'. The R & A recognised it in 1910 and for some time bogey replaced the ' ground score' of a course, but it lost much of its popularity as a club competition when Dr Frank Stableford introduced his points system in 1931.

As time went on, the increasing popularity of the game, and the number of new courses being opened . . . all with a wide variety of terrain and degrees of difficulty, the need for a standard of handicapping which would be applicable irrespective of the nature of the course became imperative.

In England the three key figures in the early handicapping debate were Dr Laidlaw Purves, Henry Lamb of the Royal Wimbledon Golf Club, and Miss Issette Pearson of the LGU. But it was the Ladies Golf Union which was instrumental in developing the first uniform course rating and assigning them to member clubs.

According to *The History of Handicapping* compiled for the EGU in 1936, Dr Laidlaw Purves set out the rules for universal handicapping (1898) which were evolved at Wimbledon. These rules may be regarded as the basis on which the British Golf Union's Joint Advisory Council have built up their system . . . the average of the best three scores over two years of medal scores. But the R & A avers that Dr Purves was more the *promoter* of an existing system than the developer. Purves is probably better remembered as the architect of the Royal St George's golf course.

Robert Browning's *A History of Golf* says of the LGU: 'Their biggest achievement was the gradual establishment of a national system of handicapping . . . it was uphill work at the start (1893), but within eight or ten years the LGU had done what the men had signally failed to do . . . established a system of handicapping that was reasonably reliable from club to club'.

In 1896 George Combe, the Honorary Secretary of the Irish Golf Union, proposed a shrewd and well devised handicapping system which was adopted by the majority of the clubs affiliated to that

Union. It set out a range of handicaps in ten classes from plus one to thirty. It also made specific allowances for matchplay, and for the first time it prescribed yardage measurements for deciding the 'Par' of a hole. This is the first time the term was used, and which *Nisbet's Golf Year Book* describes as 'perfect play without flukes'.

In 1925 the British Golf Unions Joint Advisory Committee (now CONGU) introduced a standard scratch score and handicapping scheme which was adopted by the Irish Golf Union (formed in 1891), the Welsh (1895), the Scottish (1920) and the English Union (1924), and which came into operation in the four countries in March 1926.

The scheme has since been modified on a number of occasions, but in 1982 it was decided to adopt the Australian system, which also involved the transfer of the control of all Category 1 players' handicaps back to the Club. In addition, every Club was instructed to increase the handicap of every member by one stroke and the handicap limit was raised to 28. This scheme too has been revised and a measure of flexibility has been introduced into the fixing of par for each hole in relation to its length and playing difficulty.

Nowadays of course, electronics have entered the field, and many golf club secretaries have the assistance of computers with specially designed software to maintain individual records and which print-out the results and handicap adjustments, in addition to making allowances for the variable standard scratch score system in use today.

A beautiful, but difficult downland setting.
The 372 yard 16th hole at the Mid Dorset Golf Club

1

The 'County' Scene

'A Golfing Desert'

The *Victorian History of the County of Dorset,* published in 1908 provides a fascinating insight into life in this small agricultural county.

As could be expected, hunting, shooting and fishing were the main pursuits of the moneyed classes, and there was little else but work for the others. But the county was famous for its beer, and the book records the existence of no fewer than 293 brewers and maltsters. Their product was held in high esteem, not only within the county borders, but 'great quantities of the incomparable Dorchester beer were sold in London'. As could be expected, Thomas Hardy would have had an opinion, and he expressed it in *The Trumpet Major,* alluding to it with the authority of a connoisseur:

It was the most beautiful colour that the eye of an artist could devise; full in body, yet brisk as a volcano, piquant, yet without a twang, luminous as an Autumn sunset, free from streakiness of taste but finally rather heady.

In the chapter dealing with sport and pastimes in the Victorian chronicle, a Reverend gentleman E E Dorling MA described only seven golf courses in the county, but a contemporary golf journal recorded two golf courses which were in existence in Weymouth at that time, both formed in 1894, and one which claimed a golfing history reaching back four centuries, so it is a mystery why he should have failed to mention them.

Despite prolonged research at the Weymouth Reference Library, the County Record Office at Dorchester, and by the British Golf Museum at St Andrews, no evidence could be found to substantiate the claim of the East Chickerell course to be 'the oldest in England', or the whereabouts and subsequent history of the Weymouth 'Naval' course, which was also initiated in 1894.

Forgan's *Golfers Handbook* of 1881 makes no mention of a club at Weymouth, nor is there a reference in the *Golfing Annual* prior to 1894, and in the opinion of the Director of the British Golf Museum, it is *exceedingly unlikely* that any golf was played at Weymouth prior to the late nineteenth century. But it is very difficult to dismiss the claims of prominent local residents on the basis of a lack of official records. These were the misty years of golf in England, when the game was played on a casual basis by groups of wealthy gentle men on private "links" which were often no more than small areas of rugged farm or downland, where the natural hazards provided the "sport", or the challenge to the individual's skill in maintaining the little ball "in play".

Weymouth has been a major seaside resort since the eighteenth century, and it grew in importance when sea bathing became the fashionable "cure"

H Vardon

for rheumatics and all manner of other ailments. At the height of its medicinal splendour the locals were quick to exploit the commercial aspects of the new craze, and doctors suddenly discovered that the town's Radipole Lake possessed sulphurous qualities more beneficial than the sea itself.

From about 1760 its fashion had spread among the wealthy from Bath and London, and the Duke of Gloucester and King George the Third made regular visits.

In view of all this, it would be surprising if golf was not included in the sporting pursuits of these wealthy visitors, so it is reasonable to concede at least some substance to the claim that golf had been played on the East Chickerell course for many years prior to 1894.

The arrival of the railway in 1857 introduced for the first time an influx of summer visitors from a much wider social strata who demanded much more than mere "medicinal" recreation, so adding further weight to the claim.

Jesty owned the course, but it has not been possible to substantiate (or disprove) the claim about its age

AN ARTIST'S RAMBLES ROUND ABOUT WEYMOUTH AND PORTLAND.

WEYMOUTH GOLF LINKS.

The Oldest Golf Links in England.

Open to Visitors.

Four minutes' walk from Radipole Village.

.. EAST .. CHICKERELL PARK.

Patronized by Her Majesty The Queen.

 WILLIAM JESTY,

NOTED PURVEYOR OF

Prime English Beef, Mutton, Dairy Fed Pork, etc.,

29, ST. MARY STREET, WEYMOUTH.

Branches: FORTUNE WELL (next door to the Post Office), and at 50, EASTON, PORTLAND.

All Meat guaranteed of the Best Quality, and direct from Own Farms at East Chickerell, Nottington, and Wyke Regis.

The character of the town gradually changed as a result of this egalitarian innovation, and the Georgian architecture which formed the core of this elegant watering place, became encircled by Victorian commercial and residential buildings.

In spite of the Reverend Dorling's assertion that Bridport was the first golf course to be constructed in Dorset, it is fairly certain that the East Chickerell course preceded it. Bridport is the oldest surviving golf *Club,* but its original course on the west cliff was abandoned in 1911, by which time there were eight other golf courses in the county.

According to the Reverend 'It can hardly be claimed for Dorset that the county is a golfer's paradise. There is but little golf in the county, and none of true seaside quality although the Dorset Club makes a gallant effort to provide real golf for its numerous supporters on its famous course at Broadstone.

'Within the county there are no more than seven recognised golf clubs, and it argues a lack of enterprise and enthusiasm for the game in Dorset folk that so much of the magnificent turf of its downs, and so vast an area of its characteristic sandy heath is unutilised for the Royal and Ancient game. Dorset is however a sparsely inhabited county, and it is possible that the courses it has are sufficient for the needs of its players.

'It was not until the beginning of the last decade of the nineteenth century that the wave of enthusiasm for golf, which was sweeping like a torrent over England, reached our county; and to Bridport belongs the honour of having instituted the first golf club within its borders. In February 1891, the West Dorset Club opened a nine-hole course with a circuit of about one and a half miles on some sixty acres of fine down turf on the slopes of the east cliff at West Bay. The hazards here are gorse, disused quarries, roads, and stone walls; and the best time for play is in the spring and summer months.

The opening of the original Bridport Clubhouse on the west cliff 1892

'In 1892 was formed the Isle of Purbeck Golf Club, whose links are two miles from Swanage on the north side of the road from Studland. This very hilly nine-hole course has a length of about a mile and a half; the hazards are hedges, gorse, ponds, and some artificial bunkers.

'The Lyme Regis Golf Club was initiated in 1893. Its nine-hole course is five hundred feet above the sea on the cliffs between Lyme and Charmouth.

'Golf had already been played for some time on Lenthay Common near Sherbourne, when in 1894 the course of the Blackmore Vale Club was opened a mile and a half north of the town. It was laid out on undulating ground on either side of the road which, with its high hedges, formed a hazard at more than one of the nine holes. The Club has recently gone back to links on Lenthay Common.

'The Ashley Wood Club has a downland course of nine holes, two miles from Blandford. It was opened in 1896. The turf is good and gorse is the principal hazard.

'The old Dorchester Club, founded in the same year, has now been amalgamated with the Weymouth Club under the name of the Weymouth, Dorchester and County Golf Club. The course of eighteen holes is on Came Down, two miles from the county town. The hazards are furze, chalk pits, tumuli, a pond and some ditches.

'The great course at the Dorset Club, opened in 1898, is the outcome of a prodigious expenditure of money, labour, and ingenuity. It lies about midway between Wimborne and Poole at Broadstone, partly on the eastern edge of the great heath that, under different names, extends from Corfe Mullen to Moreton, and partly in the park of Merley Hall. On the wild and hilly heath portion Tom Dunn, who designed the course at the direction of Lord Wimborne, laid out the first six and the last four holes. The thick growth of ling, gorse, and fern which, rising shoulder high, covered the sandy hillsides, was cut away, bogs were drained, and turf was laid, tees were levelled, vast putting greens and bunkers built, and after years of work, ten magnificent holes, of which it is not easy to find an equal on any inland course, appeared. It has been said by a judicious critic of Broadstone that if the vast ditch and rampart hazards were replaced by artfully arranged pot bunkers, this could be made one of the finest courses in Europe... and many may be found to agree with this dictum so far as it applies to the holes at the beginning and end of the round. But the long seventh and the five holes in the park are less enjoyable.

'The course is three and a half miles round, and the long carries required from the tees form what is perhaps the most marked characteristic of this excellent course, where the tees are like putting greens and the greens themselves of lavish dimensions. Meetings are held in the spring and autumn'.

Many of the earlier golf courses built before the introduction of irrigation, failed because they were constructed on impervious clay soils, and because of this purists believed that true golf could only be found on sandy links.

It was not until the pioneering efforts of designers like Willie Park Jnr, Colt, and Fowler, who were credited with "discovering" heathland; beginning with the highly successful Sunningdale course, that these now famous inland golf courses were accepted as being comparable with the established links courses.

Dorset has its share of heathland, and of courses built on heavy soils, some which *did* prove to be too wet, such as the original Bridport course.

Course irrigation did not begin until about 1880, and by 1884 the St Andrews Club had sunk wells beside each green to ensure a steady supply of water.

The lawnmower, although invented in 1830, was not widely used on golf courses until decades later. Sheep provided a moving hazard, but an efficient means of fertilising and maintaining a close-cropped greensward, but where they could not be used, and prior to the introduction of the mower, many courses could only be played in the autumn and winter or during droughts, because the greens were too lush.

Lining the hole with a metal sleeve to prevent damage first began in Fife at the Crail Club in about 1874, but prior to this practical innovation golfers used to tee up near the hole, with a pinch of sand taken from the hole, which became progressively deeper and more ragged. Sand boxes became a familiar sight after teeing grounds became established, but wooden tee pegs did not appear until the 1930s.

The failure of some of the other courses was mainly attributable to financial causes. Many were small private clubs with restricted memberships, and when the courses were taken over for agricultural purposes during the war, there was insufficient money available to reinstate them when hostilities ceased.

Other failures of a more recent nature may be attributed to an over-enthusiastic response to a report by the R & A on the need for more golf courses in England; to the effect of the Government's set-aside scheme; and ultimately to the current deep recession.

The boom in golf course construction was driven by a report in 1989 from the R & A which said that England needed 700 new courses if it was to meet a target of one course per 25,000 people and thus be on a par with Scotland.

A second factor was a warning from the Ministry of Agriculture and the European Commission that farmers must find other uses for land. The Government's set-aside scheme paid farmers to hive off 20 percent of surplus low-grade land.

The promise of available land and the huge potential market inundated local authority planning departments with applications for courses. One thousand were made in England, at a time when England and Wales had 2,000 courses and Scotland 450. As will be seen later, Dorset planning authorities had to deal with scores of such applications.

At the height of the boom prime sites could be sold for up to £10,000 an acre... ten times the agricultural price farmers could have previously achieved. But several of these projects foundered under enormous overheads and were never completed, and some of those that were completed quickly discovered to their cost that the worsening recession was creating mounting unemployment figures so that the money needed to make the projects pay was beyond the pockets of the average golfer. In spite of a greater-than-ever demand, most players wanted cheap, pay-as-you-play golf because they would not tolerate the interminable wait to join the established clubs, or with rising unemployment, were unable to afford the fees.

These recurrent 'waves of enthusiasm' for golf, so eloquently described by the sporting Reverend, seem to occur at irregular intervals, because the 'torrent which swept over England' in the late 1800s re-appeared again just prior to World War I. According to an article in a London newspaper in 1914 there were over 2,000 links in Britain, with over a quarter of a million members. The average cost of membership of Clubs in the Home counties was £35 a year, compared to £25 in other parts of the country; and over nine and a quarter million pounds a year was spent on golf . . . 'not including the cost of lessons . . . and all this has come about in the last 25 years'.

Early historians had referred to the county of Dorset as a golfing desert, but the population of this small, mainly agricultural county was then less than 300,000, about one half of today's figure. The boundaries did change marginally over the years, but had little effect upon the total population or the county's rateable income until the major changes which occurred in 1974, which brought Bournemouth and Christchurch into the county, greatly improving the financial scene and practically doubling the population.

A 1991 report from the County Planning Department revealed that the population of Dorset had increased by 10 percent in the last decade to 658,300, with the greatest increase in the Purbeck area and in East Dorset.

Watercolour of Broadstone c1906 by Walter Tyndale. Allowing for a degree of artistic licence it could have been part of the 7th

Dorset Golf Clubs Old and New

A common factor, and a prerequisite for the success of the oldest golf clubs in the county . . . as elsewhere in England, was the proximity of a railway station, because there were no cars, and players were usually conveyed from station to clubhouse by horse and trap. For example, J H Taylor's chosen site at Came Down was dependent upon Weymouth Council being able to persuade the Great Western Railway to extend its service and to put in a Halt, which the Company agreed to do after Dorchester added its weight to the petition. Of the other old clubs, the Isle of Purbeck was perhaps the most vulnerable. It had a small local population and very poor communications before the advent of the motor car, so it is not surprising that its early years were plagued by financial problems. Lyme Regis, Bridport and Weymouth all had convenient railway stations, and Broadstone had a Halt adjacent to the first tee.

The profiles of the golf clubs in Chapter 2 represent the bare outlines of their formation and growth, but with the clubs described here, it has been possible to flesh-out these profiles with descriptions of opening matches or ceremonies which make evocative and often amusing reading. They also illustrate the extent of the changes which have transformed every aspect of the game, including the equipment; the many forms of tuition available to today's players; the vast amount of capital now invested in the game; the construction and maintenance of courses; and the publicity, which has erased the boundaries of almost every country in the world . . . all in the space of less than one century since this particular record began.

The descriptions which follow include those of clubs which failed quickly, others which did not survive the war years, and some which plumbed the depths, then clawed their way back to solvency, due mainly to the efforts of determined members or generous benefactors. It is also interesting to note the number of planning applications on the map in Chapter 2 for yet more golf courses, which if granted will turn this one-time agricultural county into the very antithesis of the "golfing desert" referred to by earlier historians.

Four of the original seven golf clubs have celebrated their centenaries and have published histories compiled by dedicated members and we are indebted to these clubs for permission to reproduce photographs and extracts from the books. Other clubs are making preparations, some spurred on by the requests for information for the production of the club profiles included in this book, so it is to be hoped that more historical information will surface before the drafting of this book is complete.

The Reverend Dorling in *The Victorian History of Dorset* erroneously referred to all golf courses as "links", and deprecated the absence of 'true seaside quality'. Nowadays of course it is accepted that the term "links" shall apply only to the genuine sandy areas between the foreshore and the cultivated areas of land as explained in the Preface. These courses remained generally as nature designed them until about the middle of the eighteenth century when they began to be modified, firstly to include putting and teeing areas,

Willie Park

and then as the game became more popular, the technical improvements in the golf balls and golf equipment forced designers to lengthen the courses and to introduce a variety of new hazards.

A humorous if cynical observation about links courses is provided by Sir William Simpson in 1892 in his book *The History of Golf: the grounds on which golf is played are called links, being the barren, sandy soil from which the sea has retired in recent geological times. In their natural state, links are covered with long, rank benty grass and gorse . . . links are too barren for cultivation; but sheep, rabbits, geese, and golf professionals pick up a precarious living on them.*

There are no true links courses in the county because in the main the coastline is rugged, with the result that our seaside courses are on heath or clifftop downs; but the Isle of Purbeck golf course, with its spectacular views over Poole Bay, although mainly heathland, does possess many "links" characteristics.

Parkstone had not been constructed at the time of the Reverend's descriptions, but much of that land was of genuine links quality. It was set back from the sea, but it was all sand and heather when it was first laid out by Willie Park Jnr and opened for play in 1910, However, the nature of the golf course has been radically altered over the intervening years, until it now resembles a parkland course. The sand has been overlaid by fairways which have been manufactured out of imported soils and grass, and the natural heather is under increasing threat by the invasive pine, bracken and gorse.

Undated postcard. In the foreground is the hill and bunkers of Willie Park's 503 yard second hole

Isle of Purbeck

The Reverend Dorling paid particular attention to the Broadstone golf course when he described the seven original courses, but for quite different reasons, the contributors to *The Golf Annual* of 1892 produced an equally detailed description of the original 9-hole Isle of Purbeck course, which makes very interesting reading, both from a stylistic viewpoint, and because it describes a mode of play which none but the oldest readers of this book would recognise.

The announcement in *The Golfing Annual* lauds the attractions of the town of Swanage as a holiday resort, because of course the club would have to rely heavily upon the income from holiday visitors if it was to become financially viable.

ISLE OF PURBECK GOLF CLUB.
Instituted August 1892
Annual Subscription: £1.1s. Number of Members 40 President: Ralph Bankes.
Vice President: Kenneth Anderson .
Committee: Major Hawkesworth, G Burt, J R Slade,
J E Clifton, G Belben Jnr., G C Filliter, G Deveril Saul.
Hon.Sec. G R Wright, Purbeck College, Swanage.

H Sales

'In sight of the Isle of Wight and within easy reach of Bournemouth lies Swanage, one of the most picturesque little watering places on the south coast of England. Famed for its excellent sea bathing, its invigorating climate, and the beauty and variety of its surroundings, its popularity as a summer resort is yearly on the increase; but it is now able to offer the attraction of golf to visitors. A capital stretch of ground has been rented by the club, and on it a course of nine holes has been laid out in accordance with the directions of Jackson of Bembridge (The professional at the Royal Isle of Wight Golf Club).

'The right has been obtained of extending the course to eighteen holes, but the present arrangement has been so satisfactory that there is not likely to be any alteration for some little time.

'About two miles from Swanage and close by the road running from Swanage to Studland is the first teeing ground, between which and the first or 'road' hole is situated a cottage with its garden. A good drive to the right will land the ball clear of this and in position for a cleek shot down to the green. The latter stroke requires careful handling as an overdrive will reach the road. To manipulate the second or 'ditch' hole a smart drive uphill and well to the right is requisite to avoid a large hedge and ditch extending for some distance in front of it. In front of the third teeing ground is another hedge of gorse, briar, and blackthorn, and between this and the third or 'pond' hole, the ground slopes and then rises again forming a valley . Three good drives should reach the hole, but in the event of the third drive falling a little short, it will be punished either in a bunker or a cattle-pond.

'The next hole, generally called the 'farm' hole, is by no means easy, as a bad stroke is severely punished by furze, and six is a steady score.

At this point the upper and more level ground is reached, where long drives are of the greatest service. A good drive over a long bunker will reach the fifth or 'corner' hole, but an overdrive or pulled ball will be punished by one of the hedges which form the corner. The next teeing ground faces home, and a drive and a couple of good cleek shots will reach the sixth or 'first straight' hole. The seventh, or 'second straight' hole is somewhat the same. In front of the eighth teeing ground is a ditch some fifteen yards in width, thickly covered with furze and bracken. A good stroke should land between a ditch and a large bunker right across the course, and a third should reach the green. A drive of 150 yards should carry down the hill close to the ninth or 'home' hole. The whole course is about a mile and a half in length and is circular. The ground is in an elevated position, and as the soil is sandy, is never swampy.

'There is no need to refer to the climate as the Isle of Purbeck is famous for its pure, dry, and bracing air. From all points the prospect is magnificent, and very fine views may be obtained of Swanage, Studland, Poole Harbour, Bournemouth, and the Isle of Wight.

'The Club have rented a picturesque cottage with its surrounding garden, which it is intended to convert into a clubhouse. Excellent hotel accommodation can be obtained at Swanage, both at the Royal Victoria and Grove hotels, and a large hotel is about to be erected at Studland, which will be a great convenience to golfers, owing to its close proximity to the ground'.

Charming old postcard (c1909) of the cottage which became the Clubhouse of the Isle of Purbeck G C

Lyme Regis Golf Club

This undulating downland golf course adds brilliant scenic charm to its golfing attractions, so it is advisable for the visitor to make a two-day visit, one for absorbing the truly magnificent panoramic views, and the other for playing the course, so as to lessen the risk of distraction on a course which has many hazards to trap the unwary golfer.

The fifteenth tee stands 600 feet above the sea and is the perfect viewpoint for enjoying the magnificent sweep of coastline; on a clear day it is possible to see westward as far as Seaton, and eastward to Portland and the Golden Cap at Bridport.

This same vantage point offers a birds-eye view of the town and its beaches, including 'The Cobb', the jetty made famous in John Fowle's *The French Lieutenant's Woman',* and the evocative picture of the black-cloaked lady gazing wistfully out to sea in the film of the same name.

The town is steeped in history, and it was from this little harbour that Sir George Somers set sail in 1609, heading for the new American colony of Virginia, but his tiny ship was wrecked off the island of Bermuda, and he promptly annexed it for the Crown.

Seventy-six years later three ships sailed into the harbour carrying James the Duke of Monmouth to begin his ill-fated rebellion.

Two hundred years on, and in a much more settled political climate, a group of Lyme Regis gentry and four members of the Clergy formed a Club and rented forty-two acres of the wild cliff-top scrubland above Lyme Bay and Charmouth to create a golf course.

Lyme Regis 100 years ago. Harry Austin, Bob Vigors, Major General P Benson, Rita Whatmore, Betty Benson and John Whatmore re-enact the setting for the inaugural game

In keeping with tradition, they did little to alter what nature had provided, and were playing golf on the "sporting" course within a month of their decision, and continued to do so without major changes for the next seventeen years.

As part of their centenary celebrations in 1993, the Club intend to stage a "foursome" to represent the players in the first game to be played on the course; but in the photograph the gent in the smock was no golfer, he was the Ostler who looked after the horse, which all golf clubs of the day employed to pull the heavy rollers and mowers to keep the fairways in order, and with the aid of leather boots, were also used to mow the greens... there were no billiard table putting surfaces in those days!

The Golfing Annual of 1893 records the original entrance fee and the annual subscription as being one guinea each, and a family ticket cost five guineas (which included the entrance fee).

It described the course, of nine holes as being on high ground between Lyme Regis and Charmouth. 'There are good hotels and lodgings in both places. The course is about 500 feet above the level of the sea, and the view is one of the loveliest and most extensive in England. A pavilion has been erected at the Lyme end of the course and a small one at the Charmouth end, thus saving a walk of about a mile and a half.

'Visitors green charges are one shilling and sixpence a day, five shillings a week, and fifteen shillings a month.

'Lyme Regis is only about a mile and a half outside Devonshire, and partakes largely of the character and scenery of that county. There is very good sea bathing and boating, a Lawn Tennis Club, and a social Club containing reading and billiard rooms. Axminster, the nearest station is six miles off, but there is a good bus service between the two places all year round'.

The original Secretary was Sir Lionel Smith-Gordon Bart and he was followed by T G B Pares, and by T B Blathwayt in December 1899.

The first greenkeeper in 1894 was J Lake, who stayed with the Club until 1898. He was not a 'professional', but he did sell golf clubs to the members and was paid a commission, but they were ordered and paid for by the Club.

Nearby Charmouth initiated a golf club a year later than Lyme, but it was short-lived, and in 1894 their pavilion was re-sited on the Lyme Regis course, so giving the Club the unique distinction of possessing two Clubhouses. This luxury lasted until about 1928, when the eroding cliff edge advanced too close for comfort and the deteriorating building had to be abandoned.

In 1910 the 9-hole course was lengthened with the acquisition of a further sixteen acres of land, and extended to a full eighteen holes in 1930.

In addition to losing the 'new' nine holes, which had to ploughed up under the second world war *Dig for Victory* scheme, the height and the uninterrupted views described earlier had the effect of making the place an obvious choice as a strategic look-out point. The Navy moved in and seriously curtailed the Club's activities. Some golf continued to be played over the original nine holes, but there were less than fifty members left to enjoy them, and the naval golfers must have thoroughly appreciated their good fortune.

The Clubhouse became a listening post for enemy radio transmissions; a radio tower was sited on the ninth green, and on another part of the course an observation tower was built to look out across the bay for signs of the expected invasion which fortunately failed to materialise. An old Club ledger revealed that this tower was presented to the Club after the war, and was eventually sold for scrap for £85.

The Ashley Wood Golf Club

This club had a turbulent early history and came perilously close to reverting to farmland during World War II.

It was one of the founder clubs in the Dorset Union, and was represented at the inaugural Executive Committee meeting by F W Woodhouse of the brewing family. The Minutes are not helpful, but it would appear that the club resigned from the County Union shortly after joining, and then re-joined in 1933. But the club was derelict in the early 1950s when it was bought by Roy and Jackie Carey, a London couple, who sank £25,000 into *their* particular dream.

What they bought was a 'ramshackle golf club near the Blandford army camp' with fairways either overgrown with gorse and scrub, or being ploughed up by a farmer who claimed he was simply taking back his own land!

During the next seventeen years the Careys worked to clear the scrub, firstly with a mechanical flail borrowed from the American military, then with bulldozers driven by off-duty troops. When they began there was no water supply, no clubhouse sanitation and no electricity, but within three years they had a productive borehole, an electricity generator and a re-constructed clubhouse... but very few golfers, because the local players boycotted the place because of the "American invasion".

The Careys' determination bordered upon the obsessive; but everything seemed to be pitted against them, even nature itself appeared to resent the intrusion. Harvest bugs, which bored beneath the skin had to be exterminated, and then the course was invaded by colonies of rabbits which undermined the elevated tees, causing them to collapse. They were eventually brought under control by setting up hurricane lamps on the greens, with windmills attached to the tops of them to prevent the rabbits clambering over them; then at about two o'clock in the morning, when the rabbits appeared above ground in force, Carey would blast them with shotgun pellets.

Mole saboteurs worked as hard as the Careys to retain their own preserve, but they were eventually beaten by the combined effects of arsenical worms and high velocity shotgun cartridges fired into every new run and freshly turned molehill.

But after beating the bugs, rabbits and moles, the Careys faced another, even more intractable adversary... the indifference of the local golfers who objected to the Americans and to the Careys' obvious friendship with them.

A local reporter likened the club to a 'busy morgue'. However, heartbroken as Carey must have felt after his herculean efforts, he did not give up, but instead, turned his engineering skills into improving his own game. 'With swing ideas that were pure mathematics', he perfected a method which enabled him to score an authenticated 64, which is quoted in an early *Golfers Handbook* as the course record for Ashley Wood.

For the duration of the war and until their departure, the Americans from nearby Blandford practically took over the club, so whilst Carey was able to recoup at least part of his outlay, the locals did not return to the reborn club until well after the Americans had left. Finally however, they drifted back and the club prospered. The Careys eventually sold the freehold to the members, who in turn made them honorary life members of the club which they had *literally* saved from the plough.

There is no record of a professional during the formative years of the Club, but there were only forty-seven members when it was inaugurated in 1896. J Grant served the Club between 1905 and 1911, and he was followed in quick succession by G Randall (1911-17); A Saint (1919-20); J Randall (1922-26), and J Saint in 1931.

Dorset (Broadstone) Golf Club

This was the first *heathland* golf course to be constructed in Dorset, and the name of the (then) small village is reputed to have derived from the large flat stepping stones which were used to ford the stream passing in front of Broadstone Farm, the first house of any size to be built in the area.

All the old county clubs such as the Isle of Purbeck (1892); Sherborne (1894); Came Down (1896); and Ashley Wood (1896); were laid out on downland, where very little, if any earth-moving was required, so that the costs involved were relatively small. With Broadstone however, Tom Dunn, the architect, was faced with immense problems, such as the removal of sand hills and

the clearance of dense heather, gorse and fern. Fortunately he was not constrained by the financial limitations imposed by the Bournemouth Corporation four years earlier when he created the Meyrick Park golf course. Lord Wimborne wanted the biggest and the best, for a golf course which was reported to have been originally intended for the exclusive use of his family and friends.

A cutting from *The Daily Graphic* dated Thursday November 17 1898 describes the opening of the club: 'Mr Arthur Balfour (then First Lord of the Treasury) yesterday formally opened the Dorset Club's links, which have been laid out by Lord Wimborne at Broadstone. In a four some Mr Balfour and J H Taylor, the Open Champion of 1894 and 1895, beat Mr John Penn MP and James Braid by four holes up and three to play.

'First rate eighteen hole golf links are not often given away. Even the most enthusiastic players can hardly expect to often meet with this costly kind of present, for as everyone now knows, a round of the best kind of golf means a very large tract of land and an initial outlay of a round sum of money to make it fit to play on. Yet this is the gift which Lord Wimborne has, in his generosity, practically made to the golfers of Dorset and Hampshire, and it goes without saying that it is a present which they will highly appreciate. In the angle where the Somerset and Dorset branches from the South Western main line to Weymouth at Broadstone there is a considerable space of what was till quite recently waste ground covered with heather and gorse and fern. This Lord Wimborne has converted into capital links . . . the land has had to be cleared in places, drained, the turf carted and laid, bunkers erected, and the eighteen greens thoroughly made: this last a no small or cheap task considering the fact that some of them have an area of 1,800 square yards. By giving *carte blanche* to Tom Dunn of Bournemouth, and with an outlay of many thousands of pounds, that wasteland has developed into a splendid golfing course, and by way of variety five of the holes have been made in Merley Park where the country is less open and the hazards more natural. The average player will find his work cut out for him. By the time he has completed one round he will have walked about four miles . . . over a difficult up-and-down course three and a quarter miles in extent. Three of the holes are over 400 yards in length and seven more are 350 and over. The longest is 486 and the shortest 121 yards.

'The starting and finishing points are near together and close to where the two railway lines connect at Broadstone station. One artificial bunker off the tee and another at the green with a small dyke lie within the 444 yards to the first hole. The second and third holes are taken zigzag, the former uphill and the latter down again to near the first green. Here again the brook forms a good guardian to the third green which, situated in a belt of trees, is one of the prettiest spots on the links. There is a slight slope up to the fourth green, and this is the one which has cost so much labour and money to make.

'Previously the place was nothing less than a bog, but by means of excavations and enormous quantities of chalk and earth, it has been effectively drained, and now, after the astonishing expenditure of £800 upon it, a beautiful terraced green is the result. The fifth green is on high ground, with the tee below near the railway. The sixth tee, banked up to a great height, looks most formidable as the country beneath is extremely rough, and an imposing sand bunker, 100 yards or so away, stretches right and left across the hollow. Then comes the longest hole, which is the turning point. The next five holes are in Merley Park, a welcome change of scene on hot days from open heathery moor to shade beneath the trees. The thirteenth hole, though of only average length, requires experienced play as the Corfe Mullen Road runs parallel to and close by the direct line, the green being well cornered in by a bunker, trees and hedges. The fourteenth, a sporting hole with the green flanked by a deep sandpit, brings one to the high ground again, which is continued past the tumulus along a ridge where sliced balls will come badly to grief. From the sixteenth homewards it is pretty plain sailing to those confident of straight and well judged play.

'There is hardly any doubt about the Broadstone course becoming popular for it has many attractions. One is its accessibility from so many places such as Bournemouth, Dorchester, Blandford, Wareham, Swanage, Christchurch and numbers of others, even Southampton being included in the golfers' railway tickets.

'The greens are so large and of such good quality that they possess a fascination of their own apart from that attached to a most excellently laid out and beautifully situated course. For after all, though outsiders may imagine that so long as golfers get good golf they are indifferent to the scenery around, most players do take a great interest in the natural surroundings of their own links, especially, and the members of the Dorset Club will be able to point to many a delightful view; over Poole Harbour in one direction, towards the New Forest in another, and so forth.

'The Club . . . is managed by a committee nominated by the proprietor and they have in Mr Wheeler a very energetic secretary, who happens to be the only official residing actually on the spot. The membership at present numbers over 120, the club professional being Adam Johnstone'.

Johnstone stayed for just one year and was followed by Tom Dunn and James Gowan Jnr. Dunn must have moved directly from Meyrick Park, and it could have been for the purpose of "tidying up" his work on the course, but Harry Dean, whose reminiscences are included within the chapter on the County Union, recalls caddying at Broadstone when he was eight years of age, and remembered seeing both of them in the professional's shop. Gowan left Broadstone in 1904, and was replaced by H L Curtis, who seemed to have a roving commission, because he was appointed to Meyrick Park in 1901, and for a time served the Bournemouth Club (1905-15), Meyrick Park (1901-17), Broadstone (1904-09), and according to Harry Dean, he also looked after the Swanage Golf Club at the same time. Hugh Williamson spent a year at Broadstone before becoming Parkstone's first professional in 1910, and he was followed at Broadstone by Charles Corlett, who features so prominently in the chapter on the County Golf Union. He was assisted by Pennington whom Harry Dean described as being 'a lovely clubmaker'.

The heathland area of the course has not changed a great deal, but the parkland holes have been removed. The railway and the old clubhouse have also disappeared, but the modern course is still regarded by many as being the best test of golf in the county.

The original Broadstone Clubhouse (demolished 1985)

Opening of the Broadstone Golf Links 1898
The building in the background was known as the Ladies Tea House

The Early Weymouth Courses

A pictorial review of Weymouth and Portland dated 1895 mentioned a golf course on the borders of the Borough of Weymouth on the estate of W C Jesty JP, a butcher of Market Hall, with farms at East Chickerell, Nottington, and Wyke Regis.

Presumably it is this course which featured in this extract from a contemporary issue of *Golf Annual*.

Weymouth Golf Club Instituted September 26 1894
Annual Subscription, £1.1s.6d. Number of Members 70
Hon.Sec. Commander Thompson RN, Weymouth.

'The course, of nine holes, is at East Chickerell, about two miles from Weymouth Station. The hazards are roads, walls, ditches, rushes, a limekiln, gravel pits, hedges, ponds, trees, whins, and artificial bunkers. As the course lies high it commands a splendid view of Weymouth Bay etc. Visitors may play and use the clubhouse on payment of one shilling a day or five shillings a week'.

The course is described as situated on elevated ground near the head of Radipole Lake, but what follows must be regarded as open to considerable

Probably the practice putting green at the East Chickerell course c1903

doubt. The writer of the article reported that 'antiquarians' claimed that golf had been played over the ground for *four hundred years,* but had not been played upon for fifty years prior to the revival of the course by Mr Jesty.

If this were correct the course would pre-date the Royal Blackheath (1787) and the Royal North Devon (1864), which is inconceivable, but there is no doubt that a course existed, and there is every likelihood that it was in use prior to the inauguration of the Bridport course.

The most likely location of the oldest course in the county was at East Chickerell, but when J H Taylor was commissioned by the Council to find a suitable site for a municipal golf course, he did not consider the course to be suitable for extension to a full eighteen holes. When this information was conveyed to Mr Jesty he was obviously very disappointed, and the club eventually succumbed in 1912 through lack of support, mainly due to the attraction of the superior conditions at the Came Down Club.

Walter Hagen and Joe Kirkwood at Weymouth 30 July 1937.
G O Howley, A E Challen, Kirkwood, Hagen, Fred Beets, E W Hutchings
Hagen is reputed to have 'stuttered out in 36, but birdied and eagled his way home in 29'

Weymouth Council was impressed with the success of Bournemouth Council's Meyrick Park course which was attracting many more visitors to the town, and they were keen to introduce a similar facility to Weymouth.

Unfortunately Taylor could not find a suitable site close to the town, and much to the Council's chagrin Taylor recommended the site at Came

Down . . . well outside the town and inaccessible by public transport. In addition it was likely to become an exclusive private club and not the municipal amenity the Council desired. However they decided to support the plan and the amalgamation with the Dorchester Club to form the Weymouth, Dorchester and County Golf Club.

Judging from the names and titles of the committee members, the other golf club described in the *Golf Annual* must have been the so-called 'Naval' golf club, but no other details have been discovered except that H Foord was the professional at the club between 1915 and 1924.

WEYMOUTH GOLF CLUB Instituted February, 1894.
Annual Subscription: £1.1s. Number of Members, 50.
Committee: General C Horne, Col. B Gordon, Dr P Simpson,
Dr A McLean, Comdr. G Wingfield R N, Staff Paymaster
J K Mosse RN, Hon. Sec. W B Risk, Paymaster-in-Chief RN, St Elmo,
Weymouth.

'The course, of eighteen holes, is about four miles from Weymouth Station, close to Radipole village. By arrangement with the proprietor of the Belvedere Mews, players will be conveyed to the ground at 6d each in parties of four and upwards. There is a clubhouse on the ground where refreshments are provided. Visitors are admitted to play on payment of one shilling a day or five shillings a week. There is a separate course for ladies. There are several very sporting holes, and the course is about three and a half miles in circuit'.

Typical of the cricket pavilion style of early clubhouses. They were constantly being refurbished and enlarged, but being timber framed they were a fire hazard, and the cause of the loss of at least two Clubs' records

Yeovil and South Somerset Golf Club

This was the title first assumed by the Yeovil Golf Club at its inauguration on the 7th of November 1907. Its sponsors were four local businessmen who had arranged with the owner and tenant of Abbey Farm in Preston for permission to construct a 9-hole golf course.

The response to the Circular reproduced here was very good; 72 gentlemen and 30 ladies expressed an interest and a commitment to join the new club, and a total of £241.1s.0d was pledged to the 'Expenses Fund'.

At the meeting in the Town Hall, the Mayor, W M Cole, proposed the formation of a committee composed of the signatories to the letter, with Sir Spencer Ponsonby Fane GCB as President, which would make all the necessary arrangements for laying out a course and erecting a pavilion.

Three days later the committee met on the 'Links' to inspect the ground and to suggest a layout which would be discussed with a chosen professional golfer. J H Taylor and Rowland Jones 'golf professionals of note', were contacted. Taylor was unable to undertake the work, so Rowland Jones was engaged at a fee of £2.10s.0d (presumably for drawing a plan) plus expenses. Goldsmiths of Minehead were given the construction contract 'for laying out a 9-hole course on the Lower Heights at Preston', and a cheque for £1.10s.0d was drawn for the purpose (probably a first payment).

The committee engaged a Mr Tom Hawkins to 'do the Horse Rolling as required until a roller was purchased by the Club, at the rate of 12/-d per day for the man and two horses, the day counting from 7am to 3pm'.

Eighty applications were received for the post of Professional, and Robert Wilson of the Oban Golf Club and John Chambers of the Newcastle United Golf Club were shortlisted. Wilson accepted the job at a salary of £1 a week until the course was opened for play, when the amount would be reduced to 16/-d, with the usual privileges of selling clubs and balls, and coaching . . . the latter to be limited to the afternoons 'until otherwise arranged'. In the event the appointment lasted for only a year; Wilson left to join the West Wilts Club, and Charles Carter, from the London area, joined them and remained with the Club for forty-three years, during which time he became the Secretary of the West of England PGA.

The committee was empowered to spend £160 on a pavilion and its associated furnishings, and the Secretary was instructed to write to Boulton & Paul of Norwich for a quotation. However, a local company built the first clubhouse for a cost of £163 in January 1908, and fifteen ladies' lockers were added in the following month. They also decided to hire a 'portable house' at the cost of one shilling a week, presumably as a shelter for the workmen constructing the course.

In the first few weeks of the Club's formation the Secretary W Bradhurst was instructed to obtain copies of the rules of the Langport and the Dorchester golf clubs, and the President informed the meeting that he was very keen to arrange a working agreement with the Langport Golf Club, 'so that it might suffer as little as possible from the formation of the Yeovil Club'.

He wanted a joint membership agreement for their members who were resident in Yeovil and who might be inclined to leave the Langport Club; and for Langport members who might also wish to play on the new course.

This was agreed at the first AGM which was held in the Yeovil Town Hall on the 30th of January 1908. The Club also agreed to form a Ladies Committee; and the Green Committee approved Fridays as being the most convenient day for holding Ladies' competitions. In February 1913, at the sixth AGM, it was agreed to grant one guinea a year from Club funds to enable the lady members to join the LGU. The old Minutes also revealed an interesting concession, whereby the lady members asked for, and were 'allowed to appropriate one green on one afternoon during the last week of October, for a putting competition'.

The Club remained in Somerset at Abbey Farm until 1919, when they moved to the present site at Babylon Hill in Dorset.

YEOVIL,
30th October, 1907.

Dear Sir or Madam,

You may be aware that for some time past efforts have been made to obtain a Golf Course for the Yeovil district. We are glad to inform you that the project has at last materialised and obtained definite shape.

We have secured an Agreement with Mr. T. Hawkins, of Abbey Farm, Preston, permitting us to lay out a 9-hole Golf Course on a portion of his farm (by kind permission of Sir Spencer Ponsonby Fane, G.C.B.) The land has been inspected by Goldsmith, the Minehead Club's Professional, who has expressed the opinion that it is eminently suitable, and it is thought certain that the Course can be made ready for play early in the year.

You are invited to attend a Meeting, to be held at the Town Hall, Yeovil, on Thursday, 7th proximo, at 3.30 p.m., at which the Mayor of Yeovil will preside, when details of the Scheme will be laid before those present, and a Provisional Committee will be appointed for the purpose of carrying out the preliminary work and arranging for the formation of a Club.

No public advertisement of this Meeting is being made, and you are earnestly requested to make it known to any of your friends, with a view to securing their presence and co-operation.

To meet the preliminary expenses of laying out the Course, erecting a Pavilion, etc., it is hoped to obtain a sum of £250; of which amount the sums detailed overleaf have already been promised or received. As it is of the utmost importance that the Club should have a good start, it is hoped that you will kindly contribute towards this preliminary Fund. It is proposed that donors of £2 : 2 : 0 and upwards shall not be asked to pay any further entrance fees. Contributions will be received and acknowledged by Mr. W. Bradhurst, at Lloyds Bank, Ltd., Yeovil. In order that a fair idea may be obtained of the support that will be forthcoming, it will be deemed a favour if you will kindly fill up and return the enclosed slip to Mr. Bradhurst.

The scale of Entrance Fees proposed to be adopted is :—Gentlemen, £1 1s. 0d. Ladies, 10/6. Family (residents in same house), £2 2s. 0d. Sons of Members, under 21 years of age, 10/6.

The proposed Subscriptions are :—Gentlemen, £1 5s. 0d. per annum. Ladies, 15/- per annum. Sons or Daughters of Members, under 21 years of age, 10/6 per annum.

We are glad to announce that Sir Spencer C. B. Ponsonby Fane, G.C.B., has kindly consented to accept the Presidency of the proposed Club.

We are,
Yours faithfully,

A. NORMAN HAIG,
F. WHITMASH MAYO,
R. E. WELBY,
LIONEL WHITBY.

To M ....

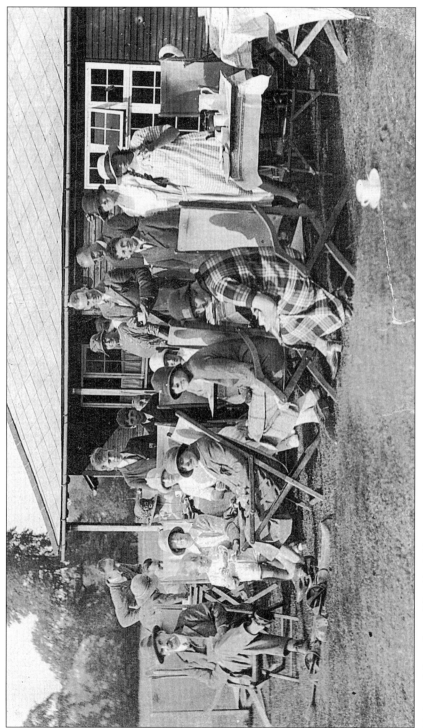

Ted Ray (left) in front of the old Clubhouse c1936

Opening of the 18-hole course in 1936
B Bradford, Lance Luffman, Abe Mitchell, James Braid, Wanda Morgan, Capt Roberts (Broadstone), Phyllis Wade, R Whitcombe, Charles Carter

Ferndown Golf Club

The development of this favoured golf club did not really begin until well after World War I, because, although the course had been constructed, and golf of a sort played on it, the war caused its closure before it had time to mature into reasonable playing condition.

A prospectus was issued by the first *Ferndown Golf Club Limited* offering founder membership to 125 investors, to buy 100 acres of land at Parley Common from Lord Wimborne. The 'Memorandum' reproduced here does not include a date, but it is reasonable to assume that it was published in 1912, because the embryo company had engaged Harold Hilton to lay out a golf course after a survey carried out by him in company with Willie Park and H S Colt.

The sketch which accompanied the document showed a lake, fed by two of four streams which traversed the boggy heathland. This was filled in when the course was constructed, but it would have been in the vicinity of the present fourteenth and fifteenth fairways.

Probably its final refurbishment prior to the new construction in 1938

Ferndown was a very small village at the time, and players would have to be persuaded to travel out from Bournemouth, so the creation of a road was fundamental to the success of the venture. However, the war put an end to both the road and the golf course, which reverted to its former boggy state, and the first company went into liquidation.

After the war a small group of members formed a new company with Sir Henry Webb as its Chairman, and they bought the land in 1920 for £12,500. They set out to restore Hilton's layout, but were forced through lack of funds to re-open the course prematurely for limited play by the members. The course was not in a fit condition and the premature opening could not have helped the situation, but at least the company did not allow green fees for a year. By that time a local journalist described the course as being in fairly good order and a daily green fee of 1/-d was being charged, but as there was no clubhouse, the company erected a shelter in which players could eat their own sandwiches.

H Hilton

Memorandum for Private circulation only.

FERNDOWN GOLF CLUB,
Ferndown, near Bournemouth.

Committee—

H. F. BESSEMER, Esq.,
Southcliffe, Bournemouth.

RAWDON V. MICHELL, Esq.,
Wainsford, Lymington.

Major L. C. ELWES, D.S.O.,
Longham House, Wimborne.

Capt. C. E. M. MORRISON,
Stornoway, Westcliffe Road, Bournemouth.

L. G. FISHER-ROWE, Esq.,
Park Cottage, Ringwood.

E. P. SUGDEN, Esq.,
Uplands, Wimborne.

The Rt. Hon. EARL MALMESBURY,
Heron Court, Christchurch.

T. E. WILLS-SANDFORD, Esq.,
Campden House, Burley.

18-Hole Golf Course on Parley Common.
An 18-hole Golf Course is to be constructed on a very fine piece of land on Parley Common, Ferndown, and a private Company is being registered called THE FERNDOWN GOLF CLUB, LIMITED, for the purpose of carrying into effect the necessary arrangements.

Accessibility of Golf Course.
Parley Common is situated five miles from the Square at Bournemouth, and a fine road is being constructed and is nearing completion, which will bring the Club House well within twenty minutes' motor run of the centre of Bournemouth, or ten minutes from the Tram Terminus at Moordown.

Motor Service.
It is intended to organise a Motor Service between Bournemouth and the Club for the convenience of Members and their friends.

Suitability of Land for Golf and Access to the Club.
The land, which extends to 100 acres or more, is beautifully undulating and eminently suitable for the purpose of Golf, and has been valued by a well-known firm of local Surveyors at the rate of £75 per acre, on the assumption that the approaches as shown coloured "red" on the enclosed plan be made so as to afford easy access from the main roads to the Course and Club House.

Purchase Price of Freehold.
The Freehold is being purchased by the Company for the sum—including the making of the approaches mentioned above—of £2,500 in cash and £2,500 in First Mortgage Debentures, being at the rate of about £50 per acre.

Nature of Soil. The soil is what is known as Bagshot sand, similar to that on which some of the finest courses are constructed.

Freehold. As the Freehold of the Course is being acquired no annual rental will be payable.

Reports from Messrs. H. H. Hilton, H. S. Colt and Willie Park. The land has been very favourably reported upon by Messrs. H. H. Hilton, H. S. Colt and Willie Park, of Musselburgh. The Course will be planned by and laid out under the supervision of Mr. H. H. Hilton, Open and Amateur ex-Champion, and Mr. A. T. W. McCaul will be responsible for the organisation of the Club.

Water for the Green, Club House, &c. Everything will be done to make the Course one of the finest in this Country. Water will be laid on to every green and a Club House will be erected containing all the conveniences which experience has shown to be essential to the comfort of Members and Visitors.

Committee. The gentlemen whose names are given at the head of this circular have consented to be the first Committee (with power to add to their number), and I am desired to invite you to become a Candidate for Membership subject to the conditions mentioned below.

Financial Liability. The Club will be Proprietary and Members will incur no financial liability whatever beyond the amount of their Annual Subscription, and Entrance Fee, if any.

Annual Subscription Gentlemen. The Annual Subscription for Original Members (Gentlemen) to the number of 100 will be £4 4s. without Entrance Fee, names being taken in priority of application.

Annual Subscription Ladies. The Annual Subscription for Original Members (Ladies) will be £3 3s. No Entrance Fee will be charged to the first 50.

Ladies and Full Membership. Ladies wishing to play on Saturdays, Sundays and Bank Holidays, may become full playing Members by paying the full Gentlemen's Subscription of £4 4s., provided they have a recognised handicap of 12 or under.

Restricted Members. Five-day Members with full privileges except the right to play on Saturdays, Sundays and Bank Holidays, will be elected at an Annual Subscription of £3 3s. without Entrance Fee for the first 100.

Your attention is also drawn to the fact that a certain number of **FOUNDERS' MEMBERSHIPS** limited to 125 will be available, particulars of which are as follows:—

FOUNDERS MEMBERSHIPS.

The Club will be the property of "The Ferndown Golf Club, Limited," who are prepared to issue to approved applicants one hundred and twenty-five First Mortgage Debentures of £100 each, amounting to £12,500, and forming part of an authorised issue of £15,000, bearing interest at the rate of 4 per cent. per annum payable annually and secured upon the Freehold Land comprising the Golf Course and the Club House and buildings, and carrying a Membership of the Club free of Annual Subscription. Such Debentures, together with their privileges, being transferable to Assignees approved by the Committee of the Club.

The Company will reserve the power at any time on giving six months notice to redeem the Debentures at par, but granting to the last holder of each Debenture a free Life Membership of the Club.

The Funds received from the issue of Debentures will be placed at the Wilts & Dorset Bank, Ringwood, in the name of Trustees to be nominated by the Committee, to be applied as follows:—

(1) Part payment of the Land £2,500
(2) Construction of Golf Course 6,000
(3) Erection and Furnishing of the Club House, Garage, and the provision of other necessary accommodation, Working Capital, &c., &c. 4,000
£12,500

The Debentures whilst ranking equally will be issued as follows:

PRESENT ISSUE, 75 Debentures at £100 each, and the later issues at such premium as may be decided upon.

A holder of more than one Debenture will be entitled to introduce one Visitor (lady or gentleman) for each additional Debenture to play without green fee.

Ladies will be eligible to take up Debentures and will be entitled to the privileges conferred by Founders' Membership whilst holding such Debentures.

Forms of application for Ordinary and Founders' Membership are enclosed.

The Reports of Messrs. H. H. Hilton, H. S. Colt and Willie Park, together with copies of the Trust Deed and Form of Debenture, may be inspected at the Offices of the Solicitors to the Company, Messrs. Jackson & Sons, Ringwood.

D. AITKEN,
Secretary (pro tem.).
The Bungalow, Dudsbury Avenue, Ferndown.

NOTE.—This form of Founders' Membership has been readily taken up, secured upon Leaseholds in many of the best known Clubs, and the Debentures usually go to a premium in a very short time. It is seldom, if ever, that the Promoters of a Club are able to offer the security of a Freehold Course in addition to the Club buildings, &c., as in this instance.

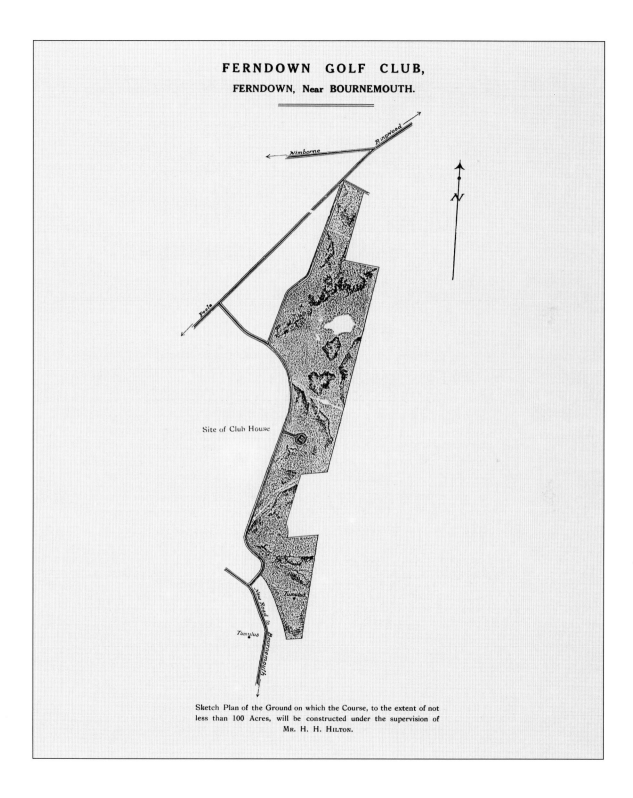

FERNDOWN GOLF CLUB,
FERNDOWN, Near BOURNEMOUTH.

Sketch Plan of the Ground on which the Course, to the extent of not less than 100 Acres, will be constructed under the supervision of Mr. H. H. Hilton.

> **D. Stewart & Son,**
> FERNDOWN NURSERIES,
> DORSET, ... 191..
>
> Construction of Golf Course on Parley Common
> Approximate Statement of Cost
>
> (1) Grassing Greens & Tees
>   approximate estimated area
>   of 21,800 sq yards @ 1½d per yd.   136. 5. 0
>
> (2) Grassing Fairways
>   approximate estimated area
>   of 210,800 sq yds @ ½d per sq yd. 437.10. 0
>
> (3) Earthwork. 231,800 sq yds. 2¼d
>   per sq yd.   2,173. 2. 6
>
> (4) Estimated Cost of 1,500 tons of manure,
>   soot, lime, bone fertilisers,   1,350. 0. 0
>   & haulage, transit &c.
>   Estimated cost of loam.   150. 0. 0
>   haulage of loam   300. 0. 0
>   £4546.17. 6

Golfers without their own transport were advised to 'take one of the green services of buses leaving Bournemouth at 9.30 and 12.30 and returning from Ferndown at 1.45 and 4.45'. Visitors were advised to alight at the top of Victoria Road and walk the 500 yards down "Colonel Burroughs Road" to the centre of the course where there was a choice of six starting tees.

A formal opening was arranged for May 21st 1921, with an exhibition match between George Duncan and Abe Mitchell, but this had to be cancelled because the McVitie and Price Tournament, in which the two were competing, had to be extended. In the event, Harry Vardon and Ted Ray opened the course in October of that year with a four-ball exhibition match against Harold Hilton and C V L Hooman the West of England Champion... which the amateurs won.

Reporting on the match, the *Daily Telegraph* journalist enthused about the 'heathery space', and 'the pure moorland air, crisp and exquisitely perfumed', but gave very little indication of the state of the course. There were very few trees on the course at that time, and it was possible to see the Isle of Wight from the clubhouse.

G S Brown, author of *First Steps in Golf* in a letter to the *Bournemouth Daily Echo,* enjoyed his first visit to the course. His description, and comparisons with famous Scottish courses were rather fanciful; but he was not alone in describing Ferndown as 'one of the finest inland courses outside the London district . . . and a second Sunningdale'. However, this hyperbole should be judged against the fact that the course was suffering from the effects of a prolonged drought . . . and neither Ray nor Vardon broke 76 in their match, on a course measuring 6,300 yards (bogey 80).

Vernon Weldon, who features elsewhere in records of Dorset golf, set a course record of 76 in December 1922, beating Ted Ray's record by two shots. The first recorded hole-in-one was achieved by F Birkett, with a wood at the 166 yard "Gibbett" hole, which was then adjacent to the clubhouse. Three years later, with the course in much better condition, but in a stiff south-east wind, the Club professional T E Steadman cut the record to 67, playing with Wren of Crichel Park and Harry Dean of Brokenhurst.

Steadman was appointed in 1922 and served the Club for four years, and was followed by J Randall, who moved from the Ashley Wood Club in 1926.

Access to the club was not easy; the lifeline road from Ensbury had been completed, but it was not in very good condition and was not adopted by the Council until 1925. Club membership had not reached 200, and the income in 1924 was only about £2,000, quite inadequate for the development of a new golf course, so in spite of injections of large sums of money by Sir Henry Webb and others, the company failed.

Undaunted by this further setback a small group of members, this time still including the indefatigable Sir Henry, but not under his Chairmanship, formed the third *Ferndown Golf Club Ltd.* and bought the course. This time, in spite of the serious national economic depression, they either found the correct formula, or were favoured by events, because their efforts were successful; the club prospered, and has continued to do so to this day.

A new 9-hole course to relieve the pressure on the Old Course, was designed by J Hamilton Stutt and opened in 1971. This allowed the changes to be

7th & 8th fairways at the time of opening ceremony 1921

made to the Old Course following the sale of land beyond what is now the fifteenth green, and which resulted in the creation of two new holes. The magnificent clubhouse, which was extended in 1989 at a cost of £250,000 stands on the same commanding site as the old building shown in the illustration, but in those early days it consisted of five Army huts, which were extended and modified over the years until, in 1936 it was replaced by the first permanent building. Another very obvious difference is the view . . . when it was opened there were very few trees on the course and it was possible to see the whole of the course from the clubhouse.

Opening of the Ferndown course in 1921. Sir Henry Webb is seated third from left

This clubhouse replaced the original wooden building and remained largely unaltered until the major extensions in 1989

The Bournemouth courses

When the county boundaries were changed in 1974, the effect was not only to practically double the population, but it bequeathed to Dorset Meyrick Park, England's first municipal golf course, and Queens Park, undoubtedly the best and most famous municipal course in the country.

Meyrick Park was originally a turbary allotment, which meant that local residents had the right to cut turves for fuel, but towards the end of the nineteenth century this practice had largely died out, and the local authority was persuaded to secure the land as a public open space.

'Lord of the Manor' Sir George Elliott Meyrick Tapps-Gervis-Meyrick, held the freehold, and in 1894 he presented 118 acres of the land to the Corporation, and stipulated that sixty acres should be set aside for golf.

A contemporary journalist described the land as a mass of knee-high whins and heather, and considered it impossible to contemplate the creation of a greensward suitable for golf. However, such was the determination to bring golf to the town, that one prominent member of the Council is reputed to have stated that 'even if the land had to be planed and French polished, the Corporation was determined to succeed in providing a park and a golf ground'.

In the event the cost of laying out the course was nearly £2,000, comprising a "Long Course" measuring 4,500 yards, and a "Ladies Course" which measured a mere 700 yards... in reality nothing but a pitch and putt course.

The concept was described by its architect Tom Dunn as the most difficult design problem he had ever encountered. By way of contrast he declared Broadstone, which he built three years later, to have been his finest creation... 'because he was not stinted for money'.

The lodge is now used for staff accommodation, but was originally a pavilion and cafe

Despite the difficult conditions and the financial restrictions, Dunn completed the construction of the course within the stipulated time . . . and almost within the budget. The new park and its golf course, named after its principal benefactor, were opened in 1894, with great pomp and ceremony, reflecting the affluence of this elegant and fashionable watering place, and of course, it was also a fitting celebration of the opening of the first municipal golf course to be built outside Scotland.

The cost and the physical difficulties involved in the construction of the park and the course were acknowledged to have been considerable, so the decision to create such a unique municipal facility reflects great credit and foresight on the part of the Corporation, especially if one considers the tremendous social gap which existed in those days between members of golf clubs and the vast majority of the local inhabitants; although it has to be remembered that the stated objective was to attract favoured visitors to the town . . . there were no working class golfers in England in those days!

The description of the colourful opening ceremonies, written by a knowledgable reporter from the *Golf* journal, makes nostalgic reading, if only because of the amusing distractions caused by overdressed spectators with their dogs which are in such marked contrast to the rigid marshalling of the many thousands of spectators who regularly flock to today's golf competitions.

The old water tower (now a listed building), which supplied water for the golf course, bowling green, cricket and football pitches. It was the first time ferro-concrete was used in such a construction. Steps were fitted and it was a popular public viewpoint for many years

Opening of the Bournemouth Corporation Golf Links

'Until last week this southern seaside resort, one of the finest recruiting grounds for invalids anywhere, laboured under the serious disadvantage of not possessing a Golf course near the town for the recreation of its many visitors. That reproach has now been removed; and Bournemouth is now in possession of one of the most picturesque greens that can be found anywhere. When one is told of the condition of the ground a year ago, and compares its description with its actual state today, it is impossible to withhold a hearty tribute of admiration for the Corporation for the public spirited policy they have inaugurated. The Meyrick Park aforetime was a howling wilderness of heather and whin, of absolutely no utility or benefit to the town, and certainly not a place wherein the citizens could recreate themselves with playing popular games. Today the eyesore has been removed. In place of heather and whin we have a clean peep of the "heichs and howes" of the rolling land, interspersed with bright green putting greens and teeing grounds, and broken up here and there by mountainous ranges of bunkers; while hundreds of the population were to be seen following eagerly in the wake of players and viewing with some wonderment the ease with which the Champion or Mr Horace Hutchinson can pick up a ball with the iron, and send it in graceful parabola to the flag.

'Actuated solely by their interest for the public good, and seeing how essential a Golf course is to the increasing prosperity of the town, the members of the Corporation have done the right thing in the right way; and each and all of them, from the Mayor downwards, deserve the hearty support and gratitude of the citizens they represent.

'The opening ceremony was performed on Wednesday November 28th. The land was formerly what is known as Poor's Common, over which certain holders had rights to cut turf. The park itself is probably worth about £100,000, and sixteen acres of the land was sold for building purposes by the Corporation. The power of sale the town has acquired by Act of Parliament, and the money goes to the development of the park. The extensive work of laying out the park, building a commodious pavilion and the settling of preliminary matters (£520 to the owners of turf rights; £700 to the cost of the special Act of Parliament etc.), has involved an expenditure of £12,000. Of this amount £9,000 is covered by the sale of the building land, leaving £3,000 to be provided by the ratepayers. With sixty acres of Golf links and about ten acres for cricket, football, bowling, etc. separated from the links by a well made road that promises in time to become a veritable "Rotten Row", the heart of the most ardent athletic inhabitant and visitor should be cheered and sustained.

Bournemouth & Meyrick Park Clubhouse

'It is true that the course is not a long one, not one fitted perhaps, to suit the play of high class amateurs or professionals, for its entire length of eighteen holes reaches to two and a quarter miles. But Tom Dunn has placed the hazards with such care and discrimination, that while the carries are not long off the tees, they are sufficiently arduous for the moderate driver, the beginner, youths and ladies, who in all probability will often desert their own course for a round on the long one. It is essentially a green however on which a player is bound to improve his iron play, for the putting greens are so placed, and the hazards guarding them so arranged, that sure and accurate lofting is the only means whereby a creditable score may be attained. The long course throughout is one hundred yards wide, and has natural and picturesque borders of heather and furze.

'Of all the links laid out by Tom Dunn, none reflects more credit on his knowledge and skill, looking at the difficult character of the work which

BOROUGH OF BOURNEMOUTH.

MEYRICK PARK GOLF LINKS.

Amateur Competition. Medal Play.

The Summer Meeting, under the auspices of the Corporation, will take place on 18th, 19th, and 20th June, 1895, when several valuable prizes, open to members of all Golf Clubs, will be competed for as follows :—

Gentlemen's Competitions.

TUESDAY, 18th JUNE.

ONE ROUND OF 18 HOLES.

First Prize, a handsome Silver Challenge Cup, presented by the Mayor, Merton Russell Cotes, Esq., F.R.G.S., for scratch play only. The winner to retain the cup for one year, and receive a prize, value £10, which he will retain.

1st Handicap Prize … …	… value	£10
2nd ditto … …	… ,,	£5
3rd ditto … …	… ,,	£3

One score is sufficient for scratch and handicap prizes.

WEDNESDAY, 19th JUNE.

1st Handicap Prize …. …	… value	£10
2nd ditto … …	… ,,	£5
3rd ditto … …	… ,,	£3

Entrance Fee for each Handicap, 5/-.

There will be a ballot for partners and the order of start, which will be posted in the Corporation Pavilion the day previous to the Competition.

Ladies' Competition on Ladies' Links.

EIGHTEEN HOLES.

THURSDAY, 20th JUNE.

Open to members of all Golf Clubs. First prize, value £5, for scratch play only.

1st Handicap Prize … …	,, £5	0	0
2nd ditto … …	,, £2	10	0
3rd ditto … …	,, £1	10	0

One score is sufficient for scratch and handicap prizes.

No Entrance Fee.

Players may choose their own Partners.

had to be undertaken. The cost of making the links amounts to £2,000.

'The park was formally opened by Lady Meyrick, who was received at the Wimborne Road entrance by the Mayor and Corporation. A ribbon stretched across the entrance was then severed and a procession was formed and, led by Mrs Meyrick, proceeded through the park to the Corporation Pavilion where an address was engrossed on vellum and had an ornamental border embodying the arms of the Meyrick family, with the motto *Be Just and Fear Not* in Welsh.

'In the afternoon a reception was held at the Royal Bath Hotel, the residence of the Mayor, when the silver challenge cup, the gift of the Mayor, was handed over to the Corporation, to be played for annually. In the evening the public gardens were illuminated and a special concert was given in the Winter Gardens by the combined bands of the Grenadier Guards and the Corporation.

'In the afternoon of the following day the new course had its genuine baptism with a match between Horace Hutchinson and J H Taylor. The crowd was large and it was by no means an easy task to keep the perfervid youth of Bournemouth from encroaching on the players. The canine population had evidently made the links their rendezvous for the day, and had the proverbial "intelligent foreigner" been a witness... taking note at the same time of the number of dogs, he might reasonably have confounded the serious Royal and Ancient game with a coursing match. The writer, who was umpire at the match, counted eighteen dogs on or near the putting green at one point. The animals were of every variety of species, from the greyhound to the douce collie and inquisitive fox terrier. Some ladies made a valiant attempt to hold their pets with a leash made from a pocket handkerchief, but were unable to hinder the dogs from a combined helter-skelter after Mr Hutchinson's ball when he was manfully trying to get the upper hand of the Champion. The town was *en fete* and so were the dogs. Usually the canine disposition when slipped from its collar is to search for a variety of amusement... but on this day there was evidently a unanimous agreement to share the fun by coursing the Golf ball. They crouched and lay in wait at the tee for both balls being sent on their mission, and not infrequently, just as the club was poised in mid-air did the frisky, gambolling charge begin, in and out between the players' legs amid a chorus of restraining yells from onlookers, caddies, vigilant policemen, and sedate Corporation officials. Verily it was a nerve-trying ordeal for both players, but they were equal to it. Taylor turned homeward 3 up, and as all the holes were halved, finished the match by 3 and 2 to play.

'At the close of the match the Mayor and Mayoress presented a purse of £6 to Mr Taylor and one of £3 to Dunn; and Messrs Hutchinson, Acklom and Haviland received a medal bearing the Corporation's arms in acknowledgement of the part they took in today's interesting proceedings'.

The charge to the public to play on the course was 6d a round, and a licensed caddie cost 1/-d. Quite a number of local residents felt sufficiently

Meyrick Park

Schedule of Duties of Greenkeeper.

To have the general superintendence and control of the Golf Courses and the Corporation Pavilion under the Borough Surveyor.

To be responsible for keeping the Golf Courses, greens and putting grounds in good order and condition, the necessary labour and implements being provided by the Corporation.

To maintain order amongst those frequenting the Golf Courses and see the By-Laws and Regulations are duly observed.

To superintend under the Borough Surveyor the keeping of the Cricket and Football ground in order and any parts of the Park which may be set apart for Archery bowls or other games.

For such services he shall be paid a Salary at the rate of Thirty shillings a week.

He is to be at liberty to teach Golf (by himself or Assistants) on the Golf Courses, provided such does not interfere with any of the above duties.

He is to be at liberty to carry on the business of Club Maker and Repairer and Vendor of Golf requisites in such place as may be provided by the Corporation.

He is at liberty to undertake engagements for advising as to, and superintending the laying out of Golf Courses elsewhere Provided that he is not absent without leave for more than two days in any week, and that he provides an approved substitute to undertake his duties during such absence.

The Engagement is determinable by a months notice on either side.

He shall commence his duties on Monday 5th November 1894.

I accept the appointment of Green Keeper to the Borough of Bournemouth on the above terms.

Dated 15th October 1894.

Thomas Dunn

strongly about the charge to write to the editor of the *Bournemouth Echo* to complain that in Scotland the charge for a round on the municipal links was only 3d and there was no justification for charging double on the first English municipal course.

It was the fashion in those early days for gentlemen golfers to wear scarlet jackets, originally to warn perambulating members of the public of the danger of flying golf balls, but they eventually became a status symbol, denoting members of the committee, or differentiating the calibre of the players; with the low handicap players sporting silver buttons, and others mere brass. They remained in vogue in many of the older clubs, including Meyrick Park and Queens Park, up to about 1908.

Many changes have been made to the course since that grand opening in 1894. The Earl of Leven & Melville donated an additional forty acres of land, and H S Colt was engaged to reconstruct the course, which the Earl inaugurated in 1925. Presumably the ladies course was subsumed in this comprehensive re-design because a description of the revised course in a booklet dated 1932 states that only two of the original greens survived. Colt's revised course increased the length to 6,000 yards, slightly longer than the present-day course which measures 5,663 yards.

This amalgamation of the two courses, in addition to creating a better overall test of golf, also relieved the ladies of the indignity of having to ask

The original Meyrick Park Clubhouse

BOURNEMOUTH CORPORATION GOLF LINKS.

Regulations for Starting.

1. Any party not ready to start immediately when its number is called, loses his turn, and must wait for the first vacancy.

2. Players coming on the ground without a number shall have their names taken down by the Starter, and vacancies shall be allotted to them in the order of their arrival at the tee.

3. In the event of unpropitious weather, or other accidental circumstances, rendering it impossible to adhere to the time as entered on the list, the Starter is empowered to dispatch matches in rotation by their numbers only, and the regulations as to time will be cancelled.

4. Any dispute which may arise must be left to the decision of the Starter.

5. A player without an opponent or who is receiving instruction cannot have a number allotted to him, nor can he be recognised as having any standing on the Green.

6. When no Starter is employed parties will start in the order of their arrival at the tee.

Application Cards can be had from the Starter, and are also to be found in the Club Houses, and at the Ticket Office at the first Tee.

Albert Davis

permission to play on the "Long" course, and in addition to having their own day for competitions, they were accorded equal status when booking for friendly games. A far cry indeed from those earlier days as this extract from the Council Minutes illustrates. In 1904 the committee of the Bournemouth and Meyrick Club asked permission from the Corporation to consider an alteration to the Rules whereby *Ladies would be permitted to play on the course, except on Wednesday afternoons and bank holidays, on the express condition that they will at all times and under all conditions allow gentlemen players to pass them on the course without being requested to do so.* Unfortunately the Council's decision was not recorded!

The most noticeable change to the overall impression of the course when compared to the year of its construction is the tree cover. When the park was opened there was scarcely a tree on the course, and a row of small firs was planted to separate the ladies course from the "Long" course.

Two Clubs established themselves at Meyrick Park; the oldest, Bournemouth & Meyrick Park was formed in 1890, but prior to the opening of the park, they played on a nine-hole course in Brockenhurst, on land belonging to the Forestry Commission, and it was then known as *The Brockenhurst & District Golf Club*. When Meyrick Park opened in 1890 the Bournemouth Club absorbed the Brockenhurst Club, but continued to play in the New Forest until 1894, when it decided to establish itself at Meyrick Park.

The second evolved from a Club founded in 1894 by a few enthusiastic golfers, including Col E W Rebbeck, J T Cutler, J E Cooper-Dean, G Bone, and Dr N Macgillycuddy. Sir George Meyrick was the first President, and F W Brewster the first Captain of the Club. It was called the Meyrick Park Golf Club, but when Queens Park opened in 1905 the members formed a company and established themselves in a very fine clubhouse adjacent to the first tee of the new course and re-named the club the Meyrick & Queens Park Golf Club. Its members played on both courses and retained its small clubhouse in Meyrick Park and this was subsequently enlarged to include rooms for a ladies club.

In 1934 the club reverted to its old title and returned to Meyrick Park.

A splinter group broke away from the main club in 1940 and formed the Meyrick Park Golf Club, but as they had no clubhouse of their own, they were allowed the use of a room in the Lodge, which was built as a pavilion when the park was created, but which was being used as a cafe.

After the war, the Council allowed the club to use the original Meyrick Park clubhouse, which had been taken over during the war to house one of the Auxiliary Services, and this lasted until 1987, when the two clubs decided to merge so that they would be better able to negotiate with the private developers following the Council's decision to offer a 99-year lease and management agreement for the golf course in return for substantial capital investment in new facilities, including a replacement public pavilion and infrastructure works.

Tom Dunn, the designer and the first professional of the original course, resigned in 1899 and there was no immediate successor, but in 1901 H L Curtis, the Broadstone professional was appointed... *and with the assistance of his clubmakers and other staff, he operated the Broadstone, Meyrick, and Queens Park courses until his death in 1917.* (According to Harry Dean, when he was one of the Assistants at Broadstone, and who later became a professional at a number of local golf courses, Curtis also ran the Swanage Club at the same time).

From the time of his death until Ernest Whitcombe's appointment in 1925, Curtis' widow operated the two municipal courses, and she then concentrated upon Queens Park, until her son Don took over.

Whitcombe spent thirty-six years at Meyrick and was succeeded by John Stirling, who became very well-known for his teaching abilities, and who stayed for twenty years before moving to Meon Valley. He was followed by John Sharkey, who now owns the Bulbery Woods and the Sturminster Marshall golf courses.

The 14th of September 1904 issue of the *Bournemouth Graphic,* reprinted an article written for the *Yorkshire Daily Observer* by *Taxameter,* 'one of the best writers on golf', who had visited Bournemouth as a delegate to a conference of journalists. It illustrates the impression the municipal golf courses had made upon the golfing public; and the success of the courses, (seemingly at no expense to the ratepayers) undoubtedly influenced other authorities to follow the lead given by the Bournemouth Corporation.

Golf in Bournemouth and District

'Ever since I first read, ten years ago, of the opening of a municipal golf course at Bournemouth, I have desired to make close acquaintance with it. In the meantime I have frequently heard of it and read about it, but had never been on the spot. A little more than a week ago however, my desire was fulfilled... I was extremely pleased with my experience there and would be glad to go back again... With the course itself I was well pleased... The Meyrick Park course is a striking example of what can be done by a little management and energy. It was largely through the foresight and pluck of Alderman A Davis... that the Bournemouth Corporation entered upon what must then have appeared a very novel scheme, namely that of running a municipal golf course.

'A large capital expenditure was sunk in the scheme, for the Meyrick Park was not the most suitable place for a golfing green in its natural state. Much digging and delving, uprooting and planting had to be done, and all this of course, meant expense. With the assistance of the late Tom Dunn..., the natural features of the park were all taken advantage of to the greatest possible extent.

'If the course lacks length, it loses little in sport or delightfulness of surroundings. On a fine day... and fine days are the rule at Bournemouth and not the exception... it is a pleasure to be alive and golfing at Meyrick Park...

'... Further evidence of the foresight and enterprise of Bournemouth Corporation is seen as we flog our little white ball across a ravine towards the third green perched on the opposite hillside. In the great expanse of greensward below us on the right, many teams of cricketers are busy with bat and ball... and devotees of "the woods" are trundling their spherical toys across the bowling green close at hand...

'So well pleased are the Corporation with the experience gained in connection with the Meyrick Park that they have laid out another public course in the Queens Park. This is not quite so centrally situated, but it will still be easy of access. Acting on good advice they have laid this course out on much larger lines, and so satisfied are they of the value of municipal golf that they are erecting a clubhouse of large dimensions at a cost of £3,000. The laying out of the new links has been equally costly, but there is no doubt that the authorities are wise in launching out freely in this direction... The situation here is also very delightful, and the surroundings are of the most pleasant character. The turf is well suited to the game, and not only will greater length be afforded, but testing and sporting hazards of various kinds will be met with on the round. Along much of the journey, the player will find the fairway bounded by stretches of heather, the purple bloom of which is fair to look upon, but whose roots are terribly troublesome to the golfer whose ball has strayed into the midst'.

It has not been possible to discover exactly why the Bournemouth Council decided to build a second golf course only nine years after the opening of the Meyrick Park course, but a contemporary journal recorded that *so popular was the game that its provision makes no demands upon the Rates.*

However, a study of the Council Minutes and of the local newspapers did not reveal a cogent reason, or even if any discussions had taken place on the desirability of building a second course. *The Bournemouth Daily Echo* as it was then called, carried very little information on the subject in its 1900-04 editions beyond the extracts from Council meetings. There was no editorial comment, and therefore no public debate.

Meyrick Park was a success, but not spectacularly so; there had been criticism from visiting golfers that the course was short, but it was generally accepted that it was an enjoyable, and in the current jargon a "sporting" course. The receipts were satisfactory, and its effect upon tourism was also satisfactory, but not sufficiently impressive to warrant the expenditure of many thousands of pounds to build another one.

It was pretty obvious however that golf had become a very popular pastime for many Bournemouth residents. The 1903 editions of the *Bournemouth Graphic* carried accounts of continuing complaints from golfers being forced to wait *for their drives off for an unconscionable time owing to the unusually large number of players,* and this was followed in April of that year by an expression of relief from a resident in the Eastern part of the town, who was *pleased to learn that the Corporation have decided to lay out a new golf course three and three-quarter miles in length on picturesque moorland ground in Queens Park.* So there was an undoubted public demand, but it is doubtful if this alone would have justified the expenditure of such a large sum of public money.

However, and for whatever reason, on February the 12th 1903, the Council Surveyor was instructed to consult J H Taylor and to report with a plan for laying out a links on Queens Park.

Taylor duly reported back on the 30th of March, and (predictably) he found the ground 'eminently suitable', and promised the 'very finest links' etc. But so many of these reports were written in such similar vein that it is difficult to suppress the cynical observation that they could all have been written by the same author, without even a sight of the grounds.

Taylor's letter is reproduced here, together with the Council's rider to add a "Rotten Row".

In September the Parks and Pleasure Grounds Committee inspected the site and subsequently recommended to the full Council that the course should be constructed ... within an estimated budget of £3,000. Using terminology not usually associated with Council officials, one of the committee members 'strongly urged the Council of the absolute necessity for a golf links'.

In the event the proposals were accepted and Taylor was commissioned to design the new course. Naturally the budget was exceeded, but the additional cost of the associated facilities more than doubled the estimates. The Pavilion cost £3,299, a Caddies Shelter £150, a Stable and Mess-House £414, and with the lake at the lower end of the park, together with the provision of water services for the course, the total extra costs added up to £4,750.

H L Curtis, who was the professional at Broadstone, was appointed to run both the Queens Park and Meyrick courses following the departure of Tom Dunn and he was allowed the use of a room in the pavilion on payment of fifty guineas a year.

The course was officially opened on the 25th of October 1905 with an exhibition match between J H Taylor, Harry Vardon, James Braid, and Alex Herd. They played two singles; Vardon against Braid, and Taylor against Herd. The matches were followed by over one thousand spectators, and ended with Braid carding 74, Vardon and Taylor 75 and Herd 77 ... against a Bogey of 82.

The new course was much longer than its counterpart, and a much more severe test of golf. It quickly eclipsed Meyrick and it attracted many important tournaments, including the *Daily Mail,* (1939) the *Sumrie* (1974/75/76), the *Martini* (1969), and the *Penfold* (1951/71/74/75/76), all very famous in their day. It also succeeded in attracting the country's finest golfers ... and the crowds which followed them ... so, although the Council was unable to charge an entrance fee, because it was still a public park, the influx of so many people must have had a beneficial effect upon the local economy and it would also have enhanced Bournemouth's reputation as a holiday centre, thereby achieving the original objective of the Council's innovative decision.

"Queens" quickly established itself as the finest municipal golf course in England, and although it is not as difficult today as it was before the 'Wessex

Way' took its toll, it is still the more popular of the two courses and it continues to attract many thousands of visitors every year.

The photograph shows the very fine municipal pavilion, which was for many years a dominant feature of the Eastern approaches to the town, until it was demolished in 1966 to make way for the construction of the 'Wessex Way'.

In the background is the clubhouse of the Meyrick & Queens Park Golf Club Ltd. which stood in two acres of ground, with facilities for tennis, croquet, bowling, and putting. This was a prestigious private club reminiscent of the original golf clubs described in the previous chapter, which played over municipal links in the formative years of the game.

The general view shows the position of the Queens Park golf pavilion before it was demolished to make way for 'Wessex Way'. To the right is the Clubhouse of the Bournemouth & Meyrick G C. Below is a close-up of the Queens Park pavilion

At the outset, before the golfing explosion opened up the game to a wider cross section of the public, the members of the private club took precedence in the choice of starting times, but as the pressures built up its members had to accept a growing equality with the 'public' players. The authoritative nature of the club diminished after the war and in 1946 the assets of the club were transferred to trustees.

The construction of the road resulted in the loss of a great deal of land, including the eighteenth green which featured in so many photographs of the famous national competitions held on the course regularly for many years, and it resulted in a drastic revision of the layout of the course, which was entrusted to the then "Director of Golf" and the Council groundstaff.

The private clubhouse was also torn down when the new road was built and in 1972 it was replaced by a modern glazed sports complex, but the club had lost its historic association with the golf course. Many of the members transferred to the Boscombe Club, which was more conveniently situated in the newly constructed municipal clubhouse adjacent to the first tee in the revised course layout. New sports facilities were introduced into the private clubhouse in an effort to recover its old prominence, but the "golf club" atmosphere had disappeared and could not be recaptured and it was finally sold in 1989.

PARKS AND PLEASURE GROUNDS COMMITTEE, 16th April, 1903.

21.—Golf at Queen's Park.

The following report was read:—

REPORT ON THE SUITABILITY OF THE GROUND AT QUEEN'S PARK, BOURNEMOUTH, FOR THE MAKING OF A GOLF COURSE.

I have had an opportunity, in company with Alderman Davis, of inspecting the ground at Queen's Park, where it is proposed to make an additional course for Bournemouth, and I herewith beg to offer my opinion of the same.

The ground, I find, is most eminently adapted for the formation of an 18 hole course of full length; in fact, it is possible to make a course there as long as can be wished, as there is ample room and to spare.

The ground itself, in its natural formation, lends itself most readily to the making of a course of great possibilities, being very undulating in character; in fact, the deep ravines that intersect the ground, add greatly to its suitability as a site for links, and will also in effect make it of a very sporting nature.

Another great advantage that the ground has in its favour is the fact that the soil is of a very porous nature, and, in places, I found that it was composed of pure sand, which, from a purely golfing point of view, is excellent, besides being very dry even in the wettest season, and is the kind of soil that lends itself to the growth of the very finest turf for golfing purposes.

It would perhaps be necessary to remove some of the trees that are at present rather thickly scattered over a certain portion of the ground, but a lot of them could be utilised in making excellent hazards, but this is a mere detail that can be arranged when the course is properly laid out, and this also applies to the heather that at present covers the ground.

In conclusion, I cannot be too emphatic in my opinion when I say that the ground you have at your disposal in Queen's Park is capable of being made into one of the very finest links that ever I saw. I would strongly urge the Corporation of Bournemouth to lose no time in putting the scheme in hand, as, when finished, it will lift Bournemouth into the very front rank of golfing centres in the South of England.

J. H. TAYLOR,
30th March, 1903.   Champion Golfer, 1894-5 and 1900.

Recommended—That the Surveyor, in consultation with Mr. Taylor, prepare plans of links at this Park, and submit same with estimates, the plan to provide for a Rotton Row.

A new municipal clubhouse and restaurant was built in 1968 alongside the new first tee, which used to be the fourth in the original layout. It is in no way comparable to the luxurious nineteenth century building, but it provides facilities for the Club and for the present-day 'pay and play' golfer. In 1991 the Boscombe men's and the Artisans Clubs amalgamated to become the Queens Park (Bournemouth) Golf Club, but the Ladies decided to retain their old title of the Boscombe Ladies Golf Club.

Fundamental changes in the administration of the two municipal courses were announced towards the end of 1992. At Meyrick Park a private hotels and leisure company was granted a 99-year licence for the improvement and management of the course, and a similar lease for the new buildings which they would have to provide, including clubhouse facilities to replace the municipal clubhouse which is in urgent need of renewal. Under the new arrangements a modern clubhouse facility will be built on the site of the present golf and squash pavilion, with the squash court roof forming a terrace overlooking the first fairway.

Glimpse of a less frenetic era. Queens Park golf course c1905

Bournemouth and Meyrick Park Golf Club is considering relocating to the new facility, and if they do, their current clubhouse will be demolished and the land returned to public open space.

At Queens Park, with its modern pavilion facilities, the Council wanted to continue to manage the golf course with its own staff, but under the terms of the Local Government Act of 1988, it was obliged to seek competitive tenders for the provision of the service for at least four, and a maximum of six years. The Council decided upon a six-year contract, and was successful in retaining the work against external competition.

John Broughton (left) and Bruce Brewer made history as the first to tee-off when the Council sanctioned Sunday play at Meyrick Park in December 1961. Queens Park followed some years later

Brownsea Island

The van Raalte family, who owned the island from 1901 to 1928 commissioned Charlie Major, a professional golfer to lay out a 9-hole golf course, and in the book *Brownsea Islander,* published by the Poole Historical Trust it is described as *in the swelling grounds of the castle where Florence* (Mrs van Raalte) *could often be seen practising her shots. They employed Charlie Major, a professional golfer, as their coach, and he stayed on as groundsman after his return from the first world war.* The book also records that the estate workers were expected to play in the band, to act as beaters for the shoots, and as caddies on the course.

The island was sold to Sir Arthur Wheeler in 1928, and a copy of the sale particulars in the Poole Reference Library contains the following description: . . . *passing at once to the west side of the castle the visitor sees before him a long stretch of lawn, flanked on the right by a noble herbaceous border, one of the horticultural glories of Brownsea, and on the left by fine trees. Beyond is rising land on which a nine hole golf course was laid out some years ago.*

A pamphlet in the library describes the course as covering several miles, with play through some fields and woods back to the start near the castle.

There are no signs of a golf course now, but it can reasonably be assumed that the grassy area between the castle and the church, part of which is now used as a open air theatre, must have formed the parkland section of it, but the route through the trees cannot be traced.

Naples Bay Golf Club

One early but untypical casualty was the course built on the Overcombe Cliffs at Weymouth in 1934 by a Mr Field-Moser who was so captivated by the views of the bay and the distant Purbecks that he decided to settle in Weymouth and build a dream golf course. He paid five thousands pounds for fourteen acres of land and engaged H S Colt, the lawyer turned golf course architect, to design a 9-hole course. In the language common to all golf course designers, Colt described the land as 'the finest site for a seaside course that I have ever seen. The situation, with outstanding views in all directions, is perfect, and the fall of the land ideal'.

He was set a very tight schedule; work began in October and the completion target was the following Easter! The layout included holes varying from about 100 to 150 yards, with 'tricky hazards of mounds and turf and parts of the course rising to about 150 feet above sea level'.

A white stone building, with sliding glass windows, a restaurant, dormy accommodation, and clubhouse facilities were included in the ambitious scheme, in addition to an adjoining 18-hole putting course and three tennis courts.

Field-Moser planned to install an innovative film machine which took action films of the golfer, then played them back for analysis, and he intended to employ a photographer to work on the course as well as providing facilities for using private bathing huts on the beach. Not many modern clubs can offer this range of facilities!

The new club, now called The Naples Bay Golf Club, was officially opened in June 1935 with an exhibition match between Don Curtis the Queens Park professional and Harry Dean, the resident professional, following which the large gathering of guests were invited into the new clubhouse for tea and dancing.

A local newspaper reporter claimed that 'there were no two golf shots alike, which the low handicapper will appreciate. One drive is across the cliff. There is a perfect reproduction in miniature of a full length 18-hole course, and only a mashie and a putter is required'.

The course was open to the public for a fee of sixpence, inclusive of a golf card, clubs and balls. The annual subscription for playing members was two guineas, and no entrance fee was charged to the first 200 members.

Such extravagance could only have but one corollary, and Field-Moser's dream turned into nightmare bankruptcy within a year. However, the club did manage to struggle on for a short while as the 1939 Golfers Handbook testifies:-

Overcombe Golf Club: mem. 49. Sec. A.J. Mayne
Greenkeeper: H. Sheppard. Par Score 30.
9 holes. Station Weymouth (2 Miles)
Visitors 2/6d per day, 7/6d per week.

Mayne, the Secretary in the above extract, became the owner, and in a magnanimous gesture, in 1955 he gave the site to Weymouth Council, on condition that the land would be kept closely mown and open to the public at all times.

Wareham Golf Club

A golf course was constructed on the common land to the north of the town in 1908, and an entry in the 1910 issue of *The Golfing Annual* described it as having nine holes; and the charges for play were two shillings a day, six shillings a week, or fifteen shillings a month.

By 1914 *Nisbet's Golf Year Book* listed the Club as having forty-one members, and the fees had fallen to one shilling for the day or eighteen holes. The Secretary at that time was Dr K J Courtney.

R Hodge was engaged as the first professional in 1910, and was succeeded in the following year by A J Cann. Harry Dean's memoirs, which are printed elsewhere in the book, recalls that he 'played Cann for the job'. Dean won the match, but tired of the job within six weeks, and Cann stayed until 1914. There is no evidence of a specially-built Clubhouse, but the records of the present Wareham Club contained a reference to permission being sought from the Parochial Church Council for permission to remove their lockers, so they must have been using a nearby Church Hall.

A study of the official Minutes of the Town Council failed to reveal any detailed discussions or the granting of permission to construct the course.

One of the promoters, a Mr Churchill who served on the Streets, Highways, and Town Walks Committee, raised the matter in November 1908. He said that the Freeholders, Leaseholders, and others with rights of pasture had no objection to the construction of a golf course, and the full Council expressed themselves in favour.

This smaller committee would have been responsible for all the detailed discussions and their records were not filed, but it is surprising that the approval of the full Council was not minuted in the records, especially as common land was involved.

Equally surprising is the lack of information as to why the golf club decided to move away from the common in 1924 to the site near Sandford Road. No mention of the move was contained in the Town Council Minutes, nor in the local newspapers of the time. Admittedly, it was a very small Club, but it was run by prominent members of the town, including Dr K J Courtney, Physician, Surgeon, and Medical Officer of Health.

The experiences of other golf clubs with courses on common land makes it reasonable to suppose that the cost of maintaining good playing conditions on land where others have equal rights of access and usage, became unsupportable where there were only a very small number of subscribing members. Sunday play was not permitted, and that would have been the most popular day for the public to make use of the common, with the resultant danger of damage to the greens. In addition, the animals of the freeholders and others having grazing rights would also have created their own, often expensive problems, and the Club would not have been allowed to fence-off the greens.

During the first world war Wareham was almost a garrison town, so it can be assumed that soldiers and their horses would have been accommodated on the common. The R & A records confirm that Cann left the Club in 1914, adding weight to the assumption that golf would have been discontinued for the duration of the war.

For whatever reason, and it might have been "Hobson's Choice", the Club moved away from the common to a small tract of land rented to them by the Drax family, the area's principal landowners.

It was a most unfortunate choice, the site was quite unsuitable for golf. Roughly triangular in shape, bounded on one side by an ancient droveway and on the others by a bog and a common dump, it would prove to be a constant drain on the meagre resources of the Club for over two decades.

The first committee, led by Dr Courtney, laid out nine holes under the direction of Joseph Howe, the Swanage Golf Club professional, and they employed two groundsmen and a young lad to begin the work of clearing the site and constructing the greens.

"Constructing" is perhaps a misnomer; the chosen site would have been roughly levelled and the disturbed areas covered with turves cut from another part of the course. It would then have been progressively rolled and mown until a reasonable putting surface was obtained. In the case of Wareham there were no suitable turves, so they had to be bought from nearby farmers.

Aerial view of the Wareham golf course with the original tract of land outlined in the foreground. In the background is the approximate site of the original Wareham golf course (1908)

Drainage ... if it was considered at all, would be left to nature and to the skill of the professional selecting the site.

The Club's records do not contain the date of the first match, but it can be assumed that golf of a sort would have been played within the first year of the move, but within that first year the committee was forced to look for a better site for the first hole, and this was to be the pattern for many years to come as they tried to cope with land which the vagaries of weather could transform into hard-baked pan in the dry summer months, and a muddy morass in the winter. The Club records testify to this, because monthly competitions could not be held on a regular basis in the first few years due to the condition of the course, and at best, the entries never exceeded ten.

A study of the records of the early years, during the period of the gradual development of the course raises the intriguing question as to why the large heavy rollers, which were used to make the fairways, were always supplied on loan by the clergymen members of the committees? Horses were hired, but the rollers were always borrowed. There is no conceivable reason why churches should own heavy rollers, so ... perhaps the clerics were adept at persuading the farmers to lend the rollers "for a good cause"?

W Richards of Bournemouth was appointed as Greenkeeper in April 1924, and together with the two groundsmen and a boy, and equipped only with hand tools, they began the slow process of transforming this totally unsuitable tract of land into a passable greensward fit for golf. Their efforts were not helped by the cattle from the nearby farm, which used to wander over the course and damage the embryo greens and fairways, especially in the wet weather. The farmer was eventually persuaded to pay for the privilege; the greens were fenced off and the cattle were allowed to graze the fairways only at the discretion of the Greenkeeper.

The committee obviously felt they were fighting a losing battle, so in March of 1925 they dismissed the Greenkeeper and the young lad, and invited Hugh Williamson, the Parkstone Golf Club professional, to inspect the course and to advise on a better layout.

Williamson brought with him Jack Pollard, who was a low handicap golfer from the Artisan section of the Club, and he replaced Richards as the 'professional'. His teaching and playing duties appeared to be confined to the hours of eight and one o'clock, after which time 'he did whatever was necessary on the course'. Additionally he had to provide tea on medal days, paint the Clubhouse and fences, and whatever other tasks the Captain required of him. He evidently did a good job because the course showed signs of genuine improvement, and his efforts were recognised by the congratulations recorded at the first AGM (which he attended). In the event Pollard spent the whole of his professional career with the Club ... and added the skills of Barman to his repertoire when the Club 'introduced intoxicants' in 1933.

The first committee meeting of the relocated Club took place on Thursday March 27 1924, probably at the home of one of the members, and a number of the people who were members of the original Club, and of the Town

Council were present, including Dr Courtney, F V Symes, the Reverend Coram, Neville Jones, Cottee (a well-known local auctioneer), and Mr Legh, who became the first Captain of the Club.

Capt Drax offered to pay for a Clubhouse, an old army hut, which was erected '100 yards east of the number 1 Tee'. This Clubhouse underwent many changes, but it served its purpose quite well until it was destroyed by fire in 1983.

In his report to the members at their first annual general meeting in the Town Hall in July 1925 , the Treasurer presented the balance sheet for the year ... and considered it to be 'very satisfactory ... in spite of there being a deficit'! The annual subscriptions were set at £2 for Founder members, £2.5s.0d for Gentlemen, and £2 for Ladies. Green fees would be 1/-d for nine holes, and 1/6d for eighteen.

Sad fate of the old army hut erected in 1924 and burned down in 1983

Predictably the meeting elected Captain the Hon Plunkett Ernle Erle Drax DSO RN as their President. Dr Courtney was elected Captain, Mr Harding Treasurer, and the Rev Coram as Secretary.

The meeting then decided to 'appeal to the Mess Presidents at the Bovington Camp for their support'.

The condition of the course led to some very odd local rules, for example, players were allowed to pick up and place the ball if 'a club laid along the ground did not touch the ball'.

Many competitions had to be cancelled due to the ground conditions, and members were reluctant to enter for the monthly medals, with the result that the committee decided to "amend" the handicaps to encourage members to play 'with a sporting chance of winning'. The new 'competition handicaps' were based on the best gross score, which would become the SSS for the course. In August 1926 Mr Tolson returned a 78, so this became the SSS; Tolson was given a Scratch handicap, and of the total of thirty members, four of them were given single figure handicaps, with the highest (40) being awarded to Mrs Harding.

The first 'external' competition was held in 1928, when the Club were hosts to the Broadstone Artisans 'and by playing off their respective handicaps they managed to be victorious'!

By 1930 the Club was in serious financial difficulties, and the committee set out to find ways of attracting additional money. They arranged a dance, and applied to the Chief Constable for permission to run sweepstakes. Pollard also introduced a sweepstake to encourage more people to take part in the monthly medals. In spite of these difficulties however, they could not defer the need to buy a motor mower, and in 1930 they bought a 24-inch Atco mower, financed by issuing £1 no-interest bonds, which would begin to be repaid by Draws after a year.

The old Clubhouse prior to the fire

There were no bunkers on the golf course, and evidently a number of the members were very keen to have them (perhaps the natural hazards had now been overcome). In any event the first bunkers were constructed on the course in 1933.

The golf course continued its gradual improvement, but the Club, like many others described here, had a hard time after the war and came perilously close to bankruptcy. The Club could not afford to pay a greenkeeper, so a core of loyal members undertook all the work of course maintenance on a voluntary basis.

The 'Half-crown' (12 $\frac{1}{2}$p) green fee of the day became especially important if the Club was to keep its head above the financial waters, but all the visitors who responded to the following advertisement in the *Bournemouth Daily Echo* were met on arrival with another notice warning them not to expect too much!

WAREHAM GOLF CLUB

9 holes: One mile from Wareham on Bournemouth/Poole road, in pleasant surroundings with lovely views of Purbeck Hills.

Five minutes walk from Wareham SR Station: on Bournemouth/Poole/Wareham bus route. (Hants & Dorset No 89)

SUNDAY PLAY. ANNUAL SUBSCRIPTION 3 GUINEAS

Green Fees 2/6d. per day: 10s. per week: £1 per month

WAREHAM GOLF CLUB

IMPORTANT NOTICE TO VISITORS

Visitors are informed that, owing to their extremely difficult position the Club were faced, at the last Annual Meeting, with a proposal that the Course should cease to function. The Annual Meeting did not accept this proposal, but were forced, with great regret, to dispense with the services of the Greenkeeper who had been with them for about twenty years. The Course is now looked after and kept in condition entirely by enthusiastic volunteers from among our small number of Members. Visitors are therefore asked to bear this in mind if the Course does not come up to the standard of the Courses of other more fortunately placed Clubs.   Honorary Secretary
                                                          15th April, 1948

Because there were no staff, the clubhouse was usually unattended and players were asked to deposit their green fees in an 'Honesty Box'.

This perilous state of affairs lasted for nearly forty years, but in spite of all their difficulties, compounded by the loss by fire of the old clubhouse, the club survived, thanks to the organising ability of the Hon Sec and the determination of a small group of members... such is the stuff besotted golfers are made of!

Wareham is one of the very few modern golf clubs to be still within easy walking distance of a railway station, with the result that the club has always had a small number of railwaymen as visitors and members. Fortunately the tradition still survives, even in this era of the motor car, and local residents can still smile at the crocodile of golfers pulling their trolleys along the roadside from the station.

The Secretary recalls a very funny incident which occurred soon after the new clubhouse was opened in 1991.

One of the railway regulars came into his office to ask whether he and his colleagues would still be welcome at the club . . . to which the Secretary promptly replied that ALL golfers, if suitably attired and prepared to respect the etiquette of the course, would certainly be welcome. Imagine the Secretary's surprise when a few days later this comedian (well aware that the Secretary had been an Army Major), knocked at his door and asked if he would mind coming out to inspect his friends, who were lined up in the corridor as if on parade!

Despite the evidence of the existence of the earlier golf club in the town, which was unearthed by the research for this book, the committee of the present club have decided to recognise the date of 1924 as the formation of a *new* golf club.

Crichel Park

The original 9-hole course was a private one, laid out in part of Lord Alington's estate for the entertainment of his family and guests, and a members club was not formed until 1932 after the course had been extended to eighteen holes.

Cyril Wren, who used to cycle to the course from Wimborne, was the resident Professional when it was a private course, but he left at about that time and was succeeded by Andrew Jolly, who was responsible for the extended design.

The course was renowned for its exceptional beauty; the park contained a wide variety of game and many specimen trees, including ash, elm, pine, walnut, yew and majestic cedars. The lake beside the twelfth hole was reputed to be very beautiful, with its swans, heron and varied waterfowl, and the highest part of the course provided magnificent views over unspoiled countryside.

Maxwell Hutchinson, writing for the popular contemporary journal *Golf*, was invited to play the course just before the war, and he was entranced by the tameness of two pheasants on the second green *who disdained to move, but waited with utmost coolness while we putted out.*

An interesting item from his article, which was written in 1938, describes an incident in a game being played by Lord Balfour. His Lordship, who was no mean golfer, was climbing up the steep bank of the sixth green when he met his ball trickling back down the slope, he expressed the opinion that *this was hardly golf,* but the writer's comment that 'with the modern ball, a good shot should take us safely to the plateau' suggests that Balfour must have been using a guttie.

Walter Hagen and Joe Kirkwood played an exhibition match against Ernest Whitcombe and Andrew Jolly when the 18-hole layout was inaugurated. Kirkwood 'stymied' his ball behind a huge fir tree on the 365 yard tenth, then played a trick shot over it to land his ball within a couple of feet of the pin.

The new holes were ploughed up during the war and were not brought back into play again and it is not known if the Club members were allowed to play on the nine 'Park' holes after the war, but the Club was not mentioned in the County Union Minute books after 1951.

Shaftesbury & County

All references to Shaftesbury disappeared from the County Union Minutes and the Record Book immediately after the war, and it is assumed that its demise was due to financial reasons. The course was on Spreadeagle Hill, not far from Shaftesbury and near the site of what is now the Compton Abbas airfield. It was one of the seven clubs which affiliated to the County Union in 1923, and the earliest printed reference to the club comes from a 1927 edition of the *Golfers Handbook:*

SHAFTESBURY & COUNTY GOLF CLUB
Membership 120. Hon. Sec. Revd R M Rees.
Professional Roy Jackson.
9 Holes. Station: Semley (5 Miles).
Visitors 2/6d. a day; Ladies 1/6d.
Hotel: Grosvenor.

Shaftesbury & Gillingham

Up in the northern part of the county there used to be a private golf course on land belonging to the Harris family of Manor Farm in Silton. It was probably "private" in the true sense of the word, and typical of many of the very early golf courses where landowners laid out a few holes on part of a farm or suitable woodland, and then played golf with selected friends. These "clubs" rarely played against other golfing societies, so it is understandable that no records survive.

It was known to have been in use just after World War I and the local archives have a number of old photographs of the family, but there were no references to golf.

The path to the first tee was reputed to be very muddy, so the owners built brick steps from the roadway to a drier approach to the tee. These steps can still be seen, in very good condition, but covered by the overgrown grass verge. Another nostalgic reminder of the old times is provided by the line of pine lockers in one of the barns which were used to house oxen. This is now called *'The Golf Room'* by the present generation of the Harris family.

Bullpits

Not many miles away from the Harris farm in the most northerly point of the county where the borders of the three shires meet, another private 9-hole golf course has been constructed on what is probably the most important historical site in the county. A fallen stone is the sole reminder of the site where King Alfred, grandson of Egbert the first king of Wessex, rallied his armies against the invading Vikings.

Lower down the steep valley, in Bourton, are the remains of an old flax mill, recorded in the Domesday Book as Long Lane Mill; and incorporated into the golf course are the relics of the hydraulics complex which fed the lake to provide power for a huge water wheel, sixty feet in diameter. Sadly this wonderful piece of Victorian engineering is no more, because it was melted down and turned into armaments during the Great War.

Bullpits was recently the subject of a protracted inter-county bureaucratic conflict about planning consents. Five of the holes are in Dorset, for which permission was granted, but when the owner applied for permission to open the course to a limited paying public, the Wilts and Somerset authorities objected.

After much acrimony the Government Inspector allowed the appeal by John Freeman, who is now permitted to open the course for a maximum of 100 rounds a week, with players restricted to using nothing stronger than a five iron.

Golf here is a return to basic principles as the plan and "course etiquette" leaflet explains.

Welcome to Bullpits Golf Course, now open after many trials and tribulations! We sincerely hope you enjoy our "little bit of fun" for although being definitely a short course, you will be hard pressed to find anywhere else like it! - it is back to the basics, just as golf was invented all those years ago.

Now due to some local politics, may we ask that you adhere to the following conditions for play:

Playing conditions and local rules

1) There is a restriction to the number of rounds that are allowed to be played per day and per week, so it is imperative that you ring (0747 840084) beforehand to ensure that all is in order.

2) For the immediate future, only iron clubs no longer than a 5 iron can be used, with no woods or metal woods please. This is basically to try as much as possible to avoid players playing too long and over the boundaries of the course. Due to the hilly nature of the course, you are strongly advised not to bring trolleys!

3) All local playing rules are described on the card - basically these are as follows:
   a) Out of bounds – On or over all course boundaries - in or over the River Stour at any point - over any area defined by white posts.
   b) Winter rules are in force at all times through the green - that means that you can clean and place the ball within 6" anywhere on the course.
   c) Water hazards and Lateral water hazards are defined with yellow and red posts and marks.

d) New and staked trees - relief can be obtained within one club length but not nearer the hole.

4) Other general conditions – Please do not play a shot near a road boundary until the road is clear. Also if there is anyone using the footpath next to the 9th fairway, please wait until they are gone before playing.

We are sorry for having to put so many clauses in, but after such a long battle to allow play, we will obviously be under close scrutiny and basically the aim is to prove to all around that Bullpits Golf Course will be an unobtrusive but much needed local facility. The main aim is to enjoy oneself, and we sincerely hope that you do just that!

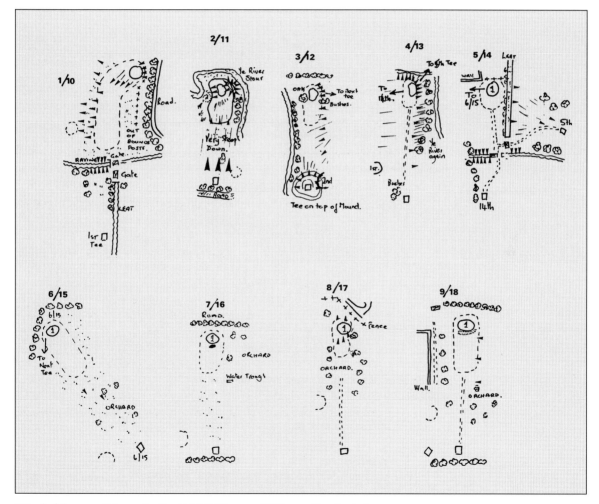

"Card of the course" drawn by David N E Thomas of "Thomas Scorebooks"

East Dorset Golf Club

Lord Wimborne's transformation of Broadstone's wild heathland in 1898, established it as the premier golf course in Dorset and until 1992 it could justifiably claim to have been the most difficult and expensive golf course construction project ever undertaken in the county. That mantle has now been assumed by the East Dorset golf course, which was officially opened on the 25th of July 1992 by Poul Schluter the Prime Minister of Denmark after two years of intense activity and incredible expenditure.

The Danish Count, Christian Lerche, bought the club from Ian Knipe in 1989 and commissioned Hawtree to create a 27-hole championship golf course.

The difficulties facing Hawtree were enormous and much more complex than a green field site would have imposed, because one of the conditions of the contract was that the existing course had to remain operative and open to the club's 650 members.

Secondly, the site of the extension had been used for gravel extraction for over thirty years, with the result that much of the land was waterlogged and unstable. The cost of reclaiming and reinstating this 'new' land was appalling... approximately equal to the cost of constructing a new 9-hole golf course.

Thirdly, there was the time scale: Hawtree is one of the largest and most experienced golf architecture practices in Europe, but the prospect of producing a 27-hole championship golf course out of such an inhospitable site, fit for play within two years, was a prospect that Martin Hawtree acknowledged to be the most difficult his company had ever experienced.

His remit was to design a course of three 9-hole loops, with each returning to the clubhouse and capable of being interchanged to produce a course of championship standard, yet be capable of providing challenging but fair golf for the average golfer, *and* to maintain play for the existing membership on at least nine holes throughout the construction process.

Hawtree were assisted by the civil engineering company Haiste Ltd. and work began in May 1990 with the reclamation and reinstatement of the unstable areas. New lakes were excavated, and an eight million gallon capacity reservoir created near the Buddens Farm estate. In order to stabilise the new ground an artificial fibrous membrane was laid over the soft sands, covered with a layer of gravel, and finally made up to the required levels with spoil excavated from the lake sites.

The construction programme consisted of two phases: the first began in May 1990 with the reclamation of the mineral site, and continued with the construction of twenty-one holes on both the new land and the existing course. Seeding and turfing was scheduled to be completed by October of that year, but the enormity of the project meant that some aspects overran into the spring of 1991. Work then began on phase two, which consisted mainly of the reconstruction of the remaining six holes on the original golf course, by which time eleven of the greens constructed the previous year

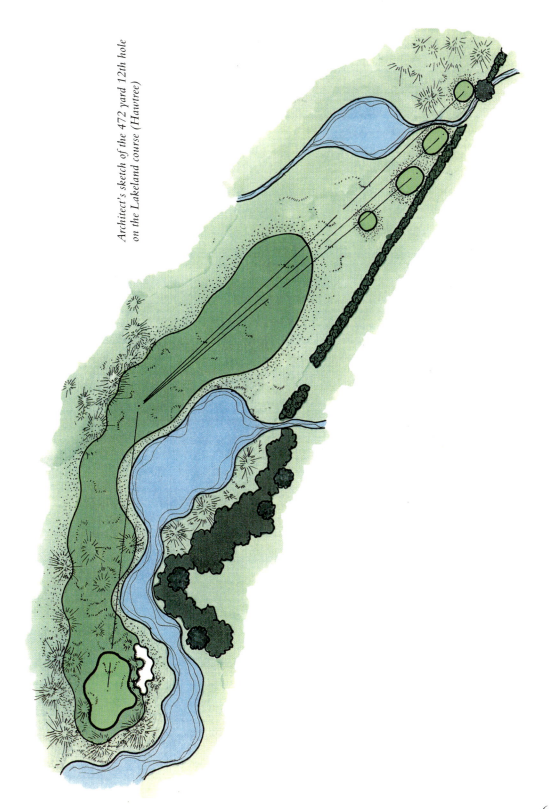

Architect's sketch of the 472 yard 12th hole on the Lakeland course (Hawtree)

were in play. By October 1991 the major works were completed, and in July 1992 the whole 27-hole complex was opened for play

When the dust of all this reconstruction work settled, the ecological and ornithological aspects attaching to all modern golf course constructions were confronted. Local ecologists advised on the ultimate objective of re-establishing the original heathland and its natural flora and fauna, which had been so ravaged by the years of devastating gravel extraction. Drainage was a considerable problem, but this is being dealt with by constructing streams, weirs and dams, designed to create small lagoons and pools. These have been planted with carefully selected vegetation and will be stocked by appropriate wildlife, which will in time attract the birds and natural predators to re-create the original heathland habitat.

The cost of the land reclamation and lake construction was in the order of half a million pounds, drainage added another £150,000, and the tree-planting programme a further £50,000 out of a total construction budget of nearly two million pounds.

It is interesting to compare the costs of today's hi-tech construction methods with the labour intensive methods employed by Tom Dunn when he created Broadstone; the time scale has been halved, but if a depreciation factor of fifty is applied, the costs are reasonably comparable. For example, the construction of Broadstone's fourth green was reported to have cost £800, so it compares favourably with £45,000 as the average cost per hole at East Dorset.

The greens are vast and undulating, akin to older style links-type greens, which require totally different putting techniques, more reminiscent of modern American golf. Bunkers abound and are designed as much for aesthetic appeal as for golf hazards; but water is the predominant feature of the aptly-named Lakeland course, although it is not too intrusive when played from the "Club" tees.

In the opinion of many of the golfers who have played it to date, it is a stern but fair test of golf, but one which demands a great deal of thought . . . or in the jargon of the day . . . 'game management'. It would appear to be the natural venue for future county championship events.

The course was inaugurated with a week of open competitions, culminating with a grand presentation ceremony and the official unveiling of a plaque set in a flower bed in front of the magnificent restaurant and clubhouse.

Poul Schluter, the Danish Prime Minister (left), with Count Christian Lerche at the official opening of the new courses in July 1992

Hyde House Country Club

Immediately below the Lakeland course of the East Dorset Golf Club and on the other side of the River Piddle, there is a private golf course, included with other recreational facilities owned by Chris Reynard, who operates an activity holiday centre based upon Hyde House, the one-time country seat of the Radclyffe family, successful wool merchants from the Bradford area.

The Radclyffe's were mentioned in the Reverend Dorling's description of the sporting activities in the county contained in the *The Victorian History of the County of Dorset,* which has been referred to earlier. Capt Eustace Radclyffe was a keen sportsman and particularly interested in Falconry, and it was primarily for this reason that he planned the trees and clearings on the Hyde House estate, to encourage the wildlife and to provide sport for his guests. He was also a keen fisherman, and contributes this description of the stretch of the River Piddle which flowed through the lower part of his estate . . . the area which has now been cleared and reinstated by Chris Reynard.

'The small stream here is particularly adapted for these fish (brown trout and rainbow trout), whose peculiarity is that they will make off downstream for the sea, but as there are a number of small mills, with the assistance of iron gratings, the downward march of these fish is retarded. By constant restocking of the highest mill dam pools, a really good supply of fish is kept up, and they grow very quickly and take the fly well'.

The house was used as a school for some time before Chris Reynard bought it in 1979 and with advice from Keith Hockey designed an 18-hole golf course in the park to add to the other activities which included water skiing, canoeing, archery, and orienteering.

About six years later he acquired a large area of wetland on both sides of the river. The land, which had at one time been arable and productive, had been neglected for years and had degenerated into a vast bog, overgrown with a matted rhododendron forest and teeming with marsh wildlife. The soil had become extremely acid, which was fine for rhododendrons, but anathema to the grasses and indigenous trees, many of which were in terminal stages of decay.

It was the most unlikely setting for a golf course, but the dream of creating an English "Augusta" spurred Chris into opening up the clogged drainage ditches and clearing out the masses of dead and decaying vegetation. An ardent conservationist, he did not contemplate felling trees, but with expert assistance, moved a great number to create the twisting fairways, losing only one tree of any substance in the process. Not all the trees were re-sited however, and nearly every fairway includes a number of choice specimens to add to the hazards of the tortuous routes between tee and green on most of the holes.

With advice from Hamilton Stutt, the parkland course and the erstwhile bog were amalgamated into eighteen holes of widely divergent character, with water as the dominant hazard.

As the wetland drained, the pH value of the soil stabilised, so permitting the finer grasses to grow, the indigenous trees to recover, and the new plantings to become established.

The course, although open for limited play by private invitation, will take some time to mature to "dream" standards, but it is *the most demanding golf experience . . . unmatched anywhere in the county,* and a return to the original concept of cross country golf, where the hazards are all of nature's making.

There are a number of very interesting golf holes within the extensive layout, many of them calling for precision and great care, but the permutations available from twenty-three holes arranged in parkland, woodland and wetland, make it possible to select eighteen holes of any desired variety and degree of difficulty to suit all categories of golfer . . . with the added bonus of playing in beautiful surroundings, totally isolated from the outside world.

However, unless you are a very good golfer, there are four essential requirements to consider before accepting the challenge of the wetland course:
1 *a bag full of golf balls,* because those which the water does not claim risk being lost in the dense undergrowth bordering every fairway;
2 *a compass* would be helpful because the twisting paths through thick forest is completely disorientating;
3 *some form of sustenance,* because the round will last *at least* four hours;
4 and finally, a *dogged determination* to complete the round . . . come what m a y !
(or alternatively, a scratch handicap would help).

There is water everywhere and trees dot every fairway, so the length of tee shot is subsidiary to the required rifle-shot accuracy, otherwise it means a dip into the bag for another ball!

Each hole has a name, but the sixth sums it all up . . . after threading though a tunnel of rhododendrons, one emerges into the light and through to a small tee; where, without exception the player , viewing the prospect for the first time, will involuntarily exclaim *"Oh God"* . . . and that is the name of the hole! (Many use a stronger expletive, but this is a refined report).

There are three options (other than the obvious one). The hole measures from 442 to 490 yards, depending upon the colour of the tee. **The very good golfer** will hit a 200 yard drive over the marsh and river to a grassy area, then a drawn shot over four bends in the river to a small green tucked between a tree and yet more water. **Mortals** will hope to find a patch of grass with the drive, play a seven iron over only two bends in the river, then pitch into the high side of the green.

It is necessary to use a boat to get to one of the other tees: and the eighteenth is all water; the lake laps tee and green, but take one more club than normally required for 170 yards, hit the bank at the back of the green, and with luck it will trickle back and offer the chance of at least one par.

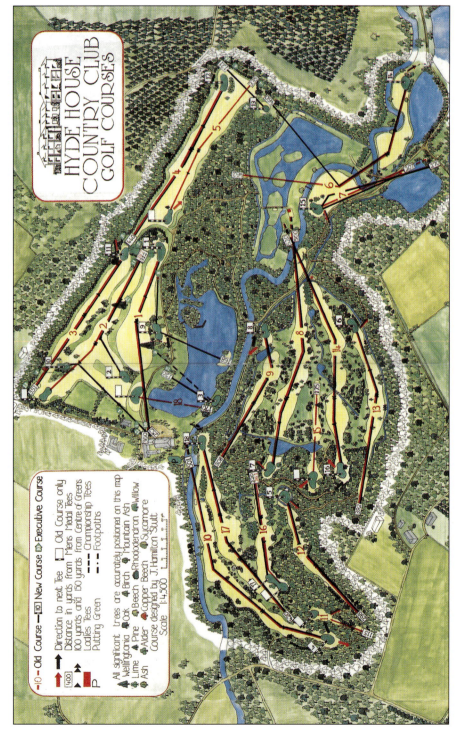

Spectacular impression of the three golf course layouts at Hyde House; of special interest to tree lovers because all species are identified

Current Developments

As the map in Chapter 2 illustrates, our "golfing desert" has bloomed into a veritable forest. The original seven golf clubs have been joined by twenty others which have become affiliated to the County Union, and there are currently twenty-six Council-approved planning applications for new golf courses or associated facilities in the county, and work is underway on a number of them.

It is doubtful if all the plans for new courses will reach fruition, but even in this bleak financial climate, with Dorset high up in the unemployment league tables, there is still a large number of young people eager to take up the sport, but unable to afford the cost of joining established golf clubs, so the need appears to be for pay-and-play academy courses and more practice facilities.

The record number of people paying to use privately-owned driving ranges and 'pay-and-play' facilities is proof of the increasing popularity of the game, which has undoubtedly been influenced by the amount of television time it now receives, and of course by the successes of British players world-wide.

Local councils have done little to meet the growing demand for public golf facilities with the result that too many of these would-be golfers are illegally using public parks, as evidenced by regular newspaper reports of injuries to the public caused by flying golf balls.

Christchurch has two municipal facilities, one of which has played a large part in introducing golfers to a Club environment. Similarly Bournemouth has two famous municipal golf courses, and although the pitch & putt course on Hengistbury Head (Holes Bay) provides a bridge between the first and final stages of becoming a club golfer, there are no public driving ranges or protected areas within the region where the absolute beginner can hit golf balls without endangering others.

Somewhat belatedly perhaps, in view of the existence of the prestigious Parkstone golf course within its boundaries, Poole Borough Council have recently published plans to create two facilities, one for a golf course of unspecified size close to the Moortown Aerodrome site off Magna Road, and the other, a starter course and driving range on land to the North of Upton Road.

In addition to the hundreds of 'do-it-yourself' tyros, private schools with golfing facilities add their graduates to the pool of potential players, all eager to get into clubs and to take part in competitive games. Canford School, which has a large "external" membership is described elswhere, and Bere Regis School also has a small course, which is available to the local public for 'out-of-term use'.

This growing waiting list of frustrated golfers is having a catastrophic effect upon the ambitions of the retired business people, who have traditionally formed a large proportion of the populations of the south coast holiday areas and their golf clubs. It is no longer possible for them to assume automatic entry, and with 'retirement' coming at a much earlier age, and not always by choice, this painful surprise is an additional severe blow to retirement plans, which had the prospect of year-round golf at its core.

Not even the low handicap newcomer can be sure of a place in the club which he has probably visited on a regular basis for many years, with the intention of joining after retirement, and there is no likelihood of any significant change in the near future. It is also unlikely that we shall ever return to the situation when the best of our county players originally came from other parts of the country, notable the Midlands and Scotland.

Prior to the 1960s not many of the county champions were "Dorset Men", but increasingly since that date, the winners have been both local and much younger. This year for example, the majority of our successful English County Champions team learned their golf in Dorset, and all benefited from the forward-looking decisions made over forty years ago by County Union committees to devote more time and resources to the encouragement and professional tuition of promising juniors.

In the current fixture list there are now sixteen competitions and matches for young golfers, whereas prior to 1954 there were none. The lists of winners at the end of this book contain proof of the success of those far sighted decisions. A few of the boys were winners at only eleven years of age and some of these featured in last year's successful English County team.

The 1955 winning SWCGA team at Broadstone for comparison with the 1992 team. Half of the players came from outside the county and the average age was over forty years

2

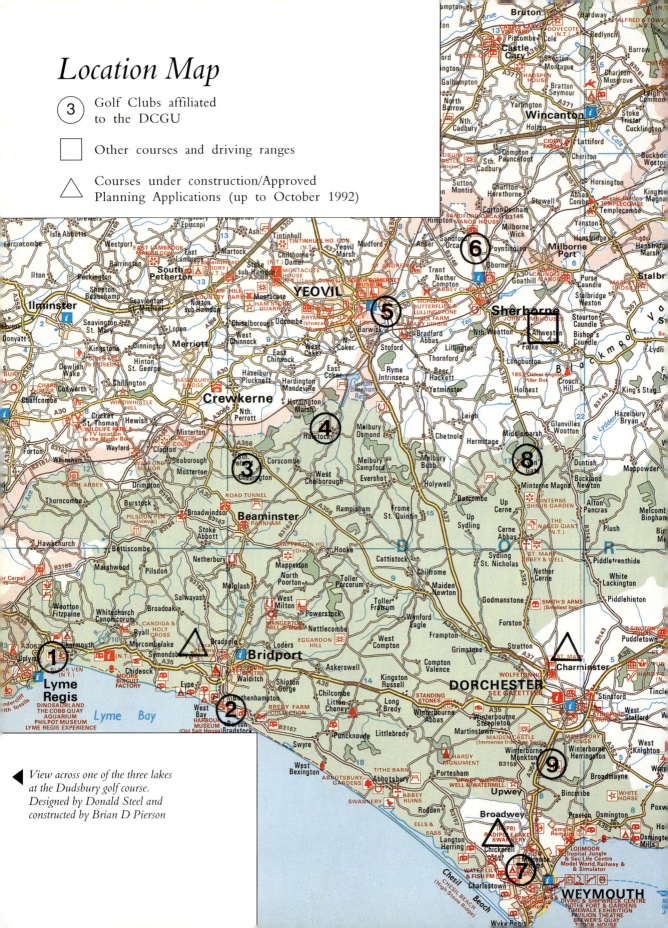

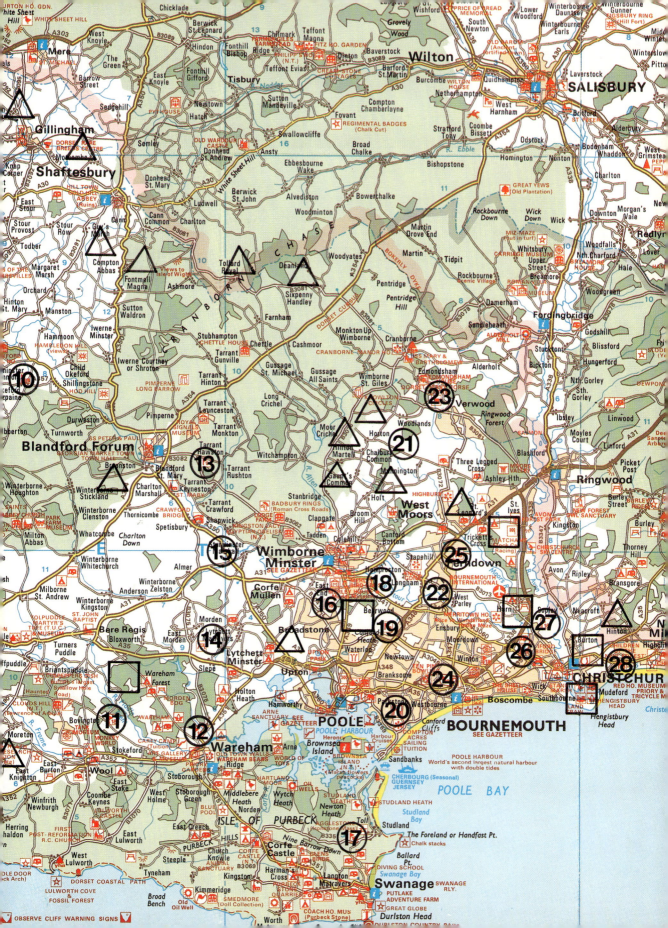

Directory of Clubs and Courses

The Clubs are listed in alphabetical order and the bold number indicates its position on the Location Map.

If the Club's history has been included in the previous chapter its inclusion here is merely a profile of the Club, with directions on how to reach it, and a description of the playing characteristic of the course which will be of interest to the first-time player or potential visitor.

Ashley Wood 1896   **13**
Tarrant Rawston, Blandford Forum
DT11 9HN
(0258) 452253
9 holes. 6,700 yards SSS 70 (18 holes)
1 mile south-east of Blandford

The announcement of the opening of the Club in the *Golf Annual* was short and to the point:

BLANDFORD
ASHLEY WOOD GOLF CLUB, Instituted April 1896
Annual subscription: £1.1s.; Ladies twelve shillings and sixpence
Number of Members: 47 Hon. Sec. Revd G C Pearce, The Tabernacle, Blandford.
A handicap Medal is played for on the first Thursday of each month.
Green Record: 39. The course, of nine holes, is situated in Ashley Wood, about two miles from Blandford Station.

Founded by a few local enthusiasts, the Club has had a turbulent history as can be judged from the account in Chapter 1 of the struggle to save it, but it is now thriving and very popular, with a current membership of 550 and very attractive and comfortable amenities.

Sited on Rawston Down, the course was originally laid out as a 2,642 yard nine holes with grass bunkers, then in 1919 the land was bought by a local farmer J Cossins, who rented it to the Club for an annual fee of 2/6d (12½p). A new club house was built to replace the old shed, which had no water, sanitation or refreshment facilities, and the Club flourished until the advent of World War II, when it was allowed to virtually disintegrate.

By the early 1950s the course was derelict and the land was already being ploughed up for return to agriculture when Roy Carey and his wife, on a visit to their son at the nearby army camp, saw it, persuaded the farmer to cease ploughing, and bought it for £10,000. He then set about the miraculous reconstruction described earlier in the book, and despite almost insuperable odds, eventually managed to get the land back into a recognisable golf course. He modernised the clubhouse, and he and his wife shared the duties of greenkeeper, professional, and steward, until the Club was re-established and attracted the support of the local golfing community.

The present course was re-designed by Hamilton Stutt in 1979 to play as an 18-hole golf course with nine greens, and it presents a tough, but fair test of golf in a beautiful setting, with lovely views over the Dorset countryside of Blandford Forum and the nearby Iron-Age fort of Badbury Rings, and is within a few miles of the National Trust property of Kingston Lacy and the old town of Wimborne.

Work is currently in progress by the Patrick Tallack organisation to extend the course to a full 18-hole layout and it is expected to be opened for play in March 1994... just two years short of the Club's centenary.

The new course will be the same length as the current one, and because the existing 9-hole layout will remain unaltered, play is not affected by the work.

A particularly attractive feature of the course is its ability to recover quickly from even the heaviest rainfall, due to the chalky sub-strata of the Downs.

Bridport & West Dorset 1891
East Cliff, West Bay, Bridport
(0308) 421095/422597/421491
18 holes 6,210 yards SSS 70
1½ miles south of Bridport at West Bay

Dorset's oldest golf club, in Thomas Hardy's *Port Bredy,* was described as having 'fine turf', with hazards such as 'quarry pits, cliffs, furze, a bog, and dry stone walls' ... but 'a pleasant sporting terrain'.
The *Golf Annual* announced the opening of the course and listed the names of the first committee:

> *West Dorset Golf Club Instituted February 1891*
> *Annual subscription: £1; family £1.10s; number of members 38.*
> *President: J Gundry. Treasurer: R D Thornton.*
> *Committee: T A Colfox, A Martin, Rev. J L Templer, A James,*
> *J T Stephens, A W H Dammers*
> *Hon. Sec. C G Nantis, Bridport. Green-West Bay.*
> *Greenkeeper: J Gerrard.*

References from the earliest Minutes of the Club described the green as consisting of nine holes on the west cliff, laid out by Ernest Ham, under the direction of A T Adams of Bellair. Ham, who came from Burnham and Berrow, became the Club's professional following the departure of Gerrard. He in turn was followed in 1924 by Arthur H Billett, who was probably related to J Billett, the professional at Weymouth between 1911 and 1913.

The Minutes also recorded the employment of 'a man to keep the ground mown and in order, at £10 a year, and two boys to be in attendance at games at the rate of 6d a day'.

The land belonged to a Major Bullen, but was rented to George Pitfield, who became a member of the Club and tried, (unsuccessfully) to obtain a 50 percent reduction in his subscription in lieu of rent!

The founder, and first President, was J P F Gundry, Bridport's leading industrialist, but he was killed in a hunting accident in the following year, and was succeeded by his son who was known as "Young Joe", the best golfer in the county at that time. He won the Club's Scratch Cup eleven times and had an officially recognised handicap of plus four!

In the first year of its history the Club had thirty-seven members and it is interesting to note that the greenkeeper was also the harbour master. The Down was used as a sheep run, and although the geological structure appeared to be conducive to good drainage, natural springs caused the course to become very wet, so it was essential to retain the sheep to keep the grass close cropped and the turf in playable condition.

At the General Meeting in February 1892 it was decided that the recognised charge for caddies should be '6d up to two rounds' and in that same year 'a cricket house' was bought and 'fixed in the ground for use as a club house. It is interesting to note that when the decision was taken to move over to the (drier) east cliff, this same cricket house was sold to the Sherborne Golf Club.

The first recorded club match was played against a side from the Weymouth and Dorchester Club. The home team comprised a clergyman, three members of the Stephens family, J Gundry, and A Whetham, but despite the obvious

The 13th green

advantage of playing on their home course, with a team including a plus-4 golfer, the home team lost!

Because of the persistent wetness of the course, the club finally decided to move across to the east cliff in 1911 to a 9-hole course measuring 2,640 yards laid out by W H Fowler from the Walton Heath Club. Nine more holes were added in 1921, presumably by Ernest Ham the resident professional, making a course of 5,255 yards.

The club became a limited company in 1947, was sold in 1953 and again three years later, and from that date until enough cash was raised to buy the course from the Pitt-Rivers Trust in 1986, the club staggered from one cash crisis to another, only just managing to keep its head above the financial waters. Nowadays however, the club is secure, and in 1989 it acquired a large tract of the farmland which formed the inland border of the course. This has been graded and sown with grass, and progressively "stone-picked", and will be used to extend the course to approximately 6,300 yards on 129 acres. A new clubhouse is to be built on the site of the present second green, so the much-loved landmark of the tiny clubhouse set into the side of the cliff beneath the "goat track" to the first tee, will disappear.

In addition to the dry stone walls and the stiff breezes which characterise this cliff-top golf course, one of the best-known features is the infamous thirteenth Port Coombe hole 'as pretty as it is deceptive'. The sunken green, which has caused so many problems for visiting golfers over the years, lies about ninety feet below the tee and is well guarded by natural hazards and bunkers. However, the love-hate relationship will not be lost in the new layout, which has been designed with help from F W Hawtree, because the hole will remain unaltered.

Another famous hole was the 365 yard sixteenth where Max Faulkner, in an exhibition match in 1952, tee'd his ball on two tee pegs. His drive not only cleared the stone wall crossing the fairway about sixty yards in front of the green, but finished ten feet past the pin!

Model of the new Clubhouse

Broadstone 1898
Wentworth Drive
Broadstone
BH18 8DQ
(0202) 693363
18 holes 6,183 yards SSS 70

16

For many years Broadstone has been regarded by many as being the premier golf course in Dorset; in the early Minutes of the County Union, and in contemporary newspaper reports, it was often referred to as the 'senior' course, and it was chosen as the venue for the first County meeting in June 1923.

This vast area of wild and hilly heathland was reputed to have been a hunting ground before Lord Wimborne decided to create a golf course and, according to contemporary writers, it cost him a great deal of money to enable Tom Dunn, son of the famous 'Old Willie' Dunn, to carve thirteen holes out of the shoulder-high dense growth of gorse, ling and fern, to create what was intended to be a private golf course.

There were no trees to provide shade when Dunn created the course, so in his original design, some relief from the sun was provided by making five holes in the grounds of Merley Park, in what is now farmland beyond the fifth green, looking towards what was then the stately home of Capt Angus Hambro.

Tom Dunn was the professional at Meyrick Park, and whilst he is known to have considered Meyrick to have been his greatest challenge, due to its dense cover of heather, gorse and pine, Broadstone was his best creation, because he 'was not stinted for men, money, or materials'.

Dunn was probably the most prolific golf course designer of his day and the first *inland* as distinct from *links* designer. His layouts were characterised as being inexpensive and serviceable, so making it possible for an increasing number of golfers from all social classes to play.

Exactly how much it cost or how long it took to create the Broadstone course is not known, but even with today's sophisticated machinery and expertise, the cost of draining the bogs and levelling out the sandy hills would still have been astronomic. Some idea of the terrain facing this early golf course designer can be seen from the water colour painted in 1906 and included in the description in Chapter 1. It is not recognisable as a specific fairway, but with the benefit of artistic licence, it could be construed as being part of the seventh, with the old windmill, which used to stand near the approach to the sixth, just visible.

The course was opened with an inaugural match between Lord Balfour (then First Lord of the Treasury) and John Penn MP, playing with Braid and Taylor. There are a number of framed prints of the event hanging in the clubhouse, some showing a train belonging to the old Somerset and Dorset Joint Railway steaming along in the background. A report of the opening ceremonies is included in Chapter 1 after the Rev Dorling's description of the course. Understandably there are one or two contradictions, but presumably the newspaper report would have been accurate.

The first professional was quoted as being Adam Johnstone, but in 1902, Harry Dean, who was then a boy caddie, reported that Tom Dunn was the professional, with Jimmy Gowan, presumably his Assistant. It is known that Dunn resigned from his position at Meyrick in 1899, so it is reasonable to assume that he took over from Johnstone.

The original clubhouse was understood to have been the hunting lodge used by guests of Lord Wimborne, but there is no mention of any such pursuits in the newspaper report. The trains halted there for the convenience of his Lordship's guests and afterwards for visiting golfers and continued to do so until 1952.

Unfortunately the attractive old building is no more; it was demolished in 1985 and a new, more functional but far less picturesque clubhouse was built alongside the eighteenth green. A modern housing development now occupies the site of the old lodge; the railway has disappeared; and the entrance is no longer through the (inevitable) 'Golf Links Road', but winds through a character-less housing estate.

The parkland holes, much criticised by the Victorian Reverend in Chapter 1, disappeared when H S Colt, who is perhaps best remembered for his Eden course at St Andrews, created six extra holes in the main heathland area of the course in 1914. Some time later W H Fowler, the creator of the Walton Heath golf course in the early 1900s, revised some of the bunkering, so finally creating a heathland entity which has stood the test of time, except for minor amendments which have enhanced the golfing aspect, such as the attractive water hazard in front of the third green, which was designed by Hamilton Stutt.

Lord Wimborne sold the course to Frank Toley, a businessman from Hanwell, Middlesex, in 1930, and it remained a proprietary club until 1952 when a lease was granted by Mrs Toley to the Dorset Golf Club (Broadstone) Ltd, with an option to purchase; this was taken up in 1973.

Much of the heath is scheduled as a Site of Special Scientific Interest, so in addition to being a marvellous golf course with many challenging holes, there are still the occasional deer to be seen, as well as a wide variety of birdlife.

Perhaps the most enduring memory that first-time visitors take away with them is the challenge of the notorious seventh which is an extremely difficult par four for any mid-handicap player.

The opening match between Mr Balfour, J H Taylor, Mr John Penn MP and James Braid. This picture shows the players on the third green, with 'Bleak House' in the background

Bulbury Woods 1989
Halls Road
Lytchett Matravers
Poole. BH18 6EP
(092945) 547
18 holes 6,020 yards SSS 69
3 miles west of Poole on A35 Poole-Bere Regis road

14

Situated on the western outskirts of Poole, with no neighbouring golf courses, the club obviously fulfilled a need because it was an immediate success; providing the facilities, the atmosphere and the intimacy unique to a private golf club, but hitherto denied to the majority of the golfers who rapidly filled up its opening membership list.

The concept began in 1987 with an outburst typical of the frustrated weekend golfer, forced to queue for a starting time at the municipal golf course, where getting up at 5-30 in the morning is a prerequisite for a game and to still allow time to do a few odd jobs around the house before nightfall!

David Holdsworth, local businessman and keen golfer, bored by the inevitable two hours of wasted time in the queue, was not in the best of moods when John Sharkey, the course professional offered some jocular advice. But getting into a local private club was a virtual impossibility, so the "jokey" 'you'll have to build your own', struck a chord... especially as Sharkey was toying with a similar idea. An earnest conversation in the privacy of the pro-shop confirmed that it was not just a joke, and within a week of that fateful meeting, the two were inspecting the Bulbury Woods Farm, which was up for sale.

John Sharkey was well qualified to assess the potential; with 140 acres of pasture and mature woodland, ample space for an 18-hole layout plus good practice facilities and access from a main road, the prospect was entirely favourable. The two formed a business partnership with Peter Osman and Eddie Halbert and bought the land with planning permission for an 18-hole golf course.

Beginning in June of 1989, the group began the task of clearing away all the vestiges of a farm structure and reshaping the land into a modern golf course layout, designed by John Sharkey. Drainage was an immediate problem, and here they sought the advice of Abbotts of Salisbury. Eight thousand trees were planted, two lakes were constructed, and two thousand shrubs and bushes were introduced to provide colour and to enhance the parkland ambience.

All this work was completed in fifteen months, and the course opened for play in September 1990.

Development work still continues, but the course is maturing well. More trees have been planted, the drainage improved and a few design changes introduced to enhance the playing characteristics.

The excellent clubhouse facilities are much appreciated by the members and are also used by the County Union for functions and committee meetings and by local business concerns for conferences.

Came Down 1896

Came Down, Dorchester DT2 8NR
(0305) 813494
18 holes 6,214 yards SSS 71
2 miles south of Dorchester

As so often happens with the older golf clubs, it is sometimes very difficult to decide upon a precise date of birth. In the references in the earlier pages of this book, attributed to the Rev Dorling, he stated that 'The Dorchester Club' was founded in 1896, but this is contradicted by extracts from the club's golden jubilee celebrations which were reported in the Dorset *Daily Echo* of the 15th of May 1956, and reproduced in the Club's history entitled *Came Down to Golf*.

'There is strong evidence to support the claims that a 9-hole course existed on Came Down from about 1886, some twenty years before the official opening of the *Weymouth, Dorchester and County Golf Club*'.

An elderly Dorchester resident interviewed by the compiler of the Came Down book recollected golf being played on a 9-hole course on Came Down in 1902 'and the tee for the first hole was in the corner of the road junction at the entrance to Came Farm, and one drove across the valley to the green, which was in a natural dip in the ground to the right of the old plateau green'.

Some few years later a company was formed to extend and improve the course, and among those associated with it were Alfred Pope, Herbert Groves, Richard Watts, Joseph Gundry and Col Brough.

When in 1904 J H Taylor advised the Weymouth Town Council that he had not been able to find any satisfactory ground for a golf links in or around Weymouth, the question of the distance of Came Down from the town was considered. Taylor stated in his report that he hoped the Great Western Railway Company might be persuaded to establish a service and put a halt in the vicinity of Came Down, and if that happened 'we would have one of the finest links in the country within minutes of Weymouth.'

Weymouth Town Council were keen to support the establishment of a golf links in order to attract visitors to the town, but they soon realised that an exclusive golf club well away from the town centre was far removed from the municipal links they first envisaged. It is interesting to record here some of the arguments which centred around the location of the golf course.

'It has not been found an altogether easy thing to convince everybody that the provision of the golf links is a vital necessity for Weymouth, and the promoters sometimes meet the objection that people who play golf should pay for it themselves. It is scarcely necessary to point out the unsoundness of the argument. Every important pleasure place has found that golf links are indispensable, and the better the links the better the class of people attracted . . . There is a large and ever increasing class of people who practically live for golf, and who shun every town that cannot provide them with the means to enjoy their sport under the best conditions. Bournemouth catered for them years ago by providing the splendid links at Meyrick Park. It paid so well that other links have just been laid out in another part of the town at enormous cost.

'It was impossible for Weymouth to lag behind under these circumstances, and it is eminently satisfactory to know that next year (1906) we shall be able to add to our other attractions, golf links which are without equal in this part of the country. Access to them by rail motor is easy, the links being only a quarter of an hour's pleasant walk from Came Bridge halt, and we have little doubt that if properly advertised, they will bring large numbers of devotees of the Royal & Ancient game to the town'.

In his book *Taylor on Golf,* the golf architect as distinct from the champion golfer always looked for *space* around his creations, and he looked askance at the growing populations around the towns even in those days. So when the Weymouth Council first sought his advice in 1904 he reported on this difficulty as over-riding all others. The Weymouth Committee were not authorised to spend money outside the borough, so it was not until after the merger had been agreed between Dorchester and Weymouth that Taylor could be provided with the funds to expand the nine holes of the Dorchester course.

The new golf club, with the unwieldy title of the Weymouth, Dorchester and County Club was opened with grand ceremony on the 17th of May 1906, followed by an exhibition match between James Braid and Taylor. As a local reporter put it 'The golf was of remarkable excellence, though the putting was not strong, due probably to the fact that the greens were very keen and not yet in perfect order'!

In 1924 the name of the club was changed to the more simple Came Down Golf Club, administered by three trustees: the Earl of Ilchester; Major J Gundry; and Capt A V Hambro MP.

The first professional at Came Down was Ernest Pursey, who had been clubmaking in South Staffordshire, and he is recorded as moving to the

Weymouth, Dorchester and County Golf Club in 1905, where he stayed for five years.

The course was radically altered by H S Colt in 1927 and the present course has not changed to any great extent since that time.

'Situated as it is on the north-facing slopes of the 400 feet high Ridgeway . . . Came Down enjoys and endures the full range of a maritime climate. Howling gales and lashing rain from the south-west, biting winds from north and east, gentle sea breezes tempering the summer heat, thunderstorms following the line of the coast, low cloud and hill fog, hoar frost and drifted snow, glorious sunshine and greens like glass, spectacular views and sunsets . . . our golf course knows them all . . .' (*Came Down to Golf* by Peter Ward).

Canford School 1985
Wimborne BH21 3AD
(0202) 841254
9 holes. 5,918 yards SSS 68 (18 holes)
Oakley Lane, off B341 Wimborne-Bournemouth Road
2 miles south-east of Wimborne

18

This lovely building, steeped in history and so closely associated with ancient Poole, is visible from all parts of this parkland golf course, where, depending upon the season, the crack of an errant golf ball against unforgiving tree, vies with the click of hockey sticks or willow against leather.

The course was planned by Peter Boult, a keen Kentish golfer, and father of a former member of the Masters' Common Room, to attract additional revenue for the school and to add a further dimension to the range of physical activities provided for the 500 pupils.

It was built by the school's groundstaff under the supervision of the architect, and modified in recent years to include an extensive tree-planting programme.

The underlying strata is gravel, so it is seldom too wet for play, but in addition to the numerous trees, there are plenty of water hazards to contend with. A stream bisects the course and two ponds at the lower end of the course yield a fair number of "lake balls" to the groundstaff!

Prior to the construction of the course the boys used to play on the nearby Broadstone course, and its close ties with the club are still maintained by Broadstone's Professional Nigel Tokely and his Assistant Andy Stuart, who provide tuition for the boys through the Golf Foundation.

At present the club is wholly administered by the school's Management Committee, but the course is not used exclusively by the school; it has over two hundred 'external' members and a waiting list. No golf competitions are held and there are no changing facilities, but plans are in hand to create a players' club, with suitable temporary accommodation, which will allow the members to conduct their own affairs within the guidelines laid down by the school and the county union. Eventually there will be more permanent accommodation and the club will have its own access. The course layout will then be revised, so that instead of a par five, the first will become the present very good par 4 seventh, which is flanked by a row of magnificent cedar trees.

The school has enjoyed success in the Hill Samuel Schools Foursomes, reaching the finals at Royal Lytham & St Annes in 1982, and they also won the West of England Public Schools Invitation Tournament at Burnham in the same year. Probably the best-known individuals produced by the school are local boys John Tyror of Broadstone and Greg Taylor of Parkstone.

Chedington Court 1992
Holt Farm
South Perrott
Beaminster
DT8 3HU
(0935) 891413
9 holes. 3,360 yards SSS 72 (18 holes)
4 miles south-east of Crewkerne on A356

This new golf course is owned by the Chedington Court Hotel, a magnificent old Jacobean style manor house built in 1840 on a site of a much older house dating from the fourteenth century.

It is not known if the name Chedington derives from William de Chedyngden, who was the 'Lord of Chedington in the Hundred of Beyminstre', or if he assumed it from the estate.

The course was designed by the hotel owners, with professional help. The greens were constructed by Mike Lock of Ilchester, with Phil Smith of South Perrott undertaking much of the ancillary work.

Construction started during the Easter weekend of 1991, and the course was opened for play eighteen weeks later, which must be something of a record.

The area extends to ninety-five acres of old pasture land, some 300 feet above sea level, with magnificent views over three counties. Great care was taken during the construction of the course to preserve the outstanding natural beauty of the parkland, which includes woodland, mature trees and old hedgerows of blackthorn and wild roses.

Bounded on two sides by Chedington Woods, the course is bisected by an ancient droveway, which is probably a relic of the days when cattle were driven from South Perrott to the market in Yeovil.

The course is quite long, and alternative tees are being constructed at most holes to provide a variation for the 18-hole layout. The greens are well constructed, drained and finely turfed, and although the fairways are wide, the nature-conscious owners aim to allow free rein to the rough at the extremities in order to encourage the summer wild flowers and insects.

The first and ninth fairways are separated by a lake, so that great care is required from the first tee and for the second shot on the ninth. The 350 yard second is a dogleg, which can be driven by the low handicap player who is prepared to risk the intervening 'out-of-bounds' area. The third green is cut into a hillside and it requires a very accurate approach. The fourth, the longest hole on the course, is 550 yards from the yellow tees, and the wide fairway invites the long hitter to "have a go". By way of contrast, the fifth has been shortened to make it easier for the average golfer to clear a ditch and the small trees on the rising fairway. This is followed by a par 4 which should not create any problems; instilling a sense of confidence for the 400 yard seventh which has a tricky uphill approach to the green. The eighth is a short 140 yards; and the ninth fairway rises away from the tee over a hill towards the lake, which hopefully caused no problems at the start of the round.

It is not an easy golf course; it plays long, but it is not repetitive, with each hole posing a different problem to challenge the most discerning golfer.

This distinctive golf course has another unusual feature, the resident Professional is a lady. She is not the only one in the county, but she is the only American; Meredith Marshall who was the Scottish Ladies Open Champion in 1986, will be playing on the European circuit.

There is no clubhouse as yet, although changing facilities are provided, and one very pleasant feature, which will be appreciated by visitors out for the day, are the picnic boxes, which may be ordered from the hotel and which will be delivered to the course.

Christchurch Golf Club 1977

27

Iford Bridge, Barrack Road
Christchurch
(0202) 473817
9 holes. 4,824 yards SSS 66 (18 holes)
On eastern boundary of Bournemouth, at Iford Bridge.

The 9-hole 'pay-and-play' Iford Bridge golf course and driving range facility was opened in 1959 and leased to H D Newbury Ltd who ran it until 1972, when it was taken back into Council control and it was operated by the Borough Treasurer's Department until 1974, when responsibility was passed to the new Borough Engineer following local government reorganisation.

With the help of the Head Greenkeeper, Jim Downer, and advice on design from Peter Troth, the Council carried out major improvements over the next fourteen years, including a new course layout in the early 1980s.

It has always been a very successful 'academy' course, and a large number of the members of the private golf clubs in the area were first introduced to the game at Iford. This tradition continues with group classes run by the resident professional Peter Troth, who has been at the course for seventeen years.

It is a parkland course, dominated by the River Stour, which forms its western boundary, and which exerts a baleful influence on most of the holes. The most difficult being a 476 yard par 5 which is reputed to be one of the most difficult golf holes in the county, with the ever-present river along the left-hand side and an out-of-bounds area to the right.

A new clubhouse was built in 1975, and in addition to the golf club, it is home to a bowling, and a tennis club, but this will be greatly improved when the current development plans reach fruition. The Council plan to extend the facility to a 27-hole golf course and driving range built by the Patrick Tallack Organisation, with a new clubhouse and car park. Work is expected to begin some time in 1993 and it will then known as The Christchurch Golf Complex.

Crane Valley 1992
Verwood
BH31 7LE
(0202) 814088
18 holes 6,400 yards
9 holes 2,060 yards
On outskirts of Verwood on B3081

23

Situated in nearly 200 acres of picturesque countryside near Verwood, the club derives its name from the River Crane which meanders through the 18-hole course.

The complex is owned by Martin Wilson, whose aim has been to provide an integrated facility attractive to golfers of all abilities. The 18-hole 'Valley' course is reserved for members and visitors with an official handicap, but the 9-hole 'Woodland', which will become an academy course as the complex develops, is open to the public on a pay-and-play basis, and in addition, there is a 12-bay driving range.

Both courses were designed to a very high specification by Donald Steel; and constructed by Brian D Pierson (Contractors) Ltd who have been responsible for an increasing number of new golf course developments in the county and are currently preparing the Royal St George course for the forthcoming Open Championship.

The 'Valley' course has the potential to rank among the best parkland courses in the area. It contains four par 5s; each of 500 yards in length, and a large lake which comes in to play on the testing third and tenth par 4s.

The river, which runs through the lower part of the course, has been used to great effect in Donald Steel's design, with the layout of the fifth, sixth and eleventh holes; the par 3 sixth in particular being a truly memorable short hole which looks good at any time of the year.

The clubhouse is set in natural woodland on the highest point on the course, adjacent to the eighteenth green, so providing outstanding views over the entire course from the bar and the large restaurant.

Limited play was allowed on both courses in the summer of 1992, and as the courses mature they will provide great pleasure, and a good test of golf for members and visitors.

Dudsbury 1992   **22**
Christchurch Road
Ferndown
BH22 8ST
(0202) 593499
18 holes 6,208 yards SSS 70
Off Christchurch Road on B3073, one mile south-west of Ferndown

When Nigel and Maggie Richards decided to diversify away from farming, they set out to create a golf club which would equal the best along the south coast. This was indeed an ambitious project, when viewed against the prestigious existing golf courses, but the completed complex, with its comprehensive facilities bids fair to realise their ambitions.

The clubhouse, with its magnificent views over the course and the Stour valley, is already established as 'The Clocktower Restaurant', and the course is maturing into a very fine test of golf with a wide variety of interesting and challenging hazards.

Designed by Donald Steel and constructed by Brian D Pierson, the 150 acre site is being enhanced by a comprehensive tree-planting programme, and includes three lakes, one of which serves as a natural reservoir for the automatic irrigation system.

One of the most challenging holes on the course for the club golfer is the par four sixteenth, where to make par requires a drive into the prevailing wind with a 180 yard carry over the corner of a lake, and then a difficult approach shot over more water and a stream which protects the elevated green.

The twelfth is equally challenging, being another difficult par four. Again the tee shot is into the prevailing wind, with a carry of some 170 yards over bunkers, but stopping short of the stream which meanders all the way through the course. The approach shot is into another elevated green which is well protected by bunkers, and depending upon the strength of the wind, requires anything from a six to an eight iron to give a chance of a par.

The 18-hole course offers an interesting challenge for all categories of golfer; and the academy course and driving range, which is available to non-members, is designed to encourage local would-be golfers to take up the game and to graduate to the main course.

The complex was opened in 1992 with an exhibition match between WPGA tour players Alison and Susan Shapcock, and Donald Steel the course designer and Chris Gotla.

East Dorset Golf Club 1978
Hyde, Wareham
BH20 7NT
(0929) 472244
Lakeland Course: 18 holes 6,580 yards SSS 75, 73, 71
Woodland Course: 9 holes 4,853 yards SSS 66

11

Cyril Corbin, a local dairy farmer was a late convert to the game of golf. He became addicted at the age of fifty, and he and his wife, in collaboration with six-handicapper Gerry Holloway, decided to build an 18-hole golf course on part of his farm, which included sixty-five acres of dense rhododendrons.

They consulted Brian Bamford the Professional at the Isle of Purbeck Golf Club, who agreed to design the course, and the work began in 1975, using farm tractors and chainsaws. The local newspaper suggested that the project warranted a mention in the Guinness Book of Records for the cheapest-ever do-it-yourself golf course!

With 650 members on the books, the course opened for play on a rainy day in March 1978 after two and a half years of construction work, which included seven miles of drains, and about forty tons of sifted soil for each green, plus a clubhouse which took a year to build.

The two friends and their wives took charge of the golf club administration and catering, and the first Professional was Paul Smith.

Eight years later the club was sold to Ian Knipe, who continued to develop the course, enlarging many of the tees, improving bunkers and planting many trees. In addition he constructed a magnificent 22-bay floodlit driving range with an extensive professional's shop, which opened in 1989.

Later that year another change of ownership occurred when the club was sold to the Danish Count, Christian Lerche for four million pounds. He added considerably to the land holding and began the transformation of the existing course under the guidance of course architect Martin Hawtree to produce a challenging 18-hole 'Lakeland' course, and a 9-hole 'Woodland' course in the rhododendron forest which had formed part of the old 18-hole Lakey Hill course.

This vast new construction programme with its fleet of earthmoving equipment, and an array of technical and environmental expertise represents the greatest possible contrast with the crude simplicity of the original concept, and it epitomises the incredible advances which have taken place in what was once the simple act of knocking a ball of feathers around the sand dunes of Scotland.

Both courses have been arranged to facilitate a combination of any of three 9-hole layouts, and the 'Woodland' course was constructed to accommodate a future extension to eighteen holes on land already in the Club's ownership.

Whilst the work on the two courses was in progress, the clubhouse was totally rebuilt to provide luxurious accommodation and restaurant facilities.

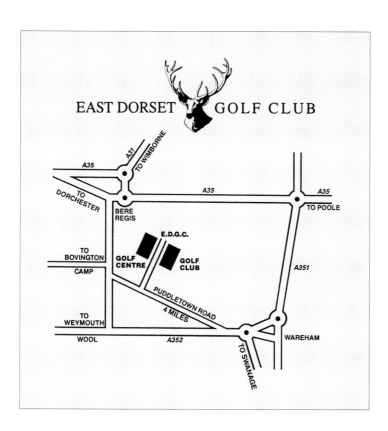

25

Ferndown 1912
119 Golf Links Road
Ferndown BH22 8BU
(0202) 872022
18 holes 6,442 yards SSS 71
9 holes 5,604 yards SSS 68
6 miles north of Bournemouth

This famous golf course, one of the best-known on the south coast, came perilously close to disappearing from the golfing scene in its early years. It twice fell into the hands of Receivers, and was almost ruined through lack of finance.

The original Club, under the Chairmanship of Rudolf de Paula, a civil engineer who lived in Ferndown, engaged Harold Hilton, the Open Champion in 1892 and 1897; a distinguished writer, and one-time editor of *Golf Illustrated* to design the Old Course.

Stewarts, the local nurserymen were responsible for the construction, but unfortunately the two years of effort to drain the boggy areas, create greens, and cut fairways through the heath, was largely wasted due to the outbreak of the Great War.

For six years the course was abandoned to nature, and when Sir Henry Webb founded a new company to buy the course in 1920 they had to virtually start from scratch to recover Hilton's original layout.

The financial situation at this time was grave; there were no funds available to create new greens, so the old ones had to be restored as cheaply as possible by the application of sifted soils and fine grass seed. But the recovery programme was not helped by the urgent need for revenue. The management was forced to allow local players, keen to avoid the journey into Bournemouth to play on the two municipal courses, to use the embryo greens, with the result that they deteriorated to such an extent that a local rule was introduced which allowed players to strike their balls at a stake driven into the 'green' in lieu of putting-out. In fact the holes were not cut until the course was formally opened in October 1921, but in the following year a severe drought inflicted severe damage to the new course and its fragile greens.

In 1926, following a second descent into Receivership, a new Club was formed, which steered the Club into solvency, and the recovery continued until the Club was bought out by the members in February 1966.

A great many changes have taken place since those early hazardous days, and the course was soon described in a well-known golfing journal as *a really fine one, providing as nearly as an inland course can, the golf to be found on first-class seaside links.*

Green fees in those early times were three shillings a day (15p), and the location was described as *six miles from Bournemouth, or a brisk three mile walk from the nearest railway station at West Moors.*

The Club and its superbly maintained golf course has become justly famous, both for its consistently fine condition and its association with the Alliss family. It is physically undemanding; with tree-lined fairways cut out of natural heathland and where all the rough consists of heather, which may be lovely to look at, but it is notoriously reluctant to release the odd wayward ball!

The Old Course has been host to the Hennessy Cup, the European Ladies Championship, and the British Ladies Open.

In 1969 J Hamilton Stutt was commissioned to construct a 9-hole course to relieve the pressure on the Old Course. It is in effect an 18-hole layout with nine greens, the tee placings giving a great deal of variety to the back nine holes and providing a very good test of golf.

Most golf courses have a "signature hole", but it is difficult to choose one for Ferndown; most visitors take away with them the memory of a beautifully presented golf course with immaculate greens.

Halstock 1989
Common Lane
Halstock
Nr. Yeovil
BA22 9SF
(0935) 891689
18 holes 4,351 yards SSS 63

The course and driving range is five miles west of Yeovil. To get there, turn off the A37 Dorchester Road at the Closworth sign, about 1½ miles from Yeovil, past the reservoir. Turn right at the tiny village green of Halstock and Common Lane is opposite and 50 yards beyond the shop/Post Office.

'Halstock Golf Enterprises' began as a driving range and club-hire facility located in an area of under-used boggy farmland accessible only through a narrow deeply rutted lane, which presented a challenge even to farm tractors.

However, convinced of the need for a starter facility for keen but cost-conscious potential golfers, two local business friends set about making the lane into a passable road. Between them they levelled the deeply rutted track and spread 1,600 tons of hardcore to make it into a passable impression of a road, which has now been surfaced to a standard where it no longer presents a challenge to even the most fragile suspension system.

The concept was born in 1987 when the economy was booming and people had the money and a desire to do something with their leisure time. Television was popularising golf, but the lack of 'academy' facilities was frustrating many thousand of would-be golfers. There was no way of getting into an established club without a handicap, and no way of getting a handicap without being a member of a club.

Local businessman Les Church was no golfer, but Bob Clifton had been an Assistant at Halesowen before becoming the Professional at Caerphilly and at nearby Sherborne. They were both keenly aware of the massive interest in golf locally and the frustration being caused by the 'Catch-22' situation; so with Les providing the finance and business acumen, and Bob the technical expertise, they built a 12-bay driving range, with rather crude pro-shop, refreshment and toilet facilities, which opened to an eager public in 1987.

They were obviously filling a need because the business flourished and they were joined by Bob's brother Roy, the Pro from the Wells Golf Club, and by young Colin Church. The demand was so great that they decided to install floodlights ... powered at first by a diesel generator ... and then at horrendous cost by mains electricity.

Early in 1988 the four partners decided to build a 9-hole golf course on the rest of the land, and using their combined skills, produced a basic, but attractive layout in the record time of five months. The next two or three winters severely tested the embryo course, and playing conditions on the temporary greens were at times horrific; however it *was* golf ... of a sort. The course gradually settled down and matured to the point when in October 1989 Halstock became affiliated to the County Union with a rating of par 64, SSS 60, and a membership made up of season ticket holders, who paid only about 60 percent of the normal green fee.

A further nine holes were built and were incorporated into an integrated course in May 1992 with a new par of 65. As yet there are no par 5s in the layout, but hopefully this may be remedied in the near future. Some of the original tees and greens have had to be rebuilt or re-sited, but all the greens have watering facilities and provision has been made for the installation of a computerised sprinkler system.

A permanent clubhouse will replace the temporary 'Portakabin', so that members will be able to enjoy all the amenities of a modern golf club.

On the course the ancient hedgerows and many magnificent oak trees were preserved and incorporated into the layout and hundreds of new trees have been planted which will eventually form attractive fairway avenues.

The course is physically undemanding; set in gently undulating beautiful countryside with views over rolling hills and woods, it is ideally suited to the needs of beginners, and it presents an incentive to the more proficient golfers to aim for a gross score close to level par. Of the eleven par 4s, six are slight dog-legs, two being virtually at right angles. Given good, dry conditions, a few of the par 4s will invite the long hitter to attempt to drive the green, but there are plenty of cunningly placed hazards to punish the wayward shots. Seven of the holes have both water hazards and 'out-of-bounds' to take into consideration.

Halstock may be a junior club within the County Union, but it was perhaps the first to set out with the object of providing the opportunity and the incentive for all those who wished to take up the game, but who were being prevented, either by finance or by the lack of nursery facilities.

Highcliffe Castle 1913
107 Lymington Road
Highcliffe-on-Sea
Christchurch
BH23 4LA
(0425) 272953
18 holes 4,689 yards SSS 63
8 miles east of Bournemouth

28

The course was originally laid out by Leslie Green, who was the first professional (1913-19) as a 9-hole course for the Rt Hon Stuart-Worley, owner of the nearby High Cliff mansion, and opened by Princess Christian on the 26th July 1913.

The next professional was P A Percival (1919-33), and he was joined by his brother-in-law Cecil Sargent as an Assistant. Sargent took over the responsibility in 1917, and in 1927 extended the course to eighteen holes.

The first clubhouse, built in 1916, incorporated the original thatched roofed cowsheds which stood on the site. This shingle-roofed building remained largely unchanged until a new clubhouse was built, on the same site, and opened by John Jacobs in 1985.

The course is physically undemanding, but great accuracy is required on some of the longer par threes. It occupies about forty-four acres and boasts very fine quality greens, many surrounded by small banks, which call for a delicate chip shot to make par.

The putter hanging over the lounge bar was presented to the club by the widow of Alf Perry, an honorary member of the club, who won the Open Championship at Muirfield in 1935.

The club is proud of two unusual records: in 1974 one of the members Jim Andrews broke his former course record of 63, set up in 1952, by going around in 62 *at the age of 70;* the British record for the oldest person holing in one was at one time held by former member T S South who holed the then 110 yard seventh *at the age of 91!*

The key to a good score on this course rests with matching par on as many as possible of the eight par threes and to hope for the odd birdie on the fours.

The old Clubhouse at Highcliffe

Isle of Purbeck 1892
Swanage
BH19 3AB
(0929 44) 361
18 holes 6,283 yards SSS 71
9 holes 2,022 yards SSS 30
3 miles north of Swanage on B3351

This Club began its life with its present title, but it has had four name changes and four owners in its one hundred year history.

The author of the Club's centenary celebration book suggests that it was probably started by the members of an elite gentlemen's club in Park Road Swanage . . . the way so many of the county's older golf clubs were initiated.

The local newspaper for August 11th 1892 promised that the *Inhabitants and visitors at Swanage may shortly expect to see the introduction of the all-popular Scotch pastime which has so great a fascination for its devotees. We understand that the golf links will shortly be ready for play . . .*

The 9-hole course on Dene Hill was duly opened in 1893, and its distinguished first President was Ralph Bankes of Kingston Lacy, who owned most of the land in that part of the Purbecks, including Corfe Castle. The Greenkeeper was R Masters, and the first recorded professional Joseph Howard (1901-29), followed by Edward Howe (1929-33).

As was the norm in those late Victorian times, the Club was formed for 'Gentlemen'; landed gentry, successful professional men, officers in the armed services, and retired civil servants. Surprisingly however the Club recognised artisans from the outset. Generally the introduction of 'Associate Membership' followed much later, but it would appear that the local artisans were allowed to use the course almost at once. They helped with the maintenance of the course, but they did not enjoy any of the members' privileges and were only allowed to play on certain days and in the evenings. The artisans section flourished until 1980, when the last eighteen members asked for and were granted membership of the Club.

1923 saw the first change in the title; the Club was in need of increased revenue from green fees and the committee decided to change the name to *The Swanage Golf Club,* and had in fact changed the headed stationery to that effect when Bankes objected. He was not impressed with the argument that Swanage was a very well known and popular holiday resort, but relatively few people had even heard of the Isle of Purbeck. They did however agree on a compromise name *The Swanage and Studland Golf Club.*

The first change of ownership occurred in 1942 when H W S Palmer from Buckinghamshire bought the course for an unknown figure. The reason for the sale was that by 1939 the Club was in financial difficulties, and the effect of the war, which practically wiped out the income from visitors, also decimated the membership. It was a familiar story; remorseless increasing demands for expenditure to maintain the course and its buildings, set against a drastically reduced income.

The Club was faced with the threat of closure, so were very relieved by the approach of their 'White Knight' who had recently moved from his hotel home on the edge of the Gerrards Cross Golf course to Bath Hill Court in Bournemouth. The Club became a limited company, and although Palmer began with a number of innovative ideas, including a move across the road to the site of the present main course, none of them materialised. However, he was persuaded by the members to apply for permission to change the name to *The Studland Bay Golf Club,* which proved to be acceptable to Bankes.

In 1951 the Club changed hands again. Palmer, who had made little impression on the course or the Club, went to live abroad for health reasons, and Kenneth Darrell-Waters, a distinguished Harley Street surgeon, bought it . . . and even tried (unsuccessfully) to buy the freehold. Mrs Darrell-Waters was Enid Blyton, probably the best-known of all childrens' book authors, whose familiar "Noddy" and "Big Ears" characters are better loved and more resilient than any of today's transient TV creations.

In the fourteen years of his tenure Darrell-Waters extended the course to eighteen holes, nine on the Dene Hill and nine on the Studland side.

1965 heralded the third and most significant event in the Club's history when H B Randolph of Wilkinson Sword fame bought it from the ailing Darrell-Waters. He began by issuing shares and forming a limited company, but in the Certificate of Incorporation the title of the Club had changed again; this time to *The Swanage and Studland Bay Golf Club!* 'HB' as he was affectionately known, created the present main course; installed automatic irrigation; built the magnificent Purbeck stone clubhouse; and he restored the original title.

The Club prospered under his direction, aided of course by the increasing affluence and mobility of the population, plus the explosion in the popularity of the game which occurred in the 1970s.

The Randolphs reigned benignly for eighteen years, but after HB's death in 1980, his son Roy soon became disenchanted with the pressures of running a large golf club, and was pleased when his brother Denys introduced the Robinson family, who became the enthusiastic fourth owners.

Leonard Robinson, a Midlands businessman and keen golfer, bought the Club in 1984, and since that date it has been run as a family business with Leonard as Chairman, Mrs Joan Robinson as Managing Director and Club Secretary, and with sons Duncan and Keith on the Board of Directors.

Just before the Robinsons took over, Ralph Bankes died and left all his lands and property to the National Trust; the largest bequest ever made to that custodian of much of this country's heritage; however, the lease on the Purbeck course which Randolph negotiated and which runs until 2005, is unaffected by the change of ownership.

A very large proportion of Dorset golfers will have played over the Purbeck golf course, so no detailed description is required. The beautiful scenic setting is unsurpassed in the county, and although golfers are sometimes accused of being oblivious to their surroundings... especially if they appear to be trying to change its contours... the playing experience here can be summed up quite succinctly: *on no other golf course could there be a better excuse for lifting your head!*

Knighton Heath 1934   **19**
Francis Avenue
West Howe
Bournemouth BH11 8NX
(0202) 5987
18 holes 6,120 yards SSS 69
3 miles north of Bournemouth at junction of A348 and A3049

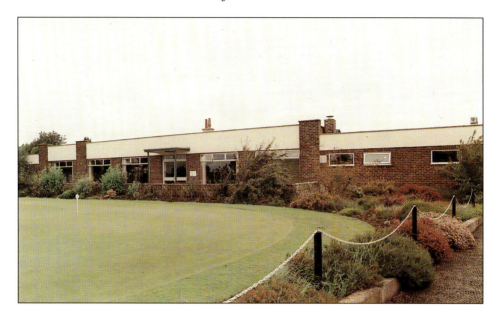

This Club, like so many others described here, has had a chequered history and financial crises. It began as the Northborne Golf Club in 1934 when Bill and Vera Freeman decided to carve a golf course out of the heathland. There were no trees, just a rolling carpet of heather and gorse, which in the summer resounded to the hum of thousands of bees.. reminiscent of earlier days when the local people "farmed" the wild honey bees on the miles of heathland which surrounded Bournemouth before Tregonwell found it and introduced the pine trees.

   In the early 1960s the Club was bought by local businessman W Knott who made the famous *Bluebird* caravans, and the Club was managed by Harold Whiting, who collected the green fees from a caravan "office". During Knott's ownership he incorporated land adjoining the nearby waterworks and abandoned the four holes cut by the Freemans. With advice from the professional Cyril Wren he laid out a new 18-hole course and began to plant the pine trees which now threaten the heather, as they do in other local heathland golf courses.

   The course was on the Hants-Dorset boundary and Knott sold the Hampshire part for the construction of the Max Factor factory and a housing estate.

   The new ownership and a new layout resulted in a new name... (New

Northborne), but its fortunes declined as the membership, understandably dissatisfied with the new regime, deserted to other clubs.

The club was sold again in 1972, but this proved to be an even greater disaster because the new owner, a local property developer, was already in serious financial straits. He could not afford to spend money on course maintenance, and although the club was run nominally by an elected committee of members, it had no powers. The club's fortunes continued to slide downhill until in 1976 the Bank foreclosed, with the objective of recouping some of the outstanding debts.

After many consultations the Bank agreed to sell the clubhouse and the course to the members if they could raise £100,000. At a hastily convened emergency meeting in a local pavilion the members agreed to an individual levy of £150 per man and £100 from every lady member . . . and that evening they pledged the astonishing sum of £30,000. A total of £96,000 was raised in five weeks, and another £1,300 was added by shrewd investment of the accumulated capital.

The salvage plan succeeded and in 1976 the members bought the club and re-named it Knighton Heath.

The first objective was to improve the condition of the course and although there were no capital reserves the decision was taken to install expensive course irrigation. The substrata of the heath is gravel and the fairways were invariably littered with loose stones, which resulted in the local joke that Northborne golfers were easily recognised by their badly scuffed golf clubs!

A concentrated effort was mounted to clear the stones; bins were placed alongside the fairways and all players were encouraged to add stone-picking to their repertoire of shots during the game!

After the clearance of the stones, the menace was finally defeated by heavy applications of *natural fertiliser* from the local sewage treatment works, which encouraged the growth of grass and increased the depth of the tilth, with the result that present-day players can indulge in the luxury of taking divots without the fear of permanent damage to wrists and clubs!

The course includes two steep climbs, and the narrow approaches to some of the greens, together with dog-legged fairways, call for much thought and accuracy with the drives. However, the greens are especially good and the course is full of variety, including a "pulpit" green, making it a very enjoyable golfing experience.

For quite some time the Club boasted the only lady golf professional in the county; Jane Miles, had an enviable County record as an amateur, and before turning Pro she worked on the course as a member of the groundstaff. The Chedington Court Golf Club near Crewkerne, and a recent member of the County Union, has also engaged a lady professional.

Pine trees, which are a feature of the Bournemouth skyline, flank many of the fairways, but a lot of the natural heather still remains; pretty to look at, but very difficult to get out of!

Lyme Regis 1893 1
Timber Hill
Lyme Regis
DT7 3HQ
(0297) 442963
18 holes 6,220 yards SSS 70
Between Lyme Regis and Charmouth off the A3502

This most westerly of the Dorset courses was laid out on forty-two acres of clifftop downs by the golfers who formed the original administration.

Very little was done to alter what nature had provided and the founders were playing golf within a month of their decision to form a Club, and continued to do so without major changes for the next seventeen years. Even today, just one year short of the Club's centenary, several of the original holes form part of the present extended layout.

Major changes to the layout were carried in 1931; the course had been purchased by the members for £2,200 in 1925, and when the residue of the land became vacant it was decided to extend the course to eighteen holes. Messrs Colt and Allison were asked to produce a design, but the committee decided in favour of a layout prepared by Major D R Nicholls, a local architect, which in addition to being £500 cheaper, also retained the original nine holes. Events were to prove the wisdom of this choice because the new nine holes were compulsorily ploughed up during the war.

After the war the re-instated course remained unaltered until a further expansion was carried out in 1982, and this is essentially the course as it exists today.

A first-time visitor would probably be advised to start from the tenth, but if played the way it was designed, the shot from the back tee on the first calls for a high degree of accuracy, because there is a very real danger of losing a wayward ball in the roadside hedge.

The second is a tight par 3, and club selection can vary from anything between a six to a one iron depending upon the wind strength and direction.

A new raised tee has recently been incorporated into the par 5 third, which calls for a straight shot, because the trees lining the fairway are unforgiving, but a long straight drive will open up the distinct possibility of a birdie.

Another par 5 follows, this time a left-hand dog-leg. The card of the course contains a diagrammatic layout, and it will indicate that the tee shot should be aimed at the tree on a mound, from which the green is visible, just short of 250 yards away.

The fifth is a 316 yard uphill right-hand dog-leg for the mid-to-high handicap golfer, but the big hitter can attack the green, but beware, it is notoriously difficult to read.

Six and seven are long par 4s, and two of the best holes on the course. Out of reach in two shots for the average golfer, and also influenced by the prevailing wind conditions. A par on either of these two holes is a very satisfying experience.

Eight is a straightforward par 3, but demanding an accurate tee shot to a two tier green surrounded by bunkers.

Nine is a deceptive hole; at 252 yards it invites attack, but the wind affects most of the holes on this course, and unless you are lucky enough to be playing in balmy conditions, then the cleverly sited bunkers will punish the shot which fails to make the green.

The back nine begins with the generous wide open fairway and a tall mast provides a marker for the tenth green.

The glorious views from the new elevated eleventh tee should not be allowed to distract you from the main purpose, because this hole demands careful shot selection. An accurate drive will open up the possibility of placing the second on a friendly grassy bank, which will encourage the ball to roll towards the flag... too far right and you will be faced with a delicate bunker shot.

A tricky 172 yard par 3 follows, with bunkers to catch a short approach shot, and a very difficult return pitch if you overshoot the green... again the prevailing sea breeze gives pause for thought over club selection.

The 514 yard dog-leg par 5 thirteenth has a wide fairway, but it too must be treated with respect. The low handicap, long hitting player can aim over the shed and the hedges, but the average golfer will follow the marker posts. The second shot will disappear from view down a steep slope, but with luck it will be resting on the apron when you crest the brow. Be sure to look out for the pin placing on the adjacent fifteenth green, it may prove to be an advantage.

The fourteenth can be a frustrating hole! Everything depends upon the wind (known locally as *The Devil's Bellows* or *Black Venn*) which gusts up and over the cliff. Be prepared to lose a ball here!

The fifteenth is one of the most spectacular golf holes in the country. The fairway is about 600 feet above the sea and provides a wonderful aerial view of Lyme Regis; it is edged by the most dramatic cliff scenery created by the ravages of centuries of ice, rain, and heavy frosts, combined with continual landslips. The area is the largest coastal mud slide in Europe, and there is an excellent museum of fossils and ammonites in the town which is well worth a visit.

The hole itself is a fairly easy . . . if the wind is kind and you have remembered to notice the pin placing when playing the thirteenth.

The four hundred yard par 4 sixteenth is regarded as being the most difficult hole on the course. A long uphill climb and (again) susceptible to wind conditions. The green is guarded by large bunkers and an 'out-of-bounds' area to punish a wayward second shot to the green.

Stay away from the left-hand side of the fairway with the tee shot on the seventeenth, but a good drive down the centre is rewarded by the prospect of a delightful second into a handsome two-tier green surrounded by trees.

A well aimed drive from the eighteenth opens up a comfortable shot to the green, but try a big one and you could find the gorse jungle to the right of the fairway . . . or the car park, which could be quite expensive! The newly planted copses, when mature, will transform this into a very pleasant finishing hole, rewarding to those prepared to respect the designer's intent.

The nineteenth beckons and you have earned your refreshment, but for all its difficulties, this is a very pleasant golf course, and one which never fails to make you want to return.

Lyons Gate Golf Club 1991   **8**
Dorchester
DT2 7AZ
(03005) 239
9 holes 2040 yards SSS 60
On A352 Dorchester to Sherborne road

A chance remark by a colleague of Noel Pires in August 1989, suggesting that it might be a good idea to convert his farm into a golf course, set the ball rolling; there were no other courses in the immediate vicinity so, aware of the need and the local interest, the crucial decision was made.

Ken Abel of the Sherborne Golf Club designed the course; planning approval was obtained in February 1990, and Noel, assisted by John Tite and the late Tom Fletcher set about building the course.

A driving range was the first objective, and this became operational on the following Easter Sunday, but unfortunately it had a very short life because it was destroyed by a violent storm in the following winter and has not been replaced. During this period the first set of greens were being constructed, and these suffered a similar fate: all the hard work was washed away by horrendous flash floods which destroyed six greens within twenty minutes.

Undaunted by this severe setback, temporary greens were laid out, which enabled the basic course to be opened in August 1990, whilst in the meantime work continued on reconstructing the permanent greens.

After all the disappointments, it was gratifying to welcome visitors from an area of about forty miles, which was convincing evidence of the need for such a pay-and-play facility, and confirmation of the original concept.

A Club was formed in August 1991 with upwards of one hundred members and the permanent greens were opened for play.

The course, remote from any built-up area is a peaceful oasis, which offers spectacular views, and wonderful seasonal displays of a wide variety of wild flowers, many of which have been chosen as the names of the holes. Plans have been drawn up to lengthen the course, but at present it is a short, undulating course, with 'Fletcher's Flight' at 323 yards the longest hole.

Meyrick Park

Meyrick Park **24**
Meyrick Park
Bournemouth
BH2 6LH
(0202) 290307
18 holes 5,663 yards SSS 68

Architect's sketch of the new pavilion at Meyrick Park

The oldest of the two golf clubs, *The Bournemouth and Meyrick Park Golf Club,* originally played in the New Forest under a different name, but transferred to Meyrick in 1894. The other, *The Meyrick and Queens Park Golf Club* was founded in 1894. In 1974 when the county boundaries were changed Meyrick Park became one of the oldest golf Clubs in Dorset.

The first recorded 9-hole 'green' to be constructed in Dorset was laid out on the west cliff at Bridport in 1891, the Isle of Purbeck course was next (1892), followed by Lyme Regis (1893) and Sherborne (1894), but then Bournemouth was in Hampshire. However, as *Sandbourne* in Thomas Hardy's Wessex, it was in Hardy country long before the bureaucratic boundary adjustments.

The Club possesses the unique distinction of being the first golf Club in England to play on a municipal course, in exactly the same way that the first-ever golf Clubs played over the public links in Scotland.

With the forthcoming change to private management it is doubtful if the old clubhouses will survive, because the new plans include a pavilion which will provide accommodation for the private clubs, and facilities for the 'pay-and-play' golfers.

The original golf courses, designed by Tom Dunn consisted of an 18-hole 'Long Course', measuring 4,500 yards, and a Ladies Course of just 700 yards.

An additional forty acres was donated in 1920 and H S Colt completely redesigned the course, incorporating the Ladies course into the men's, to produce a much better test of golf, which was in fact just slightly longer than the present layout.

The course provides a good test of golf, with a wide variety of interesting hazards, principally derived from the undulating nature of the ground, which is immediately evident from the first tee, where the drive is over a valley, to a small green cut into the hill and set at an angle.

Mid Dorset Golf Club 1990   **10**
Belchalwell
Blandford Forum
DT11 0EG
(0258) 861386
18 holes 6,503 yards SSS 71
9 miles west of Blandford Forum and one mile south of Okeford Fitzpaine off the A357

The course, nestling in the lea of the impressive Bulbarrow is worth a visit if only to enjoy the beauty and the magnificent views from one of the highest points in Dorset.

For twenty-five years the land supported a large dairy herd, and the extensive use of nitrogen-based fertilisers to produce a twice-yearly crop of silage had a devastating effect upon the wildlife, which had previously been varied and abundant, and had been hunted over for a great many years.

Planning applications for new golf courses invariably arouse intense opposition from conservationists, who object to the artificiality of manicured fairways and greens, and the use of chemical sprays. But it is a great pity that funds were not available when this golf course was mooted, to support a professionally conducted survey of the beneficial effects upon the surrounding countryside of this particular 'Change-of-Use'.

The result would have provided an emphatic and positive response to the protesters, and could have been used to allay the fears of naturalists elsewhere in the country.

The northern slopes of the Barrow once supported a local industry of moss-gathering. This was sent to Covent Garden to be used by florists and wreath-makers until Dr Beeching destroyed the rural railway system and closed Shillingstone station. In those leisurely days wildlife and animal husbandry co-existed, but unfortunately present-day intensive farming methods have driven away many of the skylarks, the buzzards and the badgers.

However, this story has a happy ending, because now that the dairy herd and the silage making have departed, the roe deer have returned and the song of the skylark is beginning to be heard again. Ancient badger setts have been protected in the golf course layout, and the local people are again looking forward to seeing the return of rare birds, which at one time were a commonplace on the hill.

So much for the nature report! The visiting golfer will appreciate the natural beauty, even if he cannot distinguish a pheasant from a lapwing, but he will certainly recognise the skill of the golf course architect and his use of the natural hazards... which are many and varied.

The course is a test for all categories of golfer, with trees, water and difficult lies to contend with. For example, the par three fourteenth is particularly challenging; played from a high tee through a gap in the coppice and over water to a green with a bunker at the back to trap any shot which fails to stop on the green.

The sixteenth skirts the edge of the hill and is bordered by punishing rough and trees, and with a difficult approach to the green... but the views are delightful!

There are three par 5s, ten 4s and five par 3s, and the layout could be described as gently undulating parkland, with steeper, more challenging holes on the south-western side of the course.

The Clubhouse is particularly well appointed, including a spacious restaurant and bar overlooking the eighteenth green.

The course was designed in 1989 by David Astill, who was the Professional at the Stevenage Golf Club, but with aspirations to be a golf course designer. Mid Dorset was his first venture, and he remains as the Course Manager, but he has since designed three others.

Moors Valley Country Park 1988   21

Horton Road
Ashley Heath
Nr. Ringwood
Hants
BH24 2ET
(0425) 479776
18 holes 6,300 yards SSS 70
8 miles north of Bournemouth off the Horton Road

Clubhouse and professional's shop under construction.

This Hawtree-designed golf course is part of a 275-acre Country Park facility owned and managed by the East Dorset District Council.

Surrounded by mature deciduous trees and Forestry Commission conifers, the park is a genuine noise-free oasis on the edge of the Verwood Forest. The complex attracts thousands of families to its conducted walks, nature trails, lakes a one-and-a-quarter mile narrow gauge steam railway layout, complete with 'Victorian' station and engine sheds, in addition to a beautifully reconstructed sixteenth century barn, which has been converted into a restaurant, shop and display area.

Not many golf courses have a steam railway alongside the fairway, but neither this nor the many other activities intrude upon the concentration of the golfer, because the course is completely isolated from the park, and there is not a house to be seen.

The golf course was a 9-hole layout for four years and although there were excellent teaching facilities and a well stocked professional's shop, there was no clubhouse. Now however, following the completion of the second nine holes, the present pro shop will be integrated into a new clubhouse which will include changing and restaurant facilities comparable with the best in the area.

A golf Club was established from the outset and affiliated to the County Union to enable players to obtain a recognised handicap. It quickly attracted a large following of 'pay-and-play' golfers, who were introduced to the basic skills by Keith Hockey, the 'Director of Golf' and his staff; then encouraged to practice and improve, and to move into the competitive environment of Club golf.

Undulating parkland, large greens, water and mature trees combine to make the course a very good test for all categories of golfer, and when the new nine holes have fully matured, the course will be well up to 'County' standards.

The course is slightly unbalanced, with three of its par 5s in the front nine; this is not the fault of the designer, but entirely due to the need to change the planned site of the clubhouse and restaurant.

The short sixteenth green is completely surrounded by water, and the lake has to be carried with the tee shot from the seventeenth, but probably the most difficult hole on the course is the 450 yard fourth. It is off-set, and at about 230 yards from the tee a line of trees juts into the fairway from the right, and with a mound on the left the average player will settle for a drive short of this bottleneck and a one-over-par five. However, the low handicap player will relish the challenge, and with an accurately placed tee shot, a par should not be a problem.

In addition to the first-class golf, there is a 14-bay floodlit driving range, ideally situated close to the first tee for a convenient 'warm-up' prior to playing.

Parkstone Golf Club 1910
Links Road
Parkstone
Poole BH14 9JU
(0202) 707138
18 holes 6,250 yards SSS 70
3 miles west of Bournemouth, off A35

20

Constructed out of the old Poole Waterworks land, Lord Wimborne commissioned Willie Park Jnr to fashion a golf course out of what a local journalist described as *a wilderness of heath and heather,* for the expressed purpose of upgrading the value of the surrounding land in order to attract wealthy residents into the area.

When the news of the sale of the waterworks installations and the proposal to create a golf course became public knowledge, there was some opposition from a section of the Poole public, 'who had not the slightest desire to have a golf course'. They also expressed the fear that the Luscombe valley would be 'closed to all but those making subscriptions'; and 'the employment of caddies would tempt young lads to earn a little more pocket money and so discourage them from attending church'. However, Lord Wimborne was a very important and powerful local figure, and the objectors were ignored.

Willie Park was one of the greatest golf architects of all time, and one of the most respected names in golf. He designed numerous courses in this country and in America; among the best known from a long list in this country being Sunningdale and Carnoustie.

As a golfer he was a perfectionist, and believed implicitly that matches were won or lost on the putting green. He was known to have practised his putting for twelve hours without a break; so it should come as no surprise to learn that he wrote *The Art of Putting,* which is said to have been largely autobiographical.

Work began on the construction of the course in June 1909, beginning at the Parkstone end of the Luscombe valley and running in a southerly direction through the Compton Acre. Two hundred and fifty workmen transformed the heath into a golf course within five months; an astonishing achievement even with that amount of labour, and the course was opened for play in 1910, eleven months after the initial clearance work began.

Contemporary sports journalists often referred to Parkstone as being Broadstone's sister course. This rather facetious allusion was only relevant inasmuch as Lord Wimborne financed them both; but there the affinity ends because, whereas he seriously intended Broadstone to be the county's 'biggest and best', Parkstone was merely a piece of real estate which he intended to improve and ultimately sell for building purposes.

In view of this stated objective it is surprising that the foremost golf course designer of the day should have been engaged for the work, and then to impose such stifling restrictions upon his undoubted design capabilities.

Park was not allowed to make the best use of the heath or the land immediately surrounding the waterworks complex. He could not include the two reservoir lakes, which should have been the most obvious focal point of any design, because the large triangle of land behind the main lake was to be reserved for building purposes; and for some unknown reason, the final settling bed in front of what is now the sixth green, was drained. In Park's layout this hole was played in the opposite direction to today's sixth, and was a right-hand dogleg par 4. With the water in place this would have been a magnificent hole in an otherwise very cramped layout. When the present third hole was

The original Clubhouse

constructed in about 1912, the hill was reduced and the spoil used to fill-in the old settling bed (referred to as a quarry in contemporary reports).

The local newspaper, reporting the official opening in 1910, praised the skill of the architect, but in fact, and for the reasons outlined, the layout did not reflect Willie Park's undoubted skill; it was unbalanced, with eleven par fours; shorter than it should have been, and with too many blind holes. The water, which was excluded from Park's canvass, remained as a pretty but peripheral attraction, until the 'medal' tee, designed by Hamilton Stutt, was constructed between the lakes in the 1970s.

By 1927, with the course now fringed with the elegant houses of rich businessmen, retired officers and ex-Government officials, Lord Wimborne announced his intention of selling the land for building development, but he agreed to give the Golf Club the first option to buy the land for £20,000 . . . on condition they agreed to preserve it as a golf course.

Six local businessmen set up a company to buy the land, but they were unsuccessful in their attempts to raise the required sum, and the course was only saved from the builders by the last-minute intervention of T W Simpson, the owner of Compton Acres, who wanted to preserve the magnificent views (which were uninterrupted by trees in those days) across the heathland to Brownsea Island and the Purbeck Hills. He offered the Company a low-interest loan of £7,500 to make up the sale figure, and so saved the course from destruction. Ironically Simpson's lovely mansion set amid the world-famous gardens, has been torn down and replaced by ugly flats, but Parkstone golf course and the lovely views have been preserved . . . hopefully for ever.

In 1932 the course underwent a radical re-design. About sixty acres of marshland were bought from Lord Alington, against the wishes of most of the members who were certain that the land could never be successfully drained. James Braid, one of the immortal Triumvirate, and the leading golf course architect of the day, was engaged to survey the land and to recommend a revised course layout. Braid's plan included the construction of four new holes in the marshland (the eighth through to the eleventh), and a major reconstruction of the rest of the course to alleviate the congestion of Willie Park's design.

Braid suffered from motion sickness and was afraid of sea travel, so although he was a prolific designer, and was sought after all over the world, he only designed two overseas courses, the Singapore Island course in 1924, and the St Andrews Golf Club, New York in 1930, both of which he designed from topographic maps.

The contractor for the work was John R Stutt, who worked in partnership with Braid on a great number of courses. Stutt liked the area and took up residence close to the course. He joined the Club in 1947 and was responsible for many improvements to the course. He eventually became a major shareholder in the Company, but he was always a supporter of the members' ambition to own the course and played a large part in the eventual transition. He was the Chairman of the Board when the members finally realised their ambition and bought the Club in 1960 for the remarkably low figure of £12,000.

Springtime is a particularly pleasant time to play at Parkstone; the views of the harbour are always spectacular, but in spring there is increased activity among the wildfowl on the lakes, and the course is ablaze with colour from hundreds of rhododendrons.

Parkstone in the early 1920s. This postcard shows the area of the old 9th, 10th, 11th and 12th holes

Queens Park
Queens Park West Drive
Bournemouth
BH8 9BY
(0202) 396198
18 holes 6,505 yards SSS 72

26

The Mayor of Bournemouth struck the first ball to open the town's second golf course on the 28th of October 1905; there is no record as to what happened to the ball, but the professionals then took over, and Braid, Taylor, Vardon and Herd gave the course its official baptism before a very large crowd.

'Queens' very quickly established itself as the premier municipal golf course in the country, and it attracted many world famous golfers (including Seve Ballesteros), to play in the national tournaments which were held on the course until about 1976. Foremost among them was the *Daily Mail;* which in the 1939 tournament resulted in a unique five-day marathon. Henry Cotton and Archie Compston were tied on 292 after four rounds, were still tied after a play-off, and again after another thirty-six holes, then Cotton won on the Saturday April 1st.

The local professional, Don Curtis had backed himself to win, but claimed that he was thwarted by the Park Superintendent, who used the bowling club mowers, which upset the 'nap' on the greens and ruined his putting technique!

Five golf clubs were established at Queens Park: The Meyrick & Queens Park (who were established in 1895 and moved to Queens in 1905); Bournemouth Artisans, who were formally inaugurated at a meeting in the Town Hall on July 3rd 1930; Boscombe (1938), who were originally formed from the 'Associate' members of the Artisans Club; The Boscombe Ladies (1953) and The Boscombe & West Hants Juniors (1962).

The Artisans Club was one of a very few autonomous artisan clubs in the country; it paid a capitation fee to the Council like all the other clubs using the course, but it was not associated with a private club. Don Curtis, the Queens Park professional was the President of the club from its inception until his death in 1983, and gave free golf lessons to its members.

The club membership was limited to sixty, and they were restricted to play before 9 am. and after 3 pm. They used the caddy shelter alongside the eighteenth green of the old course layout, and moved into their own clubhouse, (which they built themselves) near the first tee in 1951, and remained there until the new pavilion was built in 1968. The Clubs, with the exception of the Ladies, were amalgamated under the title of The Queens Park (Bournemouth) Golf Club in 1991.

When the course opened it was a very difficult bogey 75, but Don Curtis set a course record of 67 in 1936, which stood until Antonio Cerda of Argentina reduced it by one shot in the *Penfold* Tournament in 1951. The amateur record of 69 for the old course was set in 1939 by Len Loader, a long-serving member of the Artisans Club. Bill Carr, another member of the Artisans Club became a professional at the Windwhistle Golf Club in Somerset.

One of the great characters on the course for a great many years was the legendary Joe Jones, starter, secretary, and supervisor; he had lost a leg in the war, was known (inevitably) as 'Peg-Leg', and was very strict in the observance of etiquette and the Rules of Golf.

The course is not as difficult now... some of the older players rate it as being four shots easier... and it has undergone three major alterations. It is still a very good golfing challenge, and a round played to handicap would still be a very satisfying achievement. The amateur record on the revised course is 69, and was established during the Bournemouth 'Open' in 1987.

Sherborne Golf Club 1894

Clatcombe, Sherborne DT9 4RN
(0935) 814431
18 holes 5,949 yards SSS 68
1 mile north of Sherborne on the B3145 Sherborne-Wincanton Road

The 1894 issue of *The Golfing Annual* reported the opening of the course and also listed the names of the original owners and committee:

BLACKMORE VALE GOLF CLUB 1894
President: J K D W Digby, MP. Vice President: G Gordon.
Committee: C H Hodgson, A Campbell, J Douglas.
Treasurer: A J Drewe. Hon Sec. T W Wilson, The Green, Sherborne.
Greenkeeper: T R Atkinson.
Entrance Fee: £1. Annual Subscription £1. Members, about 40.
The course, of nine holes, is about a mile and a half from Sherborne. The hazards are hedges, roads, furze, and banks. The greens are good, and the tees fair.
A monthly medal (handicap) is played for on the first Wednesday of each month.

In spite of the above assessment of the course, the original choice of venue, 'somewhere on the Sandford Road', was an unfortunate one to say the least; a 9-hole layout which proved to be so poorly suited to golf and so inconvenient, that the Club moved out within a year to Clatcombe Farm. There the small group played in their red jackets for five years, before moving to Lenthay Common, where they stayed until 1908 when permission to play on the Common was withdrawn by the son of the original President (and Lord of the Manor). This was in response to a petition by the Commoners who claimed that *a flying ball might seriously injure an animal and considerably depreciate its value.* As a result, the members retraced their steps back to the fields of Mr Parsons at Clatcombe Farm, where the County Record Office confirms that a planning application was approved in 1910 for the use of three fields at Castleton for playing golf.

Following their return to Clatcombe the Club decided to drop the Blackmore Vale title and established themselves as The Sherborne Golf Club. It was at about this time that the Bridport and West Dorset Golf Club crossed the bay and sold their 'cricket house' to the Sherborne Club.

The first recorded professional was E Luscombe (1913-14), followed by J Donald (1915-24), then J Luscombe (1924-28) and P Everett (1928-31).

The site the Club had returned to was roughly the old eight holes of the present course, plus a hole which they constructed in a field to the East which later was used as a practice area. The course remained as nine holes until after World War I, but in 1936 the Club commissioned James Braid to design ten new holes on land to the south of the clubhouse and to change the old nine holes to eight of an entirely different character. This work was carried out by John R Stutt who worked in partnership with Braid on the major part of his design work.

Now, with an 18-hole course of great character and beauty, the Club was in a position to enter the premier league of county golf. But it was not to be - fate, in the shape of World War II intervened, resulting in a rapid reversion to nine holes again, with the loss to agriculture of much of James Braid's handiwork.

After the war the club members had to be content to play over the original eight holes plus the notorious fifteenth, known appropriately as 'The Gulley', which had been designed by the then Professional J W Thompson in 1941.

Fate struck another blow in 1955 when the clubhouse was burned to the ground . . . destroying all the Club's records in the process.

Preliminary survey work began in 1959 to bring back the ten holes which had been used for fattening farm stock for twenty years. There was no money available to pay a recognised course architect, so the Club set about the task on a DIY basis. Each committee member was allocated a green and with his working group of members, using their own tools and helped by the local youth club who cleared the fairways of stones, they gradually brought the course back into play over a period of about five years.

The revived, and revised course was officially opened in 1954 with an exhibition match between Dai Rees, Bernard Hunt, Peter Alliss and John Jacobs.

Extensive alterations to the clubhouse were completed in 1966; and in the following two years the committee constructed a new second hole; modified the third to relieve the congestion; and re-designed the three finishing holes. Finally, in 1985 Donald Steel extended the fourteenth with the work being carried out by Brian D Pierson.

The course, which offers golfers of all categories a variety of challenges, now sits amid surroundings of exceptional beauty, just a short distance from the historic old town, which for a short time in the ninth century was the capital of Wessex. The clubhouse, standing on a plateau nearly five hundred feet above sea level, commands fine views over the rolling countryside, pine-clad ridges and wooded coombes to the north and west.

15

Sturminster Marshall 1992
Moor Lane
Sturminster Marshall
BH21 4AH
(0258) 858444
9 holes. 2,325 yards SSS 63 (18 holes)
Off Station Road in the village

Designed and built by the same partnership which developed the Bulbury Woods Golf Club, this 9-hole golf course was opened by the President of the Dorset County Golf Union in June 1992.

Originally forty acres of farmland, the course was designed by John Sharkey; and his partner David Holdsworth designed and built the very attractive clubhouse.

The course has two par 3s and seven par 4s, and is used extensively by people from the surrounding villages, many of whom were persuaded to take up the game for the first time because of its convenience. It serves an important introductory function, and it is expected that many of the new recruits to the game will progress to membership of the Bulbury Woods Club when they have become proficient.

It is essentially a 'pay-and- play' facility, but a membership scheme is available to encourage players to obtain an officially recognised handicap. There is no doubt that such "academy" courses are an essential part of the present-day crowded golf scene, because before the advent of such basic teaching and practice facilities, it was extremely difficult and expensive for the newcomer to build up confidence and a good understanding of the fundamental aspects of the game and its etiquette, which are essential for entry to either the municipal or the private golf clubs.

Wareham 1924   **12**
Sandford Road
Wareham BH20 4DH
(0929) 554147
18 holes 5,603 yards SSS 67
1 mile north-east of Wareham on A351

Most of the land to the south and west of the old town and one-time port of Wareham ("The Gateway to the Purbecks") is marshy, so therefore the modern building development is concentrated in the northern approaches to the town, but when the golf club was formed, the land at Sandford was all farm and heathland, on part of the Drax family estates.

There are early records of golf being played 'between the old workhouse and Baggs Mill' prior to the construction of the Sandford course, and this was presumably the site of the original golf course on common land to the north of the town, which was initiated in 1908.

Right from the outset, the Sandford course presented many problems due to the poor quality of the ground. The layout was revised many times by the small ground staff, with advice initially from the Swanage professional, and later from the Parkstone professional. Eventually, after many years of care and soil conditioning they succeeded in creating a very good 9-hole course, which remained virtually unchanged until well after World War II, but it was only achieved by concentrated efforts, sometimes against almost insurmountable natural hazards and financial constraints.

Like so many other small clubs, its fortunes declined during and immediately after the war. It *almost* succumbed, but unlike some others described in the opening chapter of this book, it was saved from extinction by the enthusiasm of its legendary Honorary Secretary Eddie Darville and the determination of the small band of members who took over the responsibilities of maintaining the course after the Club was forced to dispense with the services of its greenkeeper.

In those difficult early days the clubhouse was a small tin shack, and because it had to remain unattended for most of the time, visiting players and members were asked to put their 'half-crown' (12½p) green fees into an "Honesty Box". After the game, if they fancied a cooling drink, a similar "self-service" system applied; bottles of beer were kept in a cupboard set into the wall!

Sadly the old clubhouse, and the honesty box, were destroyed by fire in 1983, and with it the Honours Boards listing the early competition winners. It was assumed until very recently that the Minute Books had also been lost, but the first one has now been discovered and will provide invaluable source material for a future comprehensive history of the club.

A new clubhouse was built in 1984, and its rebirth seemed to signal a resurgence of the old determination which had earlier saved the club from bankruptcy. Plans were laid to extend the course into the rolling countryside to the north and west, up to the edge of the Wareham Forest. The weed-filled land was of poor agricultural value, but it had great potential as a golf course, with its natural hazards of hills, stream, and trees.

There was no money available to pay for a professional golf course architect, so the members set out to explode the old adage about "anything designed by a committee". This they certainly did, and the undoubted success of their DIY efforts is reflected in a full membership and a rapidly maturing 18-hole golf course which includes a recently installed automatic irrigation system.

The Club is now considering ways of removing the congestion which remains in part of the original 9-hole layout, and also of providing room for a practice putting green near the recently enlarged clubhouse and changing rooms.

The future of the Club is now secure, and when the planned developments are complete, the course will provide challenging golf in lovely parkland surroundings.

Weymouth Golf Club 1909   **7**
Links Road
Westham, Weymouth
DT4 0PF
(0305) 773981
18 holes 6,034 yards SSS 69
A354, off Manor Roundabout (Portland & Town Centre exit)

The previous chapter describes two Weymouth golf courses near the Radipole Lake, one of which was claimed to be the oldest in England. But the 'Town Links' owes its existence to a group of five businessmen who, disappointed by the Council's decision to accept J H Taylor's recommendation to site the new golf course well outside the town, at Came Down, decided to build their own, much closer to home.

The story began in 1904 when the Town Council commissioned Taylor to survey the area and recommend a site for a golf links which would add to the town's amenities, and so attract more visitors. Bournemouth's two municipal golf courses were quoted as examples of successful municipal enterprises, which although costly to construct, were attracting many more visitors to the town and proving to be very profitable.

The most attractive site was the land at Lodmoor to the east of Greenhill, where a golf course would have made a most attractive extension to the esplanade. Unfortunately it proved to be unsuitable because it formed a natural drainage area for the River Wey, and was susceptible to flooding from the sea.

Although it is now common knowledge that Taylor favoured sites which were 'not crowded-in by communities', it is not possible to judge if this predilection for "space" affected his eventual choice, but the Came Down site must have been particularly attractive in this regard, because even today there are only one or two houses visible from the clubhouse.

In any event, the small group of Weymouth businessmen were determined to have a links more conveniently sited to their homes, and in 1905 they formed 'The Weymouth Golf Syndicate' and commissioned James Braid to design a golf course at Westham, which is just one-and-a-half miles from the Town Clock.

The first world war had a disastrous effect upon the Club's finances; the membership was decimated and a large part of the course was compulsorily ploughed up for food production. The small group found themselves in serious financial difficulties and in 1922 they sold out to the Corporation... so belatedly providing the municipal facility that its predecessors had signally failed to achieve, and at relatively little cost.

The fourteen "agricultural acres" were reinstated, and in 1934, four new holes were created on land to the west of Radipole Lane; but these and five others suffered the same fate with the advent of the second world war, and the course did not return to a full 18-hole layout until 1953, when it was opened by an exhibition match between the home professional Fred Beets and the Whitcombe brothers.

At this time 'The Weymouth Golf Club' consisted of a group of municipal season ticket holders who had formed a committee to arrange the competitions and fixtures, but in 1963, in the face of the possibility that the course might be closed due to the financial losses being suffered by the Corporation, they succeeded in obtaining a lease of the land and took control of the golf.

A third major reconstruction of the course took place in 1983 when a new road was constructed through part of the course. Although this was greatly resented at the time, the new holes, which were designed by Hamilton Stutt and constructed by Brian D Pierson, have greatly improved the "home" holes and have resulted in a better balanced layout.

Fred Beets, who joined them from Norfolk in 1913, stayed with the Club throughout his professional career, and carved out a niche for himself which will never be forgotten by the Club. He won the Dorset Professional Championship at the age of 68, and was quoted as being 'a player with good style, a first-class clubmaker and an excellent teacher with a very big stock of patience'.

During its lean years he became the Club's general factotum; and in addition to his professional duties, he acted as the secretary, greenkeeper, steward, cleaner, and whatever else was required. He was fond of recounting the time when a German bomber blew the eighteenth green to pieces after he had spent the whole day re-turfing it. On another occasion a huge crater was blown in the fourteenth fairway, but he decided to leave this as a water hazard!

Yeovil 1919
Sherborne Road, Yeovil
(0935) 22965
18 holes 6,144 yards SSS 70
9 holes 5,016 yards SSS 66
1 mile from Yeovil on A30 to Sherborne

Although the *Golfers Handbook* lists the year of origin as 1919, the original Club, under the name of the Yeovil and South Somerset Club was initiated as a 9-hole course on the Abbey Manor Estate in the village of Preston in 1908. *Whitby's Almanac* of that year gives the names of Sir Spencer Ponsonby Fane GCB as the President and W Bradhurst of Lloyds Banking House Hendford as the Honorary Treasurer. The course would then have been in Somerset.

These origins are confirmed by the recent discovery of the Minute Book belonging to the old Club and by the Honours Board for the Ponsonby Fane Trophy, which was won for the first time in 1908 by R J Luffman, brother of 'Lance' Luffman who became the Club Secretary and who was for many years the Secretary of the County Union.

In 1919 the Club moved to its present site at Babylon Hill, which was over the River Yeo and into the county of Dorset, to a 9-hole course designed by Fowler and Simpson.

Fowler made his name when he constructed the Walton Heath course in the face of much scepticism from his peers. It was among the first of the heathland golf courses but he confounded his critics and the course was enthusiastically acclaimed when it was opened in 1904. Among the many British golf courses designed by Fowler are included the Blue and Red courses of the Berkshire, The RAC, and the remodelling of the Royal North Devon, Broadstone, and Lytham St Annes courses.

Robert Wilson of the Oban Golf Club became the first professional (1907-09) and he was succeeded by Charles Carter. His Assistant at the Babylon Hill course was Stan Lambert, and Carter taught him the basic skills of club and shaft making. The heads were made out of solid blocks, and the hickory shafts turned on a lathe, then scraped and polished with a spirit mixture to bring out the grain and harden the surface. Iron heads were bought from Nicol, and Albert the old groundsman, who was Stan Lambert's father, assembled them to the shafts. Clubs were then priced at 16/-d each, or 18/-d with a bone insert in the face.

Carter stayed with the Yeovil club for forty-three years and in his time became the Secretary of the West of England PGA. He died at the age of 84.

The course was extended to eighteen holes and was opened in 1936 with an exhibition match between James Braid, Abe Mitchell, Wanda Morgan and Phyllis Wade.

The land, which was owned by the principal local landowner Wyatt Paul, was bought in 1954, when Yeovil Golf Club Ltd. was formed.

Pressure to expand the golfing facilities at Yeovil had been increasing for many years, and it became apparent that a second course was needed. Land at the top of the old course was surveyed, but abandoned in favour of part of the Newton Estate, which was accessible from the course over an old railway bridge and under the Yeovil to Weymouth railway line.

The new course was designed by the Sports Turf Research Institute and built by Mike Lock of Ilchester in lovely parkland containing numerous ancient oak trees, a millrace, a weir, and a pond; with the arches of the old Victorian railway bridge to add to the charm.

The first tee and the ninth green have been constructed on the 'home' side in order to lengthen the course to 5,016 yards, which includes two good par fives.

Players start the round in Dorset and drive over the river boundary to complete the hole in Somerset. Holes two to eight are played in Somerset, then the last hole is played back over the river into Dorset.

The lovely fifteenth century mansion in nearby Brympton d'Evercy is still occupied by a member of the Ponsonby Fane family, but sadly not for much longer because the house is up for sale, so severing the link with the founder of the Club.

Aerial view of the Bridport and West Bay Golf Clubhouse. It is understood that the name was painted on the roof when Sir Alan Cobham's flying circus used to visit the area between the wars

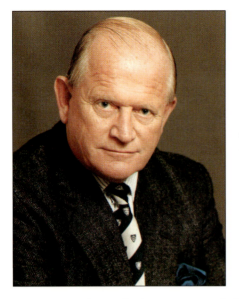

A County Union should be a union of all golfers irrespective of their standard of play; and this book, together with the 'Road Show' of Rules quiz, talks, and displays of golf memorabilia which the Executive Committee take around to the Clubs during the winter months, represents part of our plan to integrate Dorset golfers into the 'County' scene, and in the process to improve their knowledge of the game.

Our recent success at National level is proof that smaller counties like ours can compete with the larger, richer counties, but only if all our resources are carefully husbanded.

More academy facilities are needed to start the newcomer on the correct path, followed by progressively monitored programmes of coaching and competition, leading up to County appearances.

Thanks to the *Dorset Golfers Association* and to committed individuals and organisations, we have been able to fund the cost of providing improved facilities and competition experience for our younger players. But if this is to continue and expand, we must always be on the look-out for new ways and means of extending this funding and increasing the opportunities we can provide for our younger talents to be tested at all levels if we are to maintain and to improve upon the wonderful achievements of recent times.

The role of Junior Organiser at Club level is vitally important if new talent is to be recognised and encouraged. It has been all too evident in the competition scene that the Club which offers the best facilities and the greatest encouragement to its young players, invariably produces more representative players at the higher levels.

With regard to this book and its author Len Jenkins; I am reminded of the words of Bede in the *Ecclesiastical History of the English People* in AD 731, who wrote "I have assembled the facts as far as I am able to learn them from ancient documents, listening to old men talk, and my own personal knowledge". He has done a remarkable job in a very short time and has sacrificed at least a year of his own golfing time to research the work. He has unearthed many hitherto hidden facts about several of our older Clubs and has succeeded in assembling a fascinating history of the growth of golf in this county of Dorset.

Over the years the venues, the formats and the teams in the various county events have changed remarkably, but fortunately certain essential qualities have endured: the goodwill; good manners; good humour; and the sportsmanship, run like a bright thread through our game and its organisation.

A great many golfers have been proud to represent our county, and in addition to the challenge of competition, all have enjoyed the camaraderie and the good natured banter which I think is unique to our game . . . and long may it continue.

My term of office has been a rewarding experience, and I would like to thank every member of the Executive Committee, and especially our Secretary Maurice Hutchins who has a particularly demanding job to do, for their co-operation and selfless dedication.

Dr D M Holmes
President

The Executive Committee

Back row:
J Calver — *EGU Rep*
K A Abel CB DL — *Vice Pres*
K Longmore — *Pres Jnrs*
R Lawford — *I P Pres*
D Mathews — *Vice Capt*
D Lock — *I P C*

Front row:
R Norris — *Jnr Organiser*
K W Durbin — *Match Sec*
D Pratt — *Captain*
D M Holmes — *President*
M Hutchins — *Secretary*
W Hope — *Sec DGA*

Capt A V Hambro MP; the first President of the County Union

The County Union
1923 - 1992

Extracted from the Minute Books of the meetings of the Executive and the General meetings of the Union; and the records of the Accounts and Competition results which were begun in 1932.

A group of prominent members from five Dorset golf clubs met informally at the Dorset Country Club in Dorchester (now the Came Down Golf Club) on the fourth of January 1923 and decided to form a county golf union.

There is no indication in the official Minutes of any impetus or particular reason for wanting to form such a union, but it is reasonable to assume that they must have been impressed by the success of the unions in the neighbouring counties, and in particular the Devonshire Union.

The first meeting of a 'Council' took place three weeks later on the 25th of January in the same venue, and comprised Major Gundry of **Came Down** in the Chair, Major Crichton of Came Down, Capt E L James of the **Dorset** (Broadstone) Club, Major E M Morrison and J Ballantine of **Parkstone,** Major F A Stephens and O P Burdon of **Ferndown,** W Turner of **West Bay** (Bridport), F W Woodhouse of **Ashley Wood** (Blandford), and B Jackson of **Swanage** (Isle of Purbeck). They decided that 'it would be advantageous to form a county golf union to act as a central authority for determining all questions which may arise . . . and to promote the welfare and interests of the game in the county' and also 'to arrange with Railway Companies for increased travelling facilities for golfers'. In addition they decided to adopt the regulations of the Devon County Union, except that instead of having six nominated club representatives, they would have only five. This reduction probably reflected the fact that there were fewer golf clubs in Dorset, and this level of representation lasted until 1930, when it was decided that each of the eleven clubs then affiliated to the Union should be represented.

The old Clubhouse at Came Down 'where it all began'

The Council elected Capt Angus Hambro as the first President of the Union: Major Gundry as Captain: and Walter Little as Hon Secretary and Treasurer, all members of the Came Down Golf Club. They also decided that the Executive Committee would be chosen from the five other major clubs, and the first of these, which met for the first time on May 25th were Capt E L James of Dorset (Broadstone); Major Stephens of Ferndown and Cdr N H Carter of West Dorset.

In the context of a 'league table' of county unions Dorset would occupy a lowly position. It is reported that the Yorkshire clubs were the first to contemplate the formation of such a union in 1893, but their deliberations dragged on into the following year, with the result that our neighbours Hampshire have the honour of heading such a league with the formation of The Hampshire and Isle of Wight Golf Association at the Royal Winchester Golf Club in November 1893, five months ahead of Yorkshire.

The first county championship was held at the Royal Winchester Club in April 1894, and it was won by Lt "Freddie" Tait from the Aldershot Command Golf Club. The first inter-county championship (six-a-side) was played on the Royal Isle of Wight course at Bembridge in October 1895, which Hants & I o W won by 18 points to 5.

The Annual Competitions

In the first few years there were just three annual competitions and little significant change until after the war. Golf was affordable only by the wealthy middle class, and for at least a decade after the formation of the county union the competitors at the annual meetings rarely exceeded twenty. A three-day event, with entrance fees of five shillings would have been totally outside the sphere of the majority of the ordinary working man of the day because the equivalent cost would have been at least forty times greater in today's terms.

It was decided to hold the first of the annual golf meetings on the Dorset (Broadstone) course on the 11th, 12th and 13th of June 1923: the programme to be a 36-hole medal under handicap for a silver medal (entrance fee 2/6d) and a 36 hole medal for a county scratch gold medal (2/6d). On the 12th and 13th a club foursomes tournament would be held for a county shield (2/6d). On the first day there would be an optional sweepstake under handicap in the morning and afternoon rounds, with the winner taking two thirds of the sweep and the runner-up one third.

To celebrate the formation of the union four county matches were arranged for the inaugural year, against Devon, Somerset, Hants and Wilts, and it was decided that the Brokenhurst Manor Club should hold the first amateur v professional match on September 6th. The Minutes also showed that ten clubs had joined the union; in addition to the seven already mentioned, **Shaftesbury, Sherborne,** and **Lyme Regis** had joined, and **Yeovil,** whose course was in Dorset, joined in April, making eleven.

Major Gundry;
first Captain of the County
Union

Three weeks later, on the 15th of February, the Executive Committee, meeting at Broadstone, confirmed the programme, but made important amendments which must have added considerably to the costs. The winner of the 36-hole scratch competition would receive a gold medal and the runner-up a silver medal (entrance fee doubled to 5/-d). In the 36-hole handicap medal (handicap limit 18) the winner and runner-up would also receive gold and silver medals, and again the entrance fee was doubled.

In the county foursomes it was decided that clubs would enter just one couple, the winners to each receive a gold medal, and all matches would be played to a finish.

It was also decided to hold a county amateur v professionals match at Ferndown, but only if Dorset members were refused permission to play in the Hampshire competition. In the event the first of these annual competitions was held on the Ferndown course on September 3rd 1924.

The committee then selected a design for the medals and authorised the manufacture of a die at a cost of £5.12s.6d which Captain Hambro 'was given the opportunity to pay for'.

Many readers of this book will not be able to understand the Imperial monetary units used here, in the days when the old pound sterling was worth twenty shillings. "Half a crown" (12½p) was the normal stake in friendly matches for many years, and although this had doubled by the time decimalisation was introduced in 1971, it would still have bought a golf ball. The introduction of decimalisation had the effect of halving the value of the old currency, so doubling the cost of a friendly game 'at a stroke'.

The 5/-d entrance fee, or 25p in modern currency, would seem to be a trifling amount, but as it has already been explained, it would have been totally beyond the reach of the majority of the contemporaries of today's average golfer. It is also an indication of the social changes which have taken place in the golfing scene since those days, because although an ordinary worker would not have been able to afford such a fee, it is highly unlikely that he would have been eligible to join a golf club even if he could have afforded it. In those days it was "gentlemen" only, and people in trade would have had to look a round for a club with an artisan's section . . . and they were scarce in Dorset at that time.

After making a decision to print the 1923 programme and to send it out to all the affiliated clubs, Major Gundry proposed that clubs should put up all their four-handicap players to conform to the new national handicapping system, because his handicap of three had been increased to four! When viewed from this distance in time it is difficult to decide what was meant by a 'national handicapping system', because the EGU was only formed in 1924, principally to establish a uniform system of standard scratch scoring and handicapping, and it took another year or so for the system to be adopted.

Since its inception the EGU has been responsible for the standard scratch scores and the handicapping structure through a joint advisory council, which was subsequently re-christened The Council of National Golf Unions.

Walter Little;
first Secretary of the County Union

The present-day administrative structure remains fundamentally unchanged; from individual clubs, through their county unions to the EGU; and for specific matters, such as handicapping, from the EGU through CONGU to the R & A, which is the recognised ruling authority on golf.

In the absence of an official record of the first annual golf meeting in 1923, it is fortunate that a newspaper cutting of the event survives, and because of its historical interest, the report and the winners are reproduced here in addition to the inclusion in the records section of this book.

'An important step was taken towards the effective organisation of the royal and ancient game of golf in the county of Dorset by the formation of the County Golf Union, which held its first annual meeting on the course of the senior club at Broadstone last week. Every club in Dorset has affiliated to it, with the exception of the newly municipalised course at Weymouth, which is not likely to remain long outside the federation. The clubs which have affiliated are: The Dorset Golf Club; Dorchester and County GC; Ferndown; Parkstone; Shaftesbury; West Dorset; Sherborne; Yeovil (links in Dorset); Lyme Regis; and Swanage.

'The Dorset County Golf Union has been formed on the same lines as the Devon Union, to decide all questions affecting golf, and generally for the coordination of the clubs and strengthening of the game. The Union also decides the amateur championship of Dorset and it was quite in accordance with the fitness of things that the first official champion for the county should

E R Whitcombe (left) Major Gundry and Walter Little outside the Came Down Clubhouse

144

be the President of the Union, that stalwart and famous golfer Captain A V Hambro of Came Down. The gold medal which he won by two brilliant rounds of 80 and 77, will in future become the coveted prize of Dorset golf.

'Two gold medals had been given, one for the best scratch score over 36 holes, won by Capt Hambro; and one for the best handicap score, which was won by Mr S Fletcher. Two silver medals were also given, one for second scratch score, for which Major Stephens of Ferndown and Surgeon Commander Rusack RN (Came), tied, and one for second handicap score, won by Col F G Wheatley.

'The other medal competition competitors were: A K Smithells, General R M Poore, Capt Gelston, E F Rees-Mogg, W H Watkins, S F Stubbs and Lt G Belben RN.

'In the County Club Foursomes event (one couple from each club), the results were: West Dorset beat Parkstone 6 and 5; Isle of Purbeck and Came Down (w.o. for IoP; Came Down representatives not being able to play); Dorset beat Ferndown 3 and 2; Shaftesbury a bye; Swanage beat West Dorset 2 up; Dorset beat Shaftesbury 2 and 1. Final - Swanage beat Dorset 3 and 2.

'The following were the players of the individual clubs:- **Shaftesbury;** General R M Poore and Major Nixon; **West Dorset;** Commander N H Carter RN, and R G Smurden; **Parkstone;** Major C E M Morrison and C H Armstrong; **Came;** Capt A V Hambro and Major J Gundry; **Swanage;** J B Jackson and A E Lewis-Holloway; **Ferndown;** Major Stephens and V Weldon; **Dorset;** T Homer and K Smithells.'

In the first year's financial statement of the county union the total receipts amounted to £46.1s.6d: the expenditure was £20.12s.7d and there was a balance in the bank of £25.8s.11d (about £25.45p). It was resolved to hand over three pounds to the Dorset club for their Christmas Box Fund 'as a recognition to their staff for the extra work caused by the Annual Meeting of the union on their course'.

Interestingly, the Executive Council decided to hold the amateur v professional match at Ferndown on September 3rd so although there was no explanation in the Minutes, it has to be assumed that Hants were not prepared to allow the Dorset players to take part in their tournament as the Council had hoped. The competition was to consist of twelve amateurs and twelve pro's playing singles in the morning and foursomes in the afternoon; the amateurs handicap being two up. This fixture was originally scheduled to be played on the Brokenhurst Manor course, but no reason was given for the change of venue.

At this first Annual General Meeting, it was decided that in future the best sixteen scores in the scratch 36-hole medal competition should qualify for the county matchplay tournament. The winner of the scratch medal would be known as the *Champion of Dorset* and have his name recorded in a book to be kept permanently at Broadstone, and in addition, he would receive a postal order for £5.

Standard Scratch Scores

    The county union decided to fix the par scores of all the affiliated courses, and these were subsequently recorded in the Minutes of the Executive Committee meeting in September 1925: they make interesting comparisons with today's figures.

    The standard par and standard scratch scores under the EGU scheme which came into force on March 1 1926 were:-

BROADSTONE
Length Adjustment	NIL	Playing Length	5,746 yards
A.C.V★	4	Length of course	5,711 yards
Standard Scratch	74		
Par	70	GRADE C+	

CAME DOWN
Length Adjustment	NIL	Playing Length	6,093 yards
ACV	2	Length of Course	6,118 yards
Standard Scratch	76		
Par	74	GRADE C	

PARKSTONE
Length Adjustment	2	Playing Length	5,772 yards
ACV	3	Length of Course	5,517 yards
Standard Scratch	72		
Par	71	GRADE C	

FERNDOWN
Length Adjustment	NIL	Playing Length	6,516 yards
ACV	2	Length of Course	6,512 yards
Standard Scratch	78		
Par	76	GRADE C	

WEST DORSET & BRIDPORT
Length Adjustment	1	Playing Length	5,103 yards
ACV	2	Length of Course	5,079 yards
Standard Scratch	70		
Par	70	GRADE D	

SHAFTESBURY
Length Adjustment	2	Playing Length	5,792 yards
ACV	1	Length of Course	5,842 yards
Standard Scratch	74		
Par	75	GRADE D	

YEOVIL
Length Adjustment	NIL	Playing Length	5,202 yards
ACV	2	Length of Course	5,162 yards
Standard Scratch	72		
Par	70	GRADE D	

LYME REGIS

Length Adjustment	1	Playing Length	5,716 yards
Standard Scratch	72	Length of Course	5,539 yards
Par	73	GRADE D	

* Adjusted Course Value
+ 'A' where fairways are fast and give good run, through to 'E' where fairways are exceptionally heavy and there is no run at all.

The Swanage club was not included in the list because it had not complied with the Committee's request to submit their form of application, and Ashley Wood was added in 1933 with an SSS of 71.

In a note in the January 1926 meeting of the Executive Council, the EGU had asked the Committee to reconsider the scratch scores for Ferndown, Broadstone, Came Down, Lyme Regis, Shaftesbury and Parkstone; and they decided that Westward Ho! and Burnham should be adjusted to 78 and 75 respectively; in addition, a letter would be sent to the other clubs asking them to reduce their original figures by two. It would appear from this that the Dorset courses had been compared with Westward Ho! and Burnham in the calculation of the standard scores.

The scores were adjusted again in 1933: Parkstone was reduced to 71; Ferndown to 74; Came Down to 74; Lyme Regis to 72; Yeovil to 71; Shaftesbury to 73 and re-graded to 'D'; Broadstone was increased from 70 to 72; and Weymouth, which did not appear in the original list, was given an SSS of 70, with a playing length of 5,635 yards. Sherborne did not figure in the 1925 list, but it was later quoted as having an SSS of 71 and a playing length of 4,850 yards.

Amateur and Professional Alliance

C H Corlett, the professional at Broadstone, asked the Executive in October 1923 to form an amateur and professional golfing alliance. This was to be the first of a number of such approaches to be made by him on behalf of the county's professionals, but all were rebuffed by the Committee. The requests were not just unfavourably received, they were not considered worthy of serious discussion; an indication of how the status of the golf professional has changed since those early times. The managements of golf clubs, which were in the main composed of retired officers from the armed services, treated the professionals as servants of the club, and additionally, because they were classed as tradesmen, they were often treated in a very off-hand manner. All matches between members and professionals were billed as 'amateurs v professionals', never the reverse as is the custom today. Another example, which reflects the Committee's attitude is contained in the Minutes of a 1929 meeting whereby 'the Professionals' *desire* (my italics) to play the County Amateurs was not entertained owing to there being a full programme'. This was the first time since the beginning of the Minutes in 1923 that the professionals were even referred to with an initial capital letter!

Corlett's first request to form an amateur and professional alliance was refused 'owing to the limited number of professionals in the county'. We know that at that time there were twelve clubs in the Union, and presumably all employed a professional, so it is difficult to accept the reason given for the refusal. Unfortunately the PGA did not list their members by county, so it has not been possible to discover exactly how many professionals were employed at that time.

In May of the following year a deputation of county professionals met the Executive to press for the formation of a County Professionals Association, but they were rebuffed again, with the suggestion that they should approach the neighbouring county of Hampshire to ask if they could amalgamate with them.

There were no further references to the subject in the Minute Books, so it is not known if, or when such an association was ever formed. The Secretary of the PGA confirms that a South Western Section was formed in April 1909 by the four counties of Devon, Cornwall, Somerset and Dorset, but the records do not provide any information regarding an amateur and professional alliance. The SW committee of the PGA at that time had eight members from Dorset, including the three Whitcombe brothers from Came Down; F H Beets of 'The Town Golf Club' Weymouth; C H Corlett; J Randall of Ashley Wood Blandford; and Hugh Williamson of Parkstone.

To add piquancy to this account of Corlett's endeavours, we are fortunate to be allowed to reproduce extracts from a journal written in a small duplicate book by Harry Dean in 1950. Dean became an Assistant to Corlett, and went on to become a professional at a number of local golf clubs and at the Knowle Golf Club in Bristol.

The account is reproduced by permission of his daughter Mrs E Blakely; and with the exception of a very small amount of editing to correct some of the punctuation and the chronological sequence, it is presented as written, but one or two of the words were indecipherable.

It is a fascinating account of life as a golf professional in the early 1900s and it highlights the social changes which have overtaken the administration of the older golf clubs.

Charles Corlett
Broadstone 1910 – 35

'I was born in Broadstone on September the 25th 1894 and taken to Wimborne as a baby. My three elder brothers were golf caddies and they took me along with them when I was between 5 and 7 years old. I did carry clubs I well remember once for some strangers. We lost our way going from the 12th green to the 13th tee. But I ended up with nine pence and then walked home to Wimborne.

'While I lived in Wimborne I used to buy and sell firewood. I used to pay 3d. for a quarter cwt, borrow a truck, take it nearly a mile and get a profit of 1d. I always got more than my weight.

'I had to pass my home going with it, so I left the extra logs there, when

I got home later, I used to chop one small log up, take it three doors away and get ½d. for it.

'While living in Wimborne I saw the Boer War soldiers coming home, marching from the Square, over St Julian's bridge on to Blandford (1901-2)

'When I was about 7 or 8 we moved back to Broadstone. There were plenty of fields and heather about then. I went to the links on Saturdays, but I always played in the evenings. .

'At Broadstone we lived in Sandy Lane early in 1902-3. I still went to the golf links. The Pro's were Dunn and Jimmy Gowan. I was very keen to play in those days and we played for a halfpenny for 18 holes.

'We made our clubs from Nut sticks cut from a hedge for the shaft, a round block of wood 6" long and about 8 to 9 ins. circumference, made a hole in the middle with a red hot iron poker. One end was straight, the other end we made a loft for the (horn or iron?). We went over to the blacksmith, pinched a bit of iron about 30" long, 1 inch wide and one-eighth inch thick, bent the end and twisted it for loft, wrapped some rag around for a handle.

'We used corks for balls and played three little holes in the allotments at the top of Grove Road in Wimborne, about 18 yards long. My father gave me a real golf ball once (Guttie). I have never forgotten that gift. He could have sold it for 3d. 4d. or even 6d.

'Sometimes the Pro would give us some little cork balls which the ball makers would send with new balls as samples. They were about 1" in diameter.

'I left school when I was about 11 or maybe my 12th birthday. I went caddying and was given a handicap of 18. Mr Jack Beckford (+3) fixed a caddies championship. I lost in the semi-finals, and was then given a handicap of scratch. The next year I lost in the final at the 19th hole to C Wren. I had a very bad cut hand, but Dr Norman fixed it so as to play, but at the first shot it started to bleed. Wren wanted to cancel and play later, but there was a little crowd to watch. Mr Beckford was the umpire, so I said No. We were all square at the 18th hole, then Wren just went for a steady 5 at the 19th; I went for a 4 but took 3 putts. Wren told me later we both took 74 for the round.

'I was 14 years old when I met with my accident Aug. 8 1908. I had been caddying for two rounds, then I went home, had a bath and put on all new clothes, vest, pants, shirt and suit and walked to Darby's corner to meet our Sunday School treat coming from Sandbanks in a Traction Engine and three trucks. When the engine driver stopped for water I jumped up between the engine and first truck. When the engine started again I fell off on to the road under the wheels and all three trucks went over my legs and right hand. My left knee and my leg was smashed to pieces. My right hip was in a mess, my right hand had the thumb and two fingers smashed and the 3 fingers broken. I had escaped the wheels by less than 1" from going over my body.

'I was taken to Poole hospital and I had an operation at 9 o'clock and

Harry Dean

another one the next day at 11 o'clock. They told me I had 74 stitches. I was unconscious for 11 days. The doctors told me that 5 days after my accident they gave me a week to live and they were going to take my worst leg off if I did not regain consciousness within 7 days.

'I was some months in hospital and very helpless, strapped in iron cages around me. I can remember asking always whether I should be able to walk again. In the back of my mind was Golf. I think it was the hope of perhaps walking and learning to play golf again that kept me alive.

'One day I asked the hospital Doctor if there was any chance of my walking again. He told me one day perhaps (but not in these words). It was from then that I knew I would.

'Sundays was my special day, I always had the most visitors. My pal Billy Singleton was always in first. My Mother and Father were always alarmed to see me. After some weeks I was supposed to have an operation to take some skin off my back and graft on my leg. I was being prepared for the job but Nurse Black offered the skin from her arm. She was a young nurse from South Africa. I had a small piece taken from my arm "for luck", which did not take. All of her skin "took".

'A very rich man and his wife took an interest in me and just a few days before Xmas paid for me to go into a Nursing Home at Swanage for two months. I had told them that I wanted to go home first for a week, they were very angry, but they had to give way to me although the nurse told me they hoped to adopt me in time. But I told them unless I played golf it was no go. People tried to change my way of thinking, but I would not give way. When the two months was up they came to the Home and wanted me to stay a month more, but just for their sake I stayed one more week.

'Everyone was very angry except my Mum and Dad. Needless to say, after I went to their house and thanked them for all their kindness I did not see much of them again. I was asked to go to their house again by many people and was told that I should show more appreciation, but I thought that I had thanked them enough.

'As time went on I found I could walk without a stick and also could swing a golf club. My mother was very good to me, she had some shots one day.

'As time went on I went to the Golf links and was soon caddying. Then about 1912/13 the professional C H Corlett offered me to work in his shop at 4/6 a week. I gave my first lesson to Miss Carroll 1/6. I played often and Corlett charged 1/6 for anyone to play with me. He made me play quite a lot in the evenings. The other assistant George Pennington, Corlett and myself would play some holes. I was really hitting the ball a long way. Corlett made me play from scratch, he was Plus 3.

'I played quite a number of 4 ball matches against him and R C (Whabler?) Scr; Ox.& Cam. Frank Woolley Plus 3; Corlett always had a big bet on, I always thought it was £1.

'Going up to the 5th hole in one of these matches one day I was I think

4 up and playing well, when I was talking to Corlett I asked him what I had to do; he said what did I mean; I said I did not want to win and he lose the money. He just looked at me and said you play as well as you can. What a Gentleman he was. He was one of the best Golfers I ever met and the best Sportsman, he did whatever he could for me, he helped me in every way. After Harry Vardon his swing was the best I have ever seen (except putting) he must have lost a lot through that, I only ever seen him in about one match putting well, that was against George Duncan at Broadstone.

'In 1914 I went to Wareham as Pro. but only stayed 6 weeks. Corlett told me about the post and said that if I got it I should earn about £2 a week but with little playing, or I could stay with him and play for 4/6 plus 6d. per round commission. I played a round against Arthur Cann and beat him to get the job. After I had left and when he went to Wareham he made a lot of money.

'I was paid 15/- a week and profits from playing and lessons, and a small sports shop. The first day I remember I made 6/-, and for the week, about £2. This made me a full pro, but as I was only there six weeks, Corlett and the PGA decided to overlook it and I could still play as an Assistant.

'I told the Wareham secretary I was leaving and going back to Broadstone. I soon got playing again and Pennington taught me the trick of making Clubs. What a lovely clubmaker he was. He kept me at work all the time, he was very very strict, but on the other hand he would make me practice playing. He offered to pay half my expenses to play in the French Championship if Corlett would pay the other half. (They were going to play themselves), but Corlett was married and had a small family. He could not afford it otherwise he would have done so at once. That was in 1913.

I had just started working for Corlett and one night I went to a little dance. I could not dance of course, then who should come in but Mr Corlett and Mrs Corlett. What a lovely dancer Corlett was. I thought that was the secret of balance for Golf. After that I practiced until I could dance, and not only that, but could do as well or better than most. In fact my cousin and I introduced the Maxime dance at Boscombe Assembly rooms.

'I still had to wear a bandage on my leg, also my accident left my right hand with my thumb and my first two fingers smashed and of no use at all. The third finger had the top joint broke. My only good finger was my little one, and when playing golf I lock that in my left grip, so really I play with one hand.

'At the end of 1913-14 Corlett told me that Lord Allington of Crichel House had invited him to come over and play on his private Golf course for a long week-end, Friday night till Monday morning. Lord Allington had a very big house party including some Japanese Princes and lots of Lords and Ladies, also Corlett told me I was going as well. Corlett stayed at Crichel House, I stayed with the Valet, Mr Stedman. We had to play all the time but I felt very much at home playing on that nine holes after the hard Broadstone. The Stedmans had a son about 13 yrs old, he came round with us all the time, and of course, watching me, wanted to be a professional. I think he was going for training as an Engineer, but it was fixed at 14 yrs he was coming into our shop at Broadstone under Pennington to learn Golf. I remember Pennington often saying to him how silly he was to give up the chance of being an engineer to become a Pro. (What he really meant was "golf was a hard life"). Tom did very well for himself, but had he stayed in Golf he could have made a lot of money, but when war started in 1914 he joined up (as a man) although only 14 yrs old.

'The day I went into Corlett's shop I had no clubs of my own, so he told me to go to the old rack where there were a lot of old clubs and pick out a set . . . fancy having a set of clubs and a bag. The only club I remember was a jigger (I still play with a club with that loft today).

'When war started Corlett went on munitions. I was left in sole charge of the shop, Caddies etc. Although I was very lame etc. I tried to join up. The C.O. of the Dorsets, Col. Wheatley, one of our members, also on the Committee, told me at Dorchester Barracks that if they had passed me it would have wanted two men to look after me (whatever he meant I do not know). Also he told me in my condition I was no use in munitions. They gave me a green card and 3/10d. and sent me home NBG. So back to the links again. My five ambitions were:

    To be a Golf Professional
    To play in the British Championship
    To be a Freemason
    To have enough money by 40 years
    To ride from Paris to south of France in their famous Train.

'No work in so I applied to work on munitions. I was accepted, was there till 1918, had just over £100 in the bank and took a little holiday. I had only played a little all the war but was always thinking of it.

'War over, I was in digs, one day my landlady told me a Gentleman was at the door to see me (I had only left work about 2 days). I went to see who it was, none other than Hugh Williamson the Parkstone Golf Club Professional. He offered me a job, but I told him I had to have a rest first, then I hoped to go back to Broadstone. He told me he had seen Corlett and said Corlett hoped I would take the job as Broadstone was in a bad way, so I started the following Monday, although he wanted me to start next day.

'Corlett died rather young, but was never forgotten. I was Godfather to his youngest son Harold in place of G Pennington.

'I more or less took charge of the Parkstone shop, gave a lot of lessons and played. While there I qualified for the Daily Mail Finals £850. also Reg Whitcombe beat me by one shot over 36 holes for first place in the Perrier Water Shield & £100. I broke the Pro. course record of Parkstone with 68 (37&31) E R Whitcombe was second with 71. They gave me a gold watch for that.

'While there I met another real gentleman Col C E M Morrison, he gave me a cheque for £16.10 after I qualified, to pay my expenses at Westward

Edward Ray

Ho Finals. It was real bad weather. While we were there I played with George Tuck, he had just won a big match somewhere and was the northern Champion, but he never broke 80. My first day score was 86 and 80, I can't remember the second day.

'I should have played with Harry Vardon but he wired to say illness stopped him from playing.

'In the time I was with Mr Williamson I won two alliance matches, 74 entries, tied once and second once. Also played second in the Professionals Team, Ernie Whitcombe played Top.

'At Parkstone I met a Mr May, he was something to do with the King of Spain's heir that died of Leukaemia. When playing with him one day he looked at my right hand, examined my fingers and said he could operate, remove some pieces of bone and perhaps I may be able to move the joints again. I told him No. I could play Golf to scratch handicap and I felt I could play to it, so that was that.

'While at Parkstone I met and played with some very rich people. I made quite a lot of money. I was at Parkstone about 18 months, then Brockenhurst Manor Golf Club offered me the post to their club as Professional at £130 p.a. as a retainer, plus playing, teaching and shop.

'After a while a golf ball firm paid me £78 p.a. to play only with their ball, and as many free balls as I wanted to play with. I never did like the ball and I played with it only when I had to. Once on a London course I was chosen to play J H Taylor ex-champion in the News of the World match. Just before I hit off I found I had none of the balls I was supposed to play. Taylor had just told me that the Director of the firm was on the first tee waiting for us to hit off, but somehow I got by. Taylor broke the record in that round. I was 6 shots behind. You can guess the crowd we had next day for the second round.

'I was with Brockenhurst about 5½ years. I made quite a lot of money and saved most of it, I was also asked to join the Freemasons. I played in the British Open Championship, went to the continent and played in the Dutch Championship, also I played Ted Ray in a match for £25. He beat me 2 & 1 in 36 holes; we had the same scores, I was 75 & 74 and he was 74 & 75. On a 36-hole game he would have beaten me by one hole. I also played a fourball against Joyce Wethered. Her partner was a Mr Drenell (scratch). My partner was Viscount Coke, 8 handicap. We had to give them 2 up. I lost on the last green 1 down. I was round in 71.

'Taylor came to Lyndhurst for a holiday in 1924. Taylor told me that he was bringing someone to spend a holiday in the New Forest and it turned out to be Harold Beglie the famous author. He was just starting to play golf and we played together all that week. Sometime afterwards I received a book called 'J H Taylor or, the inside of a week'. It was about Taylor's early life in one half and the other half was about the week in the Forest. It was exciting to see the reference to me in the book and it was real fun playing with JH.

James Braid

'In all my professional days I cannot remember ever being nervous. I used to enjoy every shot. I used to teach a lot of well known people. Horace Vachet, E Baring, Duchess of Westminster, Lady Mary Grosvenor, Capt F Lewis, and dozens of others like that, as Brockenhurst in those days was a very rich club. Business men were not very welcome in the club. I was told by the secretary to only buy the very best for my shop. (Everyone went home to dinner at 7 in the summer)

'While at Brockenhurst I made arrangements with another Pro. to go to America, that was in 1926. We met Hagen and Kirkwood in the championship. They advised me to get in touch with them and they would get us a job when we wanted one. We also met the American Consul-General who was staying with them. But a fortnight before I was going to sail, when I was on a golfing weekend in Bristol with Don Curtis the Queens Park Golf Professional, Knowle G.C. offered me their job. Knowle was a new club with a lot of members and the terms were very good.

'The committee watched me play with Curtis and although they had advertised the post and had dozens after it, they told me they would give me only 3 or 4 days, but having sold up my home and with only a few suitcases and a set of clubs left it took a lot to change my mind. I asked my wife Yes or No she said take the job.

'I was with Knowle about 4 years. The chairman at the meeting arranging my contract told me that as J H Taylor's firm had made the course, they wrote to him for advice about a Professional to take full charge of the course, workmen, and all outside. JH told them in his letter which I read that they could not do any better. The chairman asked me to forgive him for asking Taylor without first asking me.

'The club arranged a big match to open the course, it was to be J H Taylor, E R Whitcombe, Charlie Whitcombe and myself. Morning 18 holes, Ernie and myself v Chas & JH. We lost 2 & 1. At lunch the committee sent for me and told me they would like Taylor & me to play the two Whitcombes. I went back asked JH and told him I had nothing to do with it. He looked at me and said 'Harry these two brothers, are the finest pair in the world and unbeatable, go and tell them No', but they insisted, so after a long while Taylor gave in.

'(It seemed as if all Bristol was watching the match that day)

'Taylor looked very stern; he always did when he stuck that big chin of his out. Told me I had the honour. We did not speak a dozen words the whole round, but only thought of one thing . . . winning, which we did, 2 & 1 after one of my hardest fights in Golf. I did a little more than my share, but I shall never forget Taylor, how he can fight. That was the reason I played so well, he was taking the ball of them, and leaving me to go for everything so you can see how unselfish he is. After the game he was more than pleased as he had never been on the winning side against these two Brothers.

'I taught a lot at Knowle, also I won quite a lot of alliances matches including the Gloster & Somerset Knock out Championship. The 6 rounds went

J H Taylor

68-73-71-73-69-69. Also I had a 6 against me in one of the rounds. I played a lot of big matches while I was at Knowle and met some really good golfers there, both Amateurs and Pro's.

'Just after I had won the Knock-out championship I had beaten Bob Bradbeer in the first round, Jimmy Horn in the semi-final. Had to meet Ted Buchan in the final 36 holes, he was the holder.

'Bob Bradbeer had the best score in the first round in the British Open one year. Charlie Pixton just lost the Midland championship by a shot. Jimmy Horn is ex champion of Wales.

'One day one of Pixton's members and Mr Harry Pruett came in my shop and said 'Harry I have arranged a 72 hole match with you and Pixton against Jimmy Horn and Bradbeer for £10 corners each man a side'. I told him that was asking a lot, but he said 'with your straight and steady play, and you being the captain keeping Pixton's long game in play (he was a very long hitter), you should about win'. But I had my doubts. We were to play the first 36 holes at Weston super Mare, the second half at Knowle from the back tees and a heavy clay soil. Knowle can be very long. There was nothing I could do but play, so I agreed.

'Everyone in Bristol seemed to be betting on the match, and you could have got quite long odds against us; they expected us to come back from Weston about 7 or 8 down. But after 18 we were 1 up, after 36, 2 up. The odds were about even then. Now for Knowle: after 54 we were 3 up. After lunch it started to rain, and I was the only one wearing eye-glasses. I told Pixton 'just keep with them till the rain finishes', then I would be in, but Charlie could not hold them on his own and the holes slipped away. It rained all the way round and we lost the game, but I enjoyed it except for the rain and would have liked it over again.

'After about four years at Knowle I had got everything under control. I asked to be relieved of charge of the men on the course, and to only play and teach, but the committee would not agree. The course was in really good shape and playing well; as some of the members said 'from a wilderness to a park'. I sent a letter to the captain with my resignation. My agreement was for three months, then it was back to Bournemouth with a little regret.

'I spoke for Easterbrook for the post as I was leaving and told them Sid would play for England one day (and he did), but I had the best of the Knowle job. The Pro's that came after me had a lean time. Haliburton was to follow Easterbrook, but did not stay very long.

'I came back to Bournemouth and played at Queens Park and then thought about turning amateur. Everything was working as I hoped. I was a Golf Professional, played in the Open Championship, was a Freemason, had stood on the platform in Paris (and could have ridden down south), and now finish as a Pro. at 40 years. I sent to St Andrews for my re-instatement, but I had to wait until I was 55 yrs old before it came through. We often wrote, but as one or two Pro's said, St Andrews was right; supposing they gave me amateur status and I entered for the Amateur championship and

E R Whitcombe
Came Down 1910 – 25

had the luck to beat one of the Americans. The Yanks would have said its no good playing in the British Amateur as they are playing Pro's now. So when I was too old for that I received a letter from St Andrews congratulating me on getting my amateur status. I no sooner got it than Hampshire asked me to play in a trial for them and then play against Dorset. My handicap had gone back from +3 to scratch.

'I am now 73 years old but have gone back again to 5 handicap, this is my longest handicap since a boy. When I was 67 years old I went round Meyrick Park twice in my age, but as I get older my knee is no help. I have been a member of Bournemouth some years now. The standard of play is not very high. Most of the members make themselves very old. I am afraid of getting the same, but I do a lot of exercise at home, and spend a lot of time walking, so I am really fit.

'Going back to my accident. The shock I received affected my speech. There were quite a number of letters I could not pronounce, such as 'C', 'K' and 'Q', and leaving school at 12 yrs old, I had some job on to speak properly and having to change quite a number of words. I never have been able to speak English only by thinking all the time, but I found that nearly everyone I met was only about my average and they had a lot more advantages, so I grew out of that and no-one was any the wiser. The invitations I received for dinners and people in good positions in business and otherwise, proves it.

'From Bournemouth to Weymouth. I joined the Golf Club, played from scratch, won the Jubilee cup with a record 67. I bought a large house and my wife turned it into a hotel (Linden Hall), 19 rooms. Made a little more £.s.d . . . after a few more years, back to Bournemouth to retire and to enjoy LIFE. I still play Golf, handicap 8.

'I am one of the few club-makers that made shafts from "squares" and Heads from "Blocks" "Spliced". Grips we cut from skins and started with the guttie ball. The first rubber core I saw was when Broadstone was opened in 1903 with Alex Herd, Mr Balfour, JH and Braid. Golf was played at Broadstone some years before this.

'H L Curtis was Pro. later at Queens Park, Meyrick, Swanage and Broadstone all at the same time.

'I have had three holes in one shot, and held quite a number of course records.

'I think playing against Professionals is more fun than against amateurs. Professionals class their golf against yours, hoping for some "hot" golf, but amateurs hope you will miss some shots so as they can win; except players like Ernie Millward, big Jack Santall, and just one or two more. It was real fun playing with them. I think Millward was the finest fighter I have ever played, either with or against, and a "sticker" for the R & A rules. We did not "give" much to one another. Also another amateur I played with and a good player, I used to give him three shots. Bill McGarry. Our last 5 games ended either 2 & 1 or the last green. I won 3, but had to do 2 in

C R Whitcombe
Meyrick Park 1925 – 61

71 in it. He would have made a very fine professional. He is now Manager of Ipswich Football Club and they are lucky to have him.

'I joined Bournemouth G.C. in 1950, was made an Hon. Member 197 . .

'Arthur Rowe was Hon. Sec. I presented the Club with a very old Golf Club, a Niblick well over 100 yrs old. They were very pleased indeed'.

(Harry Dean died in Southbourne at the age of 92, within four weeks of the death of his wife).

Another piece of paper found inside the book appears to be an *aide memoire* from his early years at Knowle. It is acknowledged that he did not relish the job of managing men, and at that time was not skilled at course maintenance, although he eventually transformed it into 'the best in the area'.

>   The Chargehand to walk round every morning
>   Men to take only their own tees and green
>
>   4 Men greens
>
>   1 Engine Mowing etc.
>
>   1 Special for No.18, 1, 17, 6, 2
>
>   Each man to do the apron of his own green
>
>   It is the Chargeman's own job to trim holes each day
>   Workmen not to take advice from Golfers
>   Each man to be taught what to do when golfers are playing
>   Workmen to take orders only from Chargehand
>
>   Fairways Mow more regular
>   Tee Boxes, Move every day
>   Mowing much shorter
>
>   Bunkers. Everyone want cleaning up, stones taking out
>   Edging so as to tell where they being.
>   Raking, Not over the edges into fairways.
>
>   Greens. Mown more regular.
>   Light wooden roller early mornings after switching with bamboo.
>   Cutting board used every time hole is made
>   Apron should be 10-15 ft. Mowing up and down banks of greens
>   The course cleaned up Grass mowings not left in heaps.
>   Bunker tops and around tees to be mown short.
>   Flies & insects, smells and generally dirty.

R A Whitcombe
Parkstone 1927 – 56

Notable People I have Played Golf With.
Miss Joyce Wethered. Viscount Coke, Lord Farnham, Hon. Brownlow,
Sir Christopher Magnay.Bart., Lord Wimborne, Capt. F Guest,
Major H Guest, Mr Douglas Grant, Open Championship, Deal,
Hon. Westenra, Mrs Morton Coates, Mr Horace Vachell,
Mrs Roger Cookson, Mr Frank Woolley, Mr K E Walker,
Hon H Baring, Mr E Baring, Mr Backer-Douglas, Robert Tremaine.

Professionals and Champions.
Sandy Herd, J H Taylor, Ted Ray, C A & E R Whitcombe,
Aubrey Boomer, Archie Compston, Percy Alliss, Reg Wilson,
Jack White, W B Smith, Jack Rowe, Hugh O'Neil, Charlie Reith.

Some Notable People I have Taught.
Miss Pamela Bowes-Lyon, Cousin to the Duchess of York, who became
the Queen of England. Constance Duchess of Westminster,
Lady Cheetham, Sir Leslie Scott KC, MP, Mrs Roger Cookson,
Mr H A Des Veux, Dr Gow Cook, Master W R Wills-Sandford,
Boy International, Flt. Lt. Heyward, Air Force Champion,
Sir Percy Berrill, Mr W P Lucas, Mr L Baldwin.

The young Harry Dean respected and admired Charles Corlett as a professional golfer and for his sporting and gentlemanly qualities. A native of the Isle of Man, Corlett arrived at Broadstone in 1910 via the Ravenscliff, Bradford and Chevin golf clubs, and stayed until his untimely death in 1935.

He had an excellent record as a player, including runner-up in the 1922 Belgian Open, and he just failed to win the West of England Championship on four occasions.

The members of Broadstone were equally impressed with Corlett, and on the occasion of his death one of the members composed this touching requiem:

Hugh Williamson
Parkstone 1910 – 27

Softly the wind cried round his resting place,
Faintly the moonbeams pass, then come again,
While one we love lies on earth's gentle breast,
Free from all pain.
Only the whispering leaves disturb his rest.
Beyond the heather that he loved, a light
Shines bravely forth, as if the one within
Murmured "Good Night".
For him the answer to man's endless quest,
A comrade's greeting and a welcome home.
Only for us to ask the how and when
Who stand alone.
The sun will shine on fairer hills than these,
The heather spread its glory round our way.
His voice sound clear once more within our ears,
Some other day.

South West Counties Golf Association

The letter proposing the formation has been preserved in the Association's Minute Book, and it is reproduced overleaf by kind permission of the Secretary John Lumley.

It was discussed at the county union's 1924 AGM, and Capt Hambro and Walter Little the Hon Secretary were asked to represent the county union at a meeting in the Rougemont Hotel in Exeter on the 16th of February.

At the next AGM they recommended that the county should join... and the three ex-army Majors; Morrison, Gundry and Stephens were asked to represent the Dorset Union on the Council. The subscription was £5.10s.0d, which was 10/-d (50p) for each affiliated Dorset club.

Capt Angus Hambro was elected as the first President of the Association, with C H Young of Bristol as the Honorary Secretary.

Annual golf meetings were arranged consisting of an amateur and an open championship, a county team event, and an amateur v professional event on the day following the open. Then in 1925 the first match against the Midlands Counties Golf Union took place at Burnham & Berrow, which Dorset won by 9½ to 5½.

The first amateur championship meeting was held on May 13th at Westward Ho! on the 13th of May 1924. No records of the results of the meetings were kept until 1932, but fortunately Walter Little kept a cuttings book in which he pasted the accounts of the notable golf meetings, so it is possible to describe the event.

'The first championship meeting... was of a highly successful character, there being a good entry, while the course was in first-class order. Stretched to its full length of 6,700 yards, several of the visitors found it a very big test, and did not altogether cover themselves with glory. The individual championship was won by Captain A V Hambro of Dorset, with a score for the thirty-six holes of 158. Despite the fact that he started with an eight, he completed the first round in 80, and in the afternoon knocked two strokes off this total. K F Fradgley and C G Chard were second with scores of 163'.

The team championship, played on the following day, was contested by just four counties; Devon (Fradgley, Chard and Cobley) won the event, with Dorset in second place (Hambro, Stephens and Moore). Somerset were third and Gloucester fourth. All six counties were not represented until 1927 when it was played at Burnham & Berrow over three days and Gloucester were victorious.

The now-familiar five-day event, combining the individual and the team championships began at Broadstone in June 1928, playing foursomes in the morning matches and singles in the afternoons. The open championship was still alive then, and Reg Whitcombe won the £10 prize after a play-off with Ferndown's F J Randell. E Hunter won the amateur championship, with S L Dickenson of Weston-super-Mare and Major Ruttle sharing the second place.

The first open championship was played on the 13th of October at the Came Down club and it proved to be a triumph for the Whitcombe brothers;

Horace Hutchinson

5, UNITY STREET.
COLLEGE GREEN.
BRISTOL.

November 2nd, 1923.

DEAR SIR,

It has been considered that it would be in the interests of Golf in the South West of England if an Association could be formed to be known as the "SOUTH WESTERN COUNTIES GOLF ASSOCIATION," to consist of such County Golf Unions and Golf Clubs as may be willing to become affiliated to the Association.

For the purpose of the Association the South Western Counties shall be deemed to consist of the Counties of Devon, Somerset, Wiltshire, Dorset and Cornwall.

The objects of the Association shall be, amongst other things:—

1. To uphold the laws of the game of Golf as drawn up by the Royal and Ancient Golf Club of St. Andrews.
2. To assist in establishing a uniform system of handicapping in the area.
3. To promote a greater degree of interest in County Golf Matches by arranging a South Western County Championship.
4. To promote inter Association Golf Matches.
5. To hold a meeting annually for the Championship of the South Western Counties Golf Association.
6. To decide all doubtful or disputed questions arising in the area and to promote the interests of Golf generally.

We submit that the formation of such an Association deserves the attention of all Golf Unions in the area, and suggest that a meeting of the officials of such Unions and those interested shall be held in Exeter, at the Rougemont Hotel, on Saturday, December 8th, 1923, at 3 o'clock in the afternoon.

Will you kindly give us your views on the subject and let us know if the place, date and hour of meeting suggested above will be convenient.

Kindly address your reply to C. H. YOUNG, 5, Unity Street, College Green, Bristol.

Yours faithfully,

G. TEMPLE COLE,
President Somerset County Golf Union.

T. HOLT,
President Gloucestershire & Somerset Professional Golfers Alliance.

AYLMER SOMERVILLE,
Captain Burnham and Berrow Golf Club.

Charles won with rounds of 72 and 73, Reg was second with 71 and 75, and Ernest third with 75 and 72.

The prizes were a gold medal for the amateur, or £10 for the professional; a silver medal, or £5; and a bronze medal or £2.

The report stated that the competition attracted a large number of competitors and spectators and it was played in summer-like heat under a cloudless sky. The best amateur score was that of K F Fradgley of Exeter with 79 and 76, and this would have been much improved if he had not taken 9 at the seventeenth. Capt Hambro won the silver medal and D A Turpin the bronze.

Fradgley, who was quoted in the *Golfers Handbook* as being a member of the Westward Ho! Golf Club, was the runner-up in the British and Irish National Amateur Championship in 1925.

Unfortunately the professional element of the annual meetings proved to be short-lived. In 1931 the AGM decided to cancel the open competition because of the expense involved, but in the eight years of the competition at least one of the Whitcombes featured in the first three in every one but the 1929 event, in which they did not take part.

Following the decision to discontinue the championship, C C Roberts proposed at the Association's 1933 meeting that the redundant gold medal should be given to the Hon Secretary O B P Burdon 'because it is inconceivable that he could get a medal in any other way'. (Burdon's response was not recorded!) The medal was subsequently made into a Secretary's badge of office.

Flag Foursomes

In December 1924 the Executive decided to initiate an annual amateur v professional knock-out tournament, played between one couple from each club over eighteen holes, with the final over thirty-six holes. An additional tournament, run on similar lines was also initiated, but composed of a mixed pair from each club, but there would be no handicap allowance.

At this same meeting the Executive approved a design for a trophy for the competition. It was called a 'County Flag', but it was in fact a silver miniature donated by Major Stephens of the Ferndown Club.

The first winners of this 'Flag Foursomes' as it became known, were Capt Hambro and E R Whitcombe of Came Down, and the same club won it again the following year, but this time Major Gundry partnered Whitcombe. The local newspaper mistakenly assumed that the county flag would be flown by the club as a token of the victory, but the records of the union did not mention flying a flag until at the 1965 AGM the President, G E Newton, thanked H A Wilton for the gift of a flag, and announced that it would be flown on that day and at all future county events.

The second annual golf meeting of the union took place at the Came Down Golf Club in April 1924, and thanks to Walter Little's press cuttings book, there is a record of the event.

The Flag Foursomes trophy

The gold medal winner and County Amateur Champion was Captain A V Hambro, with scores of 80 and 83, with the silver going to V Weldon of Ferndown. The winner of the 36-hole medal under handicap was C L Gordon-Steward of Came Down, with Weldon beating A V Hambro in a replay after tying for second place. The county championship knock-out tournament was won by Major Stephens, who beat Commander Carter 2 up.

The inter-club foursomes competition was held on the Came Down course in September 1924 and eight out of the eligible ten clubs took part. Ferndown won the event with V Weldon and F A Stephens, who beat Capt A V Hambro and R B Moore of the old Weymouth, Dorchester and County Golf Club by 7 and 6. Parkstone was represented by Major Morrison and Cdr G Millan; Sherborne by Capt W A Ffooks and E W Tayler; Swanage by A E L Holloway and B J Jackson; Dorset (Broadstone) by Capt Sutcliffe and A K Smithells; Shaftesbury by Major Nixon and the Rev R M Rees; and West Dorset by Major Gundry and Cdr N H Carter.

In the 1925 am-v-pro contest, played over the Came Down course, the professionals beat the amateurs by six matches to three. The report stated that two amateurs were pitted against one professional, and on this occasion the ground was very hard, 'which made play difficult and flukey'. Reg Whitcombe, then the Came Down professional 'was in irresistible form' and he 'polished off E Hunter and J B Jackson on the twenty-seventh green'.

No record of the 1925 county amateur championship meeting at Ferndown is available, but Major Stephens won the gold medal on his own course. Parkstone Golf Club hosted the 1926 championship meeting, where the scratch medal was again won by Major Stephens who beat E J Dobson in the final, and he also won the matchplay prize when he again beat his old adversary D A Turpin by 5 and 3. He was three under fours at the fifteenth, and with the win he retained his title as *Champion of Dorset.*

In the handicap section consisting of the best sixteen nett scores in the previous day's medal competition, Ellvers beat J C F Gundry.

The 1926 meeting between the amateurs and professionals took place at Came Down, and according to the local newspaper 'play was of a high order, with a win for the professionals by twelve matches to eight. Major Gundry (3) and E J Dobson (scr) fought a good match and beat the Broadstone professional by 3 & 2. Reg Whitcombe (Came Down) won both his matches. His golf in the afternoon was perfect; he was out in 38 and home in 33'.

Although not part of the county golf union, it is interesting to recall that the first competition of the recently formed Bournemouth and District Professional Alliance was played at Ferndown on March 11th 1926. Twenty-six couples took part in the 36-hole better ball competition in very windy conditions; the professionals playing off handicaps of plus three and the Assistants from scratch.

A pair of silver cups, presented by the first President Major C E M Morrison were on offer, and the result of the day's play resulted in a triple tie between A E L Holloway and R Whitcombe; M W J Bond and E R Whitcombe; and W E Mason and D Curtis.

The eventual winners were Holloway and Whitcombe of Came Down in the play-off at Ferndown on the 19th of March.

Although the programme for 1927 was fixed without the mention of any changes, the report of the meeting, held at Broadstone, indicated that the championship rules had been altered from the normal matchplay format to thirty-six holes of medal play because it was considered that matchplay was too long, and 'many could not arrange to attend a three-day tournament'. The gold medal winner was E Hunter, with T P Whitaker taking the silver.

The Minute Book did not record the results of the annual matches between the ladies and the gentlemen, although it was one of the original fixtures agreed at the first Council meeting. However in the 1928 match, when it was played at Came Down, the men prevailed by seven matches to five. The men gave six bisques to the ladies, but this was countered by the ladies having to play from the men's tees. Bisques were a common feature of men v ladies matches for many years, but the practice has now largely disappeared. It was an intriguing way to even out the physical disadvantages, which were not fully compensated by the handicapping system. It allowed the ladies to take an additional shot (bisque) at any time, either nominated prior to playing the hole, or in many cases, as and when the player chose... which led to many very interesting results.

Artisans

The first mention of artisan participation was at the 1928 AGM when the captain (E Hunter) was asked to rule on the eligibility of a member of an artisan club in the county championship meetings. The resolution did not appear in subsequent Minutes, but the matter was raised again after the war, when a suggestion to initiate an artisans' championship was rejected on the grounds that artisan members of clubs affiliated to the county union were eligible to play in the county amateur championship.

In 1928 there were only four artisan clubs in the county; those of the Isle of Purbeck, Bridport and West Dorset, Broadstone and Parkstone. After the boundary changes of 1974, Meyrick Park and Boscombe added to the number when they became affiliated as Dorset clubs. But in those very early days the status of artisans was akin to that of the professional in the minds of the autocratic managements; they too would have been regarded as tradesmen and as such would not have been welcome in the members' lounge.

Bridport did not reactivate its artisan section after the war; the Isle of Purbeck Artisans lasted until 1980; Parkstone disbanded its artisan section at the end of 1988; and Broadstone assimilated its artisans into the main club in 1976.

Ferndown Golf Club hosted the 1928 championship meeting in May when it was won by W R Wills-Sandford from Capt N H Carter who also won the handicap prize.

In the same year, the inter-club foursomes was played at Broadstone, and in the 36-hole finals on the second day the home pair (Morrison and Whittingham) started rather shakily and were two down at lunch. In the afternoon 'a magnificent Brassie shot' at the fourth by the Parkstone player C K Cotton put them three up, and they were four up going to the thirteenth. After a dramatic fight-back by the home pair, Parkstone eventually won on the eighteenth when Broadstone's putt lipped the hole but failed to drop.

Cotton, a scratch golfer, became the Secretary of Parkstone shortly after it became a proprietary club in 1928. He resigned later in the year and subsequently served as a secretary in a number of golf clubs before forming the well-known golf architects firm in 1946.

The 1929 championship meeting at Came Down was held in hurricane conditions. A serving Naval Officer, Surgeon Cdr J P Shorten won the gold medal with rounds of 80 and 81 against a 78 and a disastrous 90 by Capt Angus Hambro. In the handicap event the Commander was again successful, but it is interesting to note that in his morning round, he played off a handicap of 8, but in the afternoon's event, he had been cut to 4!

Capt A V Hambro
MP for South Dorset 1910-1922
MP for North Dorset 1937-1945
Member of the first Championship Committee of the R & A 1920.
Chairman of R & A Rules of Golf Committee 1946.
When he was appointed Captain of the R & A in 1928 he organised a moonlight party on the first tee and eighteenth green at St Andrews, with additional lighting provided by car headlamps and firework rockets!

continued on page 169 . . .

Ken Longmore

There are a number of photographs of Ken dotted through this book; as a member of the various teams, accompanying the Junior teams, or latterly as a member of the Executive, but the picture chosen here shows him at the beginning of his long and illustrious career. Aged just fifteen years, over six feet in height and nattily dressed in the fashion of the 1930s.

Born in Birmingham in 1918, he first took up the game at Ferndown at the age of twelve, but it is to Don Curtis, the professional at Queens Park, that he owes his success. He worked in his shop or on the practice ground six days a week after school, and at the age of fourteen was given his first handicap, which matched his age, but which he reduced to eleven in his first year. Such was his progress that at fifteen he partnered Curtis in a series of eight exhibition matches against Reg Whitcombe and S H Vine, and won every one!

The closest he came to winning the South West Counties Championship was in 1951 when he was runner-up to Ernest Millward, but he won everything else that the Club and County had to offer, and he has been an integral part of the fabric of Dorset golf for the last forty-six years.

Since giving up the competitive side of the game he has devoted a great deal of his time to the advancement of Junior golf. This stems from his own experiences in the 1930s when there were few facilities and not much encouragement for the younger element. He has certainly redressed the balance however, and has been responsible for many of the coaching initiatives and the organisation of Junior golf in the county. He has been the Juniors' delegate for Dorset and the South West counties since 1970, and has served on the Golf Foundation for six years.

His record in competitive golf is phenomenal; in addition to his club successes, which include seven scratch medals and eight Club championships, he won the County title four times and was runner-up on six occasions. His name has been engraved on the prestigious Wimborne Cup no less than seven times. He played in eighteen South Western championships and twice captained the county team.

On the administrative side: he has been President of the County Union; elected to the English Golf Union in 1972; served on the Executive Committee for five years and is still on the Council; has been President of the SWCGA and captain of the SW counties team; President of the SW Seniors; and currently President of Dorset Junior Golf.

Some Famous Names from

Jeanne Bisgood won five European amateur titles; made eight appearances in the English national side; three in the Curtis Cup team and two in the Vagliano Cup; won the English Ladies Amateur Championship three times; her native Surrey county title three times; and won the Parkstone Ladies Championship on no less than eleven occasions. Small wonder that she was described as the best lady golfer ever to play out of Dorset.

Jeanne hit the headlines when she beat the American champion Grace Lenscyk in the British Amateur Championship in 1949. She won the South East title the following year and made her debut as a Curtis Cup player. In 1952 the team notched up their first win over America, and Jeanne won the Astor Salver, the Roehampton Gold Cup for the second successive year, and her first European title in the Swedish Open.

1953 brought a hat-trick of victories in the Astor Salver and Roehampton; her second Surrey county title; a repeat of her 1951 success in the English Ladies Championship; and the German and Italian titles.

In 1954 she made her sixth appearance in the English national team; her third in the Curtis Cup team; and won the Portuguese title. In the following year she added the Norwegian title, and in 1957 won the English Ladies title for the third time.

One major title eluded her . . . the British Amateur; her best performance was at Broadstone in 1951 when she lost at the twenty-second hole to the eventual winner.

Pat Crow played tennis and golf for Kent before she moved to Dorset in 1946.

She won the Dorset Ladies County title ten times and won the South Western title twice, in 1954 and 1955, but failed in the hat-trick attempt in 1961 when she was beaten by the international player Ruth Porter.

Pat played a lot of golf with Jeanne Bisgood, losing to her in the quarter-finals of the English Championship in the year Jeanne won it at Queens Park.

In 1978 she completed twenty-five years of competitive golf for Dorset, but her most memorable round was with Peter Alliss in 1961 when they won the Broadstone Platters. She also partnered Dick Peach in county mixed foursomes matches, including the one at Parkstone in 1961 when Dick holed-in-one twice in the same round.

On the administrative side, she was the LGU scratch representative for the South West, and was President of the Dorset Ladies Golf Union before leaving Dorset in 1980 to live near her family in Perthshire.

Barbara Dixon moved to Dorset in 1963 and was selected to play for the county team for seven years. She won the County Championship three times between 1966 and 1970, during which time she was being coached by Doug Sewell, with whom she reached the Sunningdale Foursomes in 1970.

In 1969 she gave up her safe job in the Bank to spend a year on the amateur circuit, which began with a win at the English Ladies Championship at Burnham, which Peter Alliss mentions in his Foreword to this book. Jeanne Bisgood caddied for her, and Barbara *holed practically everything from about twenty feet,* using a putter given to her by a friend eight years previously.

Following that victory she was selected to play for England in the European Team Championship in Sweden; was runner-up in the Wills tournament; played in the home internationals (Western Gailes); in the Vagliano team in France; and was semi-finalist in the Worplesden Mixed Foursomes, playing with Tony Richmond.

Marriage in 1970, and a change of name to McIntosh, meant a move to Scotland, but the successes continued with wins at the 1971 *Scottish Evening Times* Foursomes; the Avia Division 2 Ladies Foursomes in 1972; and the East Lothian Championship in 1975.

The Ladies Golf Scene

Maureen Garrett was taught by Archie Compston at Coombe Hill, but from the age of four until her marriage in 1948 her golf was played mainly at weekends and during family holidays in Sandbanks.

She went to America in 1947 and was the first British lady golfer to play there after the war. She reached two semi-finals, and was feted everywhere she went!

In the early 1950s Maureen had the lowest handicap of any lady golfer in England (plus 3). She played for England four times between 1947 and 1953; won the French Open in 1946 and played in her first Curtis Cup match two years later, when the team lost at Royal Birkdale. She captained the team in 1960, and the Great Britain team against a Continent of Europe team in 1959.

A contemporary of Jeanne Bisgood, the pair were a formidable force in British golf, and romped away with the scratch and handicap titles in the second division of the Avia Foursomes at the Berkshire in 1979.

In 1982 Maureen crowned her illustrious career when she was appointed President of the LGU, and was honoured in America with the Bobby Jones award for distinguished sportsmanship in golf... the first non-American woman ever to have achieved that distinction.

Esme Stuart-Smith learned her golf from Earnest Whitcombe at the Bournemouth club and he insisted that until she achieved a single-figure handicap, she should learn to *manufacture* shots by playing with a half-set of clubs.

She reached the single-figure target in the early thirties and became a member of the Hampshire ladies team.

After the war, and as a member of the Parkstone club, Esme won the Dorset Ladies Championship four times between 1948 and 1965, and reached the final of the Parkstone Ladies Championship four times. She twice reached the final of the South Western Championships, and played in the Open and the English Championships. But her most memorable achievement was at Hunstanton in the British Championship of 1946 when she beat the favourite at the twenty-first hole... *but the next round proved to be a bit of an anti-climax!*

Jane Sugden comes from a sporting family, both parents were good golfers and Jane played with them during school holidays at St Enodoc. She partnered her father in the Worplesden Foursomes in 1954, and her husband John in 1967. Then in 1976, she reached the semi-final of the Burhill Family Foursomes playing with her son Christopher.

Jane played golf for England for three successive years from 1953; and in that year played for the Great Britain & Ireland team against Canada; and the Vagliano Cup team in France. She was a semi-finalist in the English Championship in 1954; twice Northamptonshire Champion and Champion of Dorset five times.

She captained the Dorset LCGA in 1977 and 1978; was a member of the ELGA Scratch Score Committee from 1978 to 1985; an English Selector from 1986 to 1990; Chairman of the English Selection Committee in 1988; and the English representative on the British International Selection Committee in 1989 and 1990.

Ray Lawford

Ray went into professional golf straight from school; he became an Assistant to Ken McIntyre at Broadstone and intended to progress to professional status, but after four and a half years he had earned virtually nothing as an Assistant, so he gave it up for a more secure future as a house painter. Peter Alliss in his Foreword to this book, suggests that Ray could have had a bright future as a professional if he had belonged to one of the more fashionable home counties Clubs. In the event he applied for and obtained his reinstatement to the amateur ranks and joined the Broadstone Artisans Club, where his father had been a founder member.

He marked his return to the amateur ranks in 1955 in spectacular fashion; at the age of twenty in the County championships he beat the Broadstone and former Cambridge captain Ian Campbell-Gray in the semi-finals, and in the 36-hole final beat R E Garrett by seven and six after being six up at the half-way mark, to become the youngest County champion. In the same year, as if to underline his return to golf for its own sake, he tied with Dick Peach in the final of the South Western Counties Championship on his home course, and won the 18-hole play-off, going out in 38 and matching it on the return half.

Dorset won the South Western title that year after being in the doldrums for about ten years, and they went on to dominate the county golfing scene for the next four years.

Ray Lawford played in four SWCGA championship-winning sides, including 1966 when the competition was played at Ferndown and he won his second individual title. He also won the Wimborne Cup in successive years, and in 1970 won his second county title, beating Graham Butler in the final. In the following year he *almost* did it again, but lost to Teddy Garrett, the son of R E Garrett, whom he beat to win his first title in 1955.

Ray was elected Captain of Dorset in 1973-4; South Western Counties Captain in 1976 and President in 1989, the same year that he was invited to become an England Boys Selector; he became the Captain of his Club Broadstone in 1978; and President of the County Union in 1990.

An historically important decision was taken by the Executive Committee at their 1929 meeting at Came Down, when they resolved *to ban the use of steel shafted clubs from every Golf Club in the county*... and there is no record of this resolution ever having been rescinded!

The Director of the British Golf Museum at St Andrews confirmed that steel shafted clubs were available in this country from as early as 1891, and the question of their eligibility was submitted to the R & A in 1911 and 1913. The USGA approved their use in 1926 and the R & A gave their approval in 1929... the very year that Dorset outlawed them! What a pity that the subsequent discussions of the Union were not fully minuted, because at this remove it is not possible to discover when the steel shaft became an approved addition to the golfers' armoury in Dorset. We do know however, that British golfers did not rush to adopt the new shafts. Advertising was not such a potent force in those days and golf equipment suppliers reported very poor sales for many years.

Another item of historic interest occurred at the Executive committee meeting held at Ferndown on February 8th 1929, when the Committee expressed its thanks to the Came Down Golf Club for their resolution to appoint the Captain of the Union an honorary member of their club during his term of office.

Mr D E Matthews, the Came Down Golf Club Manager checked through the old Minute books and confirmed that at a committee meeting on January 29th 1929, with Major Crichton in the Chair the meeting decided '(a) That the Captain for the time being of the Dorset Ladies Association be *ipso facto* an honorary member of the Came Down Golf Club. (b) that the Captain of the Dorset County Golf Union for the time being, an honorary member of the Club'.

Mr Matthews' search through the Minute books subsequent to that date failed to find any resolution rescinding the decision, so presumably the arrangement is still in being.

Membership of the EGU

Walter Little read out a request from the English Golf Union at the meeting of the Executive at Came Down in February 1930 for Dorset to join. The entrance fee was to be £5.5s.0d and the subscription £2.10s.0d. The Executive decided to ask each club in the Union to contribute 15/-d for the first year if the General meeting agreed. In addition, the EGU asked for a guaranteed annual sum of £25 to support the Board of Greenkeeping Research, with the suggestion that the Union could obtain the money from an annual subscription from the clubs of from one to three guineas.

There had been two previous propositions from the EGU which the Union had declined, but at the General meeting in November 1931 it was decided it was time for Dorset to join the thirty other counties in the English Union.

The Hants and Isle of Wight Golf Association which was founded at the Royal Winchester Golf Club in November 1893, was the first County Union in England. Yorkshire, which had been discussing the formation of a union for almost a year, did not make the decision until April 1894.

Prior to joining the EGU a competitor had to be born in the county to qualify for playing in the amateur championship, but this had to be amended following an EGU circular in March 1931 which stated that the player could either be (1) born in the county (2) a member of an affiliated club in the county for two years or (3) have been resident in the county for two years.

Saunton hosted the 1930 South West Counties Golf Association meeting in lovely May weather. The day's play consisted of three county matches, singles and foursomes, in which Wilts defeated Cornwall; Devon beat Glos; and Somerset beat Dorset.

The team championships were continued at Burnham and Berrow two days later and Somerset topped the league table, with Dorset next to last, but disappointment was expressed at the absence of Devon, the previous winning county.

The report of the 1931 am-v-pro match at Parkstone makes very interesting reading because the professionals were being asked to play under very considerable handicaps.

The weather was excellent and the greens were reported to have been in very good condition, but the contest was decided on somewhat novel lines ... 'the professionals having to meet two or three rivals, with the local professional Reg Whitcombe heading the list, and play against their better ball. This was a very severe test, especially at the short holes'.

'Whitcombe played golf worthy of a Ryder Cup man, and returned a score of 69; but even this was not good enough, his three rivals proving a bit too strong for him. Whitcombe was one up at the turn and all square at the fourteenth. But on the sixteenth R M Chadwick holed out from the edge of the green to win for his side.

'Whitcombe's chance of squaring the match ended when he sliced his tee shot at the eighteenth. C H Corlett was the only professional to win against three opponents, but he had to return a round of 66 to do so, but the beaten trio had a better ball score of 67'!

The Dorset Regiment, which at that time was based in Dorchester, applied for and were admitted to membership of the County Union in 1932. However, the membership was short-lived, and they resigned three years later, giving as the reason that 'they were now stationed too far away'.

The Curator of the Dorset Military Museum provided the information that in 1935 the 1st battalion was in India, and the 2nd battalion, although in Dorset, was preparing to leave for Palestine. But the regimental quarterly magazine reported that the annual golf meeting was held in August 1935 and that golf continued to be played at least until 1936. The Dorsets were amalgamated with the Devonshire regiment in 1958.

At the November 1931 meeting it was decided to introduce county colours in the form of ties, to be awarded at the Captain's discretion. The ties were to be obtained from R Lemon and Sons of Sherborne, and the Secretary was instructed to print a form which the Captain would sign and send to all who were awarded the ties. This would then have to be presented to Messrs Lemon, who would have to register the individual's name and address. The cost of the tie was 6/6d (32½p).

The design of the tie has been attributed to R L Close of the Ferndown club, and it is interesting to note that players were obliged to wear the ties when playing in any of the county union matches.

The 1932 championship meeting was held at Ferndown. The Came Down player C L Gordon Stewart won the gold medal and G E Newton, playing on his home course, took the silver and he also won the handicap prize with an aggregate of 153 nett.

A brief history of the annual amateur v professional competition is contained elsewhere in the text, but a particularly interesting meeting was held at the Came Down Golf Club in 1932, which is worth reporting because it again illustrates the brilliance of Reg Whitcombe's golf, even against the quite formidable odds of better-ball matches against two and three very good amateurs.

On this occasion the professionals won the day, but in the majority of the early meetings the odds were stacked against them. 'Each professional played the better ball of at least two amateurs, and a feature of the day's golf was the wonderful play of R A Whitcombe, who holds the West of England and South Western Championships. In the morning when the amateurs won by seven points to six, Whitcombe beat the better ball of P S F Stubbs, Major Gundry, and H S Stringer by 4 & 3; in the afternoon, when the pro's won by 7½ to 5½, he beat the best ball of Capt Carter RN, W Stanford, and P S F Stubbs by 4 & 2'.

Walter Little, the Came Down Secretary, who had been the Hon Secretary and Treasurer since the formation of the county union, decided that he would retire at the end of 1932, and in the following year, when the county championship meeting was held at Came Down, the President of the union, O B P Burdon, presented him with an inscribed silver cigarette box in appreciation of his services. In his tribute the President stated that the union would not have been started but for the efforts of Walter Little.

Although Walter Little had been re-elected at the 1930 meeting, there had been a long discussion about appointing a Secretary 'who could be more in touch with the Captain'. So his resignation presumably came as no surprise. Sadly he died in 1936.

At the 1933 championship meeting at Came Down the clubs entering the team championship event were reduced to four players, the three best gross scores to count over thirty-six holes of medal play, but clubs could enter more than one team. In the individual competition G Glass-Hooper won the gold medal and A Dore the silver. Glass-Hooper also submitted the lowest handicap score, but was not allowed to accept the prize because he had already won the gold medal.

H (Lance) Luffman of Yeovil was appointed as the new Hon Secretary and he remained in the post until ill-health forced his retirement in 1967.

Lance Luffman

The First Ten Years

Thirteen clubs had affiliated, including the Dorset Regiment, and the Crichel Park Golf Club joined in 1934.

Records of the accounts before 1932 are not available, but at the beginning of the tenth year the Union had £35.10s.9d in the bank, and the balance sheet at the end of the year showed a total expenditure of £28.17s.0d. The largest items in the account were the cost of the gold medal at £2.5s.0d (silver 7/6d), and the subscriptions to the EGU at 10/-d per member club. At the end of the year the cash-in-hand amounted to £52.13s.3d.

The competition programme was not a particularly crowded one; it began in April with the amateur v pro match, which that year was played on the Ferndown course and resulted in a win for the amateurs by $18\frac{1}{2}$ matches to $13\frac{1}{2}$.

The County amateur championship at Came Down was won by G Glass-Hooper from A Dore of Broadstone Artisans, and the team event was won by Swanage . . . in half a gale!

In the 1933 SW team championship, played at St Enodoc, Dorset were one off the bottom. Devon won the event from the unfortunate Somerset team who won the same number of matches but lost by just one and a quarter points.

The Union had achieved its aim of organising the game and the clubs' participation in local and inter-county golf; it had joined the English Union, and the South Western Counties Association, and had set the standard scratch scores for all the affiliated golf clubs in the county.

Walter Little, the Secretary and leading light in the founding of the Union in 1923, also survived the first ten years, but only just; he resigned at the end of 1932.

Into the War Years

The rules governing south west counties matches were amended in 1933, so that all matches had to finish on the eighteenth and the number of players for both the singles and foursomes matches should be ten. In the following year the Union decided to insist that the order of play in the inter-county matches should not be posted in advance, but handed to the secretary in a sealed envelope in response to complaints that counties were making last-minute adjustments to their team pairings to match the strength of the opposition.

The Ashley Wood Golf Club rejoined the county union in 1933, leaving Crichel Park as the only club remaining outside. The reason they gave was that they intended to wait until their eighteen holes were complete. They obviously had second thoughts about this because they were represented by Lt Col Chesney at the 1934 AGM and the financial records show that the club continued to pay its affiliation fees up to 1952.

In June 1934, after exhaustive discussions with the county clubs, it was agreed that affiliated unions should accept an increase in their subscriptions to the EGU. It was originally proposed to increase the amount to between 15/-d and £1.2s.6d (75p-£1.12½p), but the committee was very careful to ensure that the clubs would not be financially embarrassed by the proposed increase. They were prepared to withdraw from the EGU if there was any fear of a club resigning from the county union. In the event all the unions affiliated to the EGU agreed to the subscription being increased to ten shillings (50p). A doubling of this figure was proposed in the following year, but predictably this received short shrift, but it was obvious that the EGU was in dire need of extra financial support.

Major Morrison, another of the founder members, resigned as President of the county union in 1935 due to ill health, and he was followed by Capt N H Carter RN (Retd) of the West Dorset Club.

In 1937 it was decided to hold a draw to effect an equitable share-out of the smaller annual fixtures among the nine minor clubs because they had been pressing the Executive for some time for a greater involvement in the tournament fixtures. As a result, Weymouth, Swanage and Shaftesbury shared the smaller fixtures in 1938, and the fixtures for 1939 were scheduled to be shared between Sherborne, Crichel Park and Ashley Wood;

with Lyme Regis, Bridport and Yeovil sharing the fixtures for 1940.

Present-day members of these clubs may have difficulty accepting that their courses were not considered good enough for the more important county fixtures, but a number of them were only 9-hole courses at that time. In addition, so many improvements have been made to the county's golf courses in a relatively short time in the wake of membership buy-outs and following many years of virtual stagnation under autocratic and conservative private managements. These changes reflect the very considerable technical and social changes which have revolutionised the golf scene, in this country and throughout the golfing world.

In 1938, what we now recognise as the last of the old order of things, the amateurs beat the professionals by 11½ games to 8½. The gold medal for the county amateur championship was won by E J Nicholl, with G Glass Hooper taking the silver medal; and the team championship was won by Northborne (E J Nicholl, P Stuart-Smith and B Asker). In the South West Counties Association championship at Saunton, L C Lake of Devon won from E J Poole of Somerset; and the team championship was won by Devon. The Dorset team comprised G E Newton (Captain), G Glass-Hooper, C Mayo, J S Ruttle, F F Laugher, J A Elliott, R L Close, D Arnott, F W Prentice, J F Lewis, R A Rapp, H L Luffman and J F E Santall.

In the mens foursomes at Swanage, the Ferndown pairing of M R Gardner and G E Newton beat J T Clegg and L H Joham of Crichel Park. The flag fours at Shaftesbury was won by Crichel Park (L H Joham and A Jolly) from Glass Hooper and W B Dunnett of Came Down.

The 1939 programme, arranged at the AGM in Came Down scheduled the amateur v professionals match to be played at Northborne in March; the county championship and team championship at Ferndown in April; the mixed fours at Ashley Wood in May; the mens fours at Sherborne in September; and the flag fours at Crichel Park at the end of September.

We know now of course that the non-golfing German dictator's unfriendly actions drastically upset these democratically arranged plans, with the result that golf, and the general social scene has never been the same since.

Incidentally, it may surprise readers to learn that although Germany was by no means a golfing nation, Hitler did in fact donate a trophy when they hosted the Olympic Games in 1936. They wanted to include golf, although it was not a recognised Olympic sport. In the event, five countries competed for the trophy, which was won by T J Thirsk and A L Bentley for England.

The doomed 1939 programme got as far as the SWCGA Championship at Saunton before the red inked *'Cancelled . . . War'* appeared in the record book. E J Poole of Somerset won the individual prize from J W D Goodban of Devon; and Gloucester won the team prize. The professionals beat the amateurs (for only the second time); and G Glass Hooper won the amateur championship; with F F Laugher beating P T Helm for the silver after a play-off. The team championship was won by Ferndown; and the mixed fours at Ashley Wood in May was won by Lyme Regis; the runners-up being Came Down.

The Union's finances at the end of 1939 showed a bank balance of £81.16s.4d, and the books for that year were balanced at just over £129, which included the cost of the medals at £3.13s.6d.

The Post-War Scene

The fourteen clubs affiliated to the union in 1939 all paid their ten shillings subscription throughout the war, although of course all county golf was suspended for the duration. The balance sheet at the first post-war AGM, held at the Crown Hotel in Weymouth in 1945 showed cash reserves down to just over £46.

There were a few new names among the club representatives, but no changes at the 'top table'. C C Roberts was still the Chairman and G E Newton the Captain, with Lance Luffman still acting as Hon Sec. Ten clubs were represented at the meeting out of what had now become *thirteen* affiliated clubs . . . the missing one being Shaftesbury.

There was no official comment about the absence of Shaftesbury, but it did not appear in the records again, and all our researches have failed to produce any records or past members with knowledge of the reason for the club's demise. Unfortunately the *per capita* method of union levy had not been introduced at that time, so it is not possible to discover the number of members, but it can only be assumed that its demise was due to financial reasons.

They played on Spreadeagle Hill, on what is now National Trust land near the Compton Abbas airfield, and members of that flying club assert that the outline of the course can still be seen from the air. The land is riven by deep valleys, and the hills are exposed to south-westerly winds, so it must have been a difficult course to play, especially in the winter. Shaftesbury joined the county union in 1923, and in the 1926 assessment was given a standard scratch score of 72 and a Par of 73 . . . a very difficult 5,716 yard golf course!

At the 1945 AGM the Minutes of the previous meeting held in 1938 were read and approved; the annual report and accounts were accepted; and the meeting got on with the business in hand as if nothing had happened to interfere with their placid administration. ***No mention was made of the war,*** and the most important item on the agenda was the inflated price of the gold medal for the championship winner, due to the high cost of gold and the imposition of the iniquitous Purchase Tax!

The pre-war cost of the medal had been £2.10s.0d, but this had now practically trebled to £6.18s.6d. However, the representatives voted overwhelmingly to preserve the tradition, and the Secretary was authorised to buy the 1946 medal. In fact the tradition existed until 1977, the year before Graham Butler broke all the records with his tenth win.

In the following year, and again at the Crown Hotel. Major Ruttle was elected President following the resignation of C C Roberts, who had decided to return to his native New Zealand.

Support for the EGU

In 1946 a discussion about another plea from the EGU and the Board of Greenkeeping Research revealed some interesting statistics about golf in the county, and with it the first suggestion of a *per capita* charge for the members of county unions.

The letter from the EGU dated August 26 1946 stated that 'a composite subscription is desirable and that the joint requirements of the EGU and the B of GR can be met by each county union paying at the rate of £4.6s.0d per affiliated Club'.

As with any such organisation, the EGU in its formative years had to struggle to survive on meagre resources. Clubs and county unions recognised the need for a national administrative body, but all requests for additional financial support were strongly opposed, both at club and county level. For example, the doubling of the fees from 5/-d to 10/-d in 1934 was only half what the EGU had asked for, yet their accounts at that time showed an income from just over 1,000 clubs to have been only £260. Although a doubling of the subscription was agreed in 1936, few of the counties actually paid up, and during the war years, the subscription reverted to the old figure of ten shillings.

Lance Luffman announced that there were approximately 1,700 playing members among the thirteen affiliated clubs. The DCGU needed about 30/-d per club, consequently a levy of 1/-d per playing member (men and ladies) should provide the required funds to meet the new rate required by the EGU and B of GR and also the DCGU expenses.

The members decided '(a) that this meeting instructs their delegate to the EGU special meeting of the Council on November 6 to oppose the principle of a composite subscription to the EGU and B of GR, (b) that in the event of the composite subscription at the rate of £4.6s.0d per club being passed at the above meeting, this meeting agrees that the DCGU shall subscribe as decided by the majority and that the money required to meet the above increased subscription and also for the running of the Dorset Union shall be met by the Dorset Clubs paying their subscription for 1947 at the rate of 1/-d per playing member (men and ladies) per Club, this 1/-d per playing member replaces the two guineas subscription in previous years'.

In the following year's meeting, and resulting from that special meeting of the EGU, they decided that the subscription to the English Union would be based at 30/-d (£1.50p) per club. The idea of a composite subscription to include the B of GR was defeated; the Board preferring clubs to negotiate their own individual subscriptions.

The EGU sent a letter to all clubs, asking them if they would subscribe £2.2s.0d annually for a loose-leaf 'Rules of Golf and R & A Decisions', but predictably there was no support!

The estimated expenses for the county union in 1948 were assessed at £60, and the total county membership was in the region of two thousand.

The first 25 years

The silver jubilee AGM was held at the Kings Arms Hotel in Dorchester, with Major Ruttle in the Chair, but he made no mention of this milestone in the history of the union.

It was decided to update the rule book and to add a fourth member to the Executive Council, namely a Deputy President. The Broadstone representative proposed that the Captain should be non-playing, and that the county championship event should remain as a one-day event. Both propositions were heavily defeated and in the following year the championship, played at Ferndown, became a three-day event . . . a surprising decision at a time when petrol rationing was still in force.

There were thirteen affiliated clubs, and the expenses for the year were estimated to be about £60; championship entrance fees were expected to be in the region of £10, so leaving £50 to be obtained from the member clubs.

Steel shafted clubs were banned by the Executive Committee in 1929: Club representation of the Council was increased from five to ten: and in 1931 the county joined the EGU.

Walter Little, the founding Honorary Secretary died in 1936.

G E Newton resigned as Captain in 1948 after twelve years in the post which included the linkage between the pre-and post-war administration, and he was replaced by R E Garrett of Ferndown. Newton was subsequently appointed Deputy President, the first holder of a new office which was required under the revised regulations.

Lyme Regis was added to the rota in 1950 to stage the larger events, and since the war, the programme had begun to be spread more widely to include some of the courses previously regarded as being unsuitable for holding the major tournaments; for example Northborne staged the amateur v professional event in 1947, and the mens foursomes went to Yeovil in 1948. Came Down was added to the list to stage major events in the 1950 AGM.

At the 1951 AGM the Committee welcomed the Wareham club into the fold. The Minutes also revealed that Dorset had won the SWCGA Championship held at Ferndown, and had won the first two places in the stroke play championship prior to the county matches. The Chairman (Ruttle) also announced that for the first time Dorset had entered a team for the English Counties Championships to be held at Formby. The county repeated its SWCGA win in the following year when it was held at Trevose, and a special mention was made of E B Millward who won the championship for the second time, in addition to winning the English championship at Burnham.

Wareham's entrance into the county union was unfortunately balanced by the demise of the Crichel Park Golf Club. When *per capita* charges were introduced in 1950, the membership of Crichel Park stood at eighty, and this was unchanged in 1951, so the financial situation must have been grave.

G E Newton

Presumably the club was unable to carry on, especially with the added burden of course and equipment maintenance which had accumulated during the war years.

As with Shaftesbury, which failed to survive the war years, it has not been possible to find any records of the club in spite of investigating all the known sources including the Crichel Park Estate Office and local historians.

Two new tournaments

A new handicap tournament, to run concurrently with the inter-club mixed and the mens foursomes, was played for the first time in Yeovil in 1953. The scratch event continued unchanged but the handicap event was intended to be restricted to the clubs participating in the scratch competition. The first winners of this new event were Mrs R L Close and A W Wood of Ferndown.

A Juniors championship was inaugurated at the 1953 AGM, open to boys under eighteen with handicaps of twenty-four or less. The conditions of eligibility were that the boys must live or be at school in the county; be a member of a club affiliated with the DCGU; or who were born in the county, provided that they had not played in a championship meeting of another county. It would be played over eighteen holes of medal play and the winner would be known as *The County Boy Champion*.

The first match was held at Parkstone in April 1954 and was won by D Marriott of Broadstone with a score of 82 from J R Morton of Yeovil with 84. The winner of the handicap section was J Bolton of Parkstone with a nett score of 69. The under-fifteen gross event was won by I G Birch of Came Down with 97.

John Morton, now 54 years of age and currently captain of his Yeovil Club, recalls the occasion, and remembers travelling to Parkstone on a 'Royal Blue' coach. The driver did not know the exact whereabouts of the Parkstone club, so he was obliged to walk several miles carrying his golf clubs and clothes. It was a very hot day, and he eventually arrived at the course with little time to spare, and feeling hot and exhausted.

He had to carry his own clubs of course, and remembers playing 'a lad called Tarver, whose father, Col George Tarver caddied for him'. After the game he remembers Col Tarver's generous condolences and admitting that if he had been allowed to help John with club selection etc. there was no doubt that he would have won.

The Captain of the Union that year was E J Nicholl, and he had the delicate and difficult task of informing the County Ladies Captain Mrs Arkell that the Executive had turned down her request that girls should be allowed to compete in the event.

A suggestion that an artisans championship should be introduced was discussed in 1954, but it was rejected on the grounds that artisans who are amateurs and members of artisan clubs in the county were eligible to play in the county amateur championship.

Amateurs v Professionals

The annual competition was one of the original fixtures arranged by the Executive Committee at their meeting in February 1923, but there is no doubt that it was a patronising gesture on their part to compensate for the apparent refusal of the Hampshire County Union to allow Dorset members to compete in their similar event.

The format was twelve amateurs and twelve professionals playing singles in the morning and foursomes in the afternoon, with the amateurs allowed a handicap of two-up.

The odds were weighed heavily against the professionals, who were asked to play against the better ball of two and sometimes three very good amateur "gentlemen" golfers, who were, in those early days, the cream of the county's amateur players and the administrators of the original seven golf clubs.

It is not known if those first professionals received any out-of-pocket expenses for the away matches, but they certainly would not have owned a car, so would presumably have had to rely on their amateur partners for transport. The prize for the rare early wins has not been recorded, but thanks to a contemporary report of a meeting in the early 1930s, the winning pro received £5. The odds against a professional win were demonstrated in the 1931 match at Parkstone, when they were asked to play against three amateurs. Reg Whitcombe's sub-par score of 69 was not good enough; and despite Broadstone's Corlett's excellent 66, his score was only one better than the better-ball of his three opponents. The par for the Parkstone course at that time was 71. Such were the odds that the professionals only managed to win twice in twenty-five years!

After World War II the social barriers crumbled and the game became accessible to a wider range of people, including those in trade and regarded as unacceptable in the pre-war private golf clubs. The social status of the professional golfer also improved, and they began to look for better remuneration for the pleasure of playing with the amateurs . . . and also against less punitive odds.

In 1958, after discussions with Percy Alliss at Ferndown, the format was changed to a 36-hole pro-am medal play tournament, and in order to celebrate the golden jubilee of the Weymouth Golf Club, the first revised fixture was played on the Weymouth course in 1959. The Corporation presented a cup for the winning amateur and the golf club offered increased money prizes for the professionals. Fittingly, the first professional winner was the home professional F H Beets, who collected £15, and Percy and Alec Alliss collected £5 each for joint second. The 'Weymouth Cup' was won by L C Emmett.

Under the revised format the competition became known as the 'Dorset Close Championship', and it ran for twenty-one years, when it became a strictly amateur event known as the Dorset Stroke Play Championship. However, during this period the Isle of Purbeck professional Brian Bamford enjoyed a fine run of five consecutive wins, but in 1977 Graham Butler halted the run with a phenomenal performance when he established a course record of 67 at Ferndown and won both Parkstone and Weymouth cups... and he audaciously repeated the feat in the following year!

The Whitcombes

1956 was a sad year for British golf, for the county, and for the Parkstone Golf Club in particular, because Reg Whitcombe, the only south western counties golfer ever to win the Open Championship, died after a long and distressing illness.

This history is a record of the activities of amateur golfers within the county union, but the Whitcombe brothers were an integral part of Dorset golf for many years, and they featured in a number of the amateur v professional tournaments included in the union's calendar; so it is fitting that at least a mention of their great golfing achievements should be included. In this chosen piece out of the many available from the time, the somewhat fulsome appraisal of the *Observer* sports reporter writing in 1924, has an ironic ring, and his personal analysis of the golf swing will probably produce a wry smile... if only it was that easy to keep one's head down!

'*Three Famous Brothers* Nothing more remarkable in golfing history has been witnessed than the sudden and dramatic rise to fame of the three brothers Whitcombe. In the case of Reginald, perhaps it is rather reflected glory, because he has not accomplished the brilliant things that stand to the credit of his two brothers. Still, he is a sound and capable golfer, who, blessed with a little luck, may some day be rubbing shoulders in the higher walks of golf with the rest of the family.

'The dash into the limelight of Charles and Ernest is without precedent in golf, and there can be no question that the performances of these sons of an old yeoman family of the West Country are the outstanding feature of this year's British professional golf. They are born golfers as distinct from the made, their attitude in the manner of hitting the ball clearly showing that they have gone through no laborious processes to bring them to their present state of efficiency.

'Now what is the secret of the Whitcombes golf? It is I think, summed up in one word "control". *Be on the course at whatever cost* seems to be their motto. There is much in common with the Whitcombes methods, they adopt the interlocking grip, which prevents either hand roving and getting out of position during the course of the swing, and their method of taking the club up and bringing it down again is simplicity itself. There is nothing to think of except looking at the ball, and this being purely automatic, nothing can go very wrong.

'A distinct feature of their attitude towards the ball... is that they keep their heads down for a longer period after the ball has gone than the majority of golfers... the main characteristic of J H Taylor... copied by the Whitcombes to their benefit'.

F Beets
Weymouth 1913 – 85

The three Whitcombe brothers

Introduction of 'Bob-a-Nob' scheme

The annual EGU subscription for members of the county union had remained at 6d (2½p) for a number of years, increasing only minimally after the war, but there had been increasing pressure for more financial support, which resulted in 1957 in the introduction of a per capita charge of 1/-d a member, which was immediately dubbed the 'bob-a-nob' charge; a vernacular saying which will be lost upon the readers who had no experience of the old money, but the shilling was commonly known as a bob.

This innovative scheme produced an income of £5,350 for the EGU, compared to just less than £2,000 in the previous year. A scheme similar to the bob-a-nob had been compulsory in Scotland since 1957, and in Ireland the rate was three shillings per head, but the system did not become compulsory in England until 1961.

In the words of the President the county 'did not distinguish itself' in the 1958 SWCGA event at Burnham, which was won by R C Champion of the host club. At that year's General meeting Major Ruttle announced that, as in future the event would be staged on courses in Devon, Cornwall and Somerset, Dorset would start with the disadvantage of always having to play away from home.

The reason given for the proposition to eliminate from the rota the two Dorset courses, Ferndown and Broadstone, was that by tradition the championship should be held on true links courses, effectively Burnham & Berrow, Westward Ho!, Saunton, St Enodoc, and Trevose, thus excluding Dorset, Gloucester and Wiltshire. The proposition was carried and was not reversed until ten years later, when Ferndown again hosted the championship.

It was generally felt that the reason given for the banning of the Dorset courses was somewhat specious because Broadstone had been the venue for

Percy Alliss
Ferndown 1938 – 63

181

the third championship meeting in 1926, and again in 1928, 1932 and 1936, while Long Ashton, as far removed from a true links course as can be imagined, hosted the second championship in 1925.

A more likely reason was that in 1955, after a very dry spring, the championship meeting at Broadstone was played in very hot and sunny conditions. Course irrigation was unknown in Britain in those days, so Broadstone presented the competitors with a challenge of manipulative skills and physical endurance.

At the end of the week the steep banks, punishing heather and long hard walks produced a group of protesting footsore and weary golfers, few of whom were nursing a desire to play it again! To add to their discomfort, was the negative aspect of playing for an already lost cause. Dorset had won the team championship by the Friday evening regardless of any result on the final day; and in the event produced a record individual match score which has never been matched. They also produced the first three finishers

The county team at Burnham in 1958
Back row: T Deighton, R Southcombe, M R Gardner, A J Horsington, W Southcombe, K Longmore
Front row: H Wilton, R G Peach, T R Jenkins, F G R Vowles, H C Neilson, R Lawford

in the individual championships, Ray Lawford winning his first SW championship after an 18-hole play-off against his County Captain Dick Peach, with Ian Campbell-Gray in third place.

Dorset won again in 1956 at St Enodoc after a nail biting finish against Somerset on the final day. The winner of that match would also be the team champions, and Dorset prevailed by the slenderest of margins; winning a one-hole victory on the final green in the last foursome match of the day. Ray Lawford and Dick Southcombe were the heroes of the hour, and Dick Peach won the individual championship.

The nett result meant that Dorset had won the team championship on five out of six years from 1951 to 1956, and on each of those occasions produced the individual champion. The missing year (1953) Dorset was last in the list and did not win a single match . . . such are the vicissitudes of golf.

When the decision was reversed and Ferndown again hosted the SW championship in 1966, Dorset responded by winning the team prize for the first time since 1956, and Ray Lawford won his second individual title.

1955 marked a change by the EGU in the format of the English county championship finals to determine the 'Champion County of England'. Prior to this, each county who wished to enter nominated three players (four between 1927-37 and thereafter again reduced to three) who each played thirty-six holes of stroke play, with the aggregate score of the three to count. As more counties entered it became impractical to accommodate the numbers for thirty-six holes on one day, so the country was divided into four groups, Northern; Midland; South-Eastern; and South-Western. Each group would run a 36-hole medal qualifying competition for six nominated players from each county in the group, the aggregate scores of all six players to determine the winning county. In the South-Western region it was decided to use the SW individual championship as the qualifying competition, six players being nominated by each county prior to the start of the championship. Thereafter there would be a knock-out competition for the winners of each group, eighteen holes of singles and foursomes for teams of six; semi-finals one day and finals on the following day.

Dorset won the SW group at the Broadstone championship meeting of 1955, and thus had the honour of being the first SW county to participate in the final stages of the first championship meeting to be played to this new format at Formby.

The county lost its semi-final match to Worcestershire by six matches to three; and they in turn lost in the final to Yorkshire who had beaten Surrey in the other semi-final by seven matches to two.

The format of the final has since been changed to a three-day round robin event, so that players who make a long journey to participate have the opportunity of playing throughout the week.

Major Ruttle, who had been President since 1946, resigned in 1958, and G E Newton of the Ferndown Golf Club was voted into office.

R E Garrett, Major Ruttle's son-in-law and a distinguished member of

Victor and vanquished. Ray Lawford's first SWC win at Broadstone 1955

the county union, had died, and in his valedictory speech as President, the Major announced that his daughter Maureen Garrett had presented a silver salver in memory of her husband, to be awarded to the winner of the qualifying rounds in the championship. The first name to be engraved on the new trophy was that of Ken Longmore of the Parkstone Club with a consistent 74 + 74 on the Ferndown course.

In the following year Maureen Garrett achieved the unique honour of being appointed the captain of Middlesex; of England; and of the Great Britain team, all in the same year: and Major Ruttle proudly confided to the meeting that she had been asked to captain the Curtiss Cup team to play America in 1960.

Associate Memberships

Major Gardner of Yeovil, the 1958 captain, proposed the formation of an associate membership of the county union, open to all male members, for a fee of £1, which would entitle the member to one day's free golf at each club in the county. The proceeds from the fees would be used to assist and to train juniors towards county standards. The proposal was endorsed by the meeting and they would be known as *The Dorset Union of Golfers.*

The income from the 'county card scheme' as it became known was a most important source of finance for the County Union because, in addition to providing funds for promoting junior and colts golf, it allowed the union to subsidise members of the county team, particularly for the SW counties week. Prior to this the team members had to pay their own expenses; a situation which clearly could not continue because the younger players in their late teens and early twenties could not afford to be away from their jobs and they were the backbone of future county teams. It was recognised that good young players had to be nurtured if the county team was to remain competitive with its rivals in the South West region. Dick Peach recalls that eight members of the 1956 team which he captained were over forty and he in his mid-thirties was the second youngest player. How different is the situation today, when it is not unusual to field a county side where half the players are under twenty and there is rarely one over thirty. Such has been the effect of the explosion in the game of golf during the past twenty-five years.

The formation of the new association had a marked effect upon the finances of the county union; the membership was extended to 200 in 1960 and again in the following year, adding £226 to the coffers, and true to their declared objective, the committee decided to promote more boys' competitions and to introduce a training programme for juniors under the stewardship of G H Kendall (Parkstone). This was further extended in 1965 to include clinics given by John Stirling the professional at Meyrick Park.

Juniors v Seniors foursomes competitions were arranged at New Northborne (as it was then called), Broadstone and Ferndown; and trophies given by K Robshaw of the Parkstone club, and the *Daily Telegraph,* were

continued on page 186 . . .

R E Garrett

Twice county champion, one of the longest hitters in the game, the most good humoured and friendly man, such are the recollections of Ted Garrett's contemporaries.

In the 1951 county championship he beat the redoubtable Ernest Millward at Parkstone, succeeding again in 1954 against the equally tough Ken Longmore, then in the following year he was runner-up to Ray Lawford at Broadstone. He and Miss C Bannister were twice runners-up in the inter-club mixed foursomes in 1952 at Broadstone, and in 1954 at Yeovil they lost to Pat Crow and Dick Peach in the scratch event. He also won the county handicap medal competition at Parkstone in 1951; and in very good company, featured in the men's inter-club foursomes on three consecutive occasions, winning with George Newton at Lyme Regis in 1947, losing to Millward and Austreng in 1948, and winning again with Newton at Weymouth in 1949.

He served as a Major in the Royal Artillery during the war, and was for a time stationed near Chesil beach, then to Africa and Italy. He escaped the bullets, but without his knowledge in Africa fell foul of an insidious but nonetheless fatal virus which just over a decade later was to be the cause of his death.

He met Maureen Garrett in 1946 when Maureen decided to take a French conversation course in preparation for her defence of the French Open title, and they were married a year later.

Ted was descended from a very old firm of Blandford tailors and his mother was for a time in the 1920s the Lady Secretary of the Ashley Wood Golf Club. After the war he joined House & Sons, estate agents, and was made a partner after qualifying as a surveyor and auctioneer.

He was of fairly average height and build, but he was able to hit the ball tremendous distances (a trait his son Teddy has inherited). He was also recognised to be a very steady putter... not given to 'nerves', and perhaps more importantly in a county not famed for its foursomes play, he enjoyed the format and was particularly good at it.

The virus he picked up in Africa affected the muscles of the heart, and he was to suffer numerous serious heart attacks in the latter years of his life. Maureen recalls one particularly spectacular one which caused her to abandon her attempt at the British Open at Gleneagles in 1957. Ted was part of the county team at the SW championships in Saunton and he suffered a massive heart attack on the golf course. Maureen chartered a private aircraft and flew to a nearby RAF station and stayed with him at the team hotel for a few days until, against medical advice, she insisted on having him moved to Barnstaple hospital. He 'recovered' but was ill for a year and he died at University College Hospital in London after cheerfully reassuring Maureen that he was being treated by 'the Ben Hogan of heart specialists'... but even the great Hogan could not perform miracles at every appearance.

competed for at Parkstone. In 1964 Kendall reported a very successful year's results, with 22 entries for the championship at Broadstone, which his son Robin (age 17) won with a gross score of 76. He ended his report with the observation that 'young Peach (14) is now down to 7, and Teddy Garrett can hit the ball almost as far as his father could'. So within six years of Major Gardner's innovative idea, over 50 percent of the entries for the boys championship at Yeovil had a handicap of 12 or under... quite a success story!

In the 1960 inter-club scratch mixed foursomes, R G Peach the Parkstone golfer, playing on his own course with Mrs Pat Crow, achieved the unique distinction of holing-in-one twice in one round: at the 160 yard second and 158 yard fourteenth holes. They also birdied the short seventh from Mrs Crow's tee shot, thus aggregating four strokes for the three short holes played... to end the semi-final match on the fourteenth green.

At the end of the 1962 meeting Major Ruttle expressed his satisfaction that the 1963 County Championship would be held at Lyme Regis... 'an up-and-coming club'!

In that same year Major Gardner suggested the formation of *The Dorset Captains Golfing Society,* but in accepting the proposition as worthy of further consideration, the meeting expressed doubts about their ability to fit it into an already full fixture list.

Richard Southcombe

The definition of a 'male playing member' came up for discussion at the 1964 meeting. The question was posed by G Tice of Broadstone, and the detailed answer given was that 'this should include all male members, including country members, and that a member who belonged to two or more clubs should pay his subs at each club'. According to the EGU rules, juniors under eighteen years were exempt, but Major Ruttle (EGU President), said that the EGU would welcome the suggestion that juniors be included in the subscription.

It may surprise readers to learn that printed fixture cards were not introduced until 1965, when one thousand were printed as an experiment in response to a suggestion by G H Kendall, who produced a sample of the Devon Union card. A cogent argument in favour of adopting the cards was the opportunity they offered to clubs to advertise their 'open' meetings.

A county flag was donated to the union in 1965 by H A Wilton 'to be flown at all county events'. This was a genuine flag, not to be confused with the flag trophy, the silver miniature donated by Major F A Stephens of the Ferndown Club in December 1924.

Lance Luffman, who had been the Secretary and Treasurer since 1932, was experiencing difficulty in travelling to all the events, so at the 1965 AGM it was decided to appoint Richard Southcombe, a fellow member of the Yeovil club, to act as joint secretary. However, this situation lasted for only one year because Luffman was forced to retire through ill health, and he died three years later in 1968.

Coaching for Juniors

G H Kendall, in resigning from his five-year stewardship of the county juniors in 1966, gave a glowing report of the success of the coaching and training schemes. W G Peach won the Dorset boys championship at Broadstone with a record gross 74 from N J Robbins (76), and in the handicap section S Leach won from E J S Garrett; all sixteen year-olds. The youngest competitor was N B Josling (15) with a nett score of 82.

Peach was selected for the English boys team for the annual match against Scotland after a stroke-play trial for potential candidates. This international match preceded the British boys' championship and was held at Moortown, Leeds.

In the editorial of the September issue of the English Golf Union's fixtures list Lt Col K A Nash, the Secretary of the EGU, commented upon how much fun it was to watch the antics of the parents on these occasions, and then made the following cryptic observation: *Mr R G Peach, who represents Dorset on the Council and Executive Committee of the EGU, saw his son Bill hit a good one from the first tee ... and then went back home to Dorset. Bill got into the team and won both his matches. Peach Senior is this year's Dorset Champion ... so he knows the form ...*

Bill Peach was selected for the English team again in 1967 at Western Gailes.

It will be a source of some amusement to readers, used to the huge amounts of money now available to all top sportsmen, to learn that at the 1967 meeting it was decided to award three pounds to the professional partner in the flag foursomes!

Graham Butler of Ferndown won the county championship in 1967 on the Parkstone course, beating Dr D M Holmes 2 and 1, and he also won the inter-club flag foursomes, playing with his professional Doug Sewell. The Garrett Salver was won by Ray Lawford from W G Peach at the second extra hole.

Individual coaching for five juniors was introduced to overcome the problems of the 'County Pro' having to visit the boys' home clubs. The first five to be nominated for Doug Sewell's clinic were Nigel Green of Came Down, Doug Owers of Weymouth, G Archer of Ferndown, N Robbins of Yeovil and M Swift of Sherborne. In the following year seven juniors were selected and E Garrett and D Owers were selected for coaching under the EGU scheme.

Following a proposal by Graham Butler, the age limit for Colts was reduced to twenty-three to conform to the EGU rules.

Channel League

The Union applied to join the Channel League in 1971, which meant that two more county matches (Monmouth and Somerset) would be added to the fixture list because the county already played friendly matches against the other counties in the league. The County had applied to join on a number of occasions, but their applications were not supported, however this time they were successful and they played their first fixtures in 1972.

In his report of the year's successes, the President, R G Peach congratulated Graham Butler on his record seventh win in the County Championships; but he also had the unpleasant task of announcing the death of Col Mike Gardner of the Yeovil Club.

continued on page 190 . . .

Col Mike Gardner

In a golfing career spanning half a century, Mike Gardner was more fortunate than most in having the two foremost professionals of the time as his tutors. At the age of seven his first lessons were with Abe Mitchell, and when the family moved to Bournemouth he was put in the hands of Reg Whitcombe. When he matured many observers commented that from a distance it was difficult to tell the difference between him and Whitcombe, they were so alike in stature and golfing styles.

With this background it is not surprising that, at nineteen years of age, and playing off a handicap of two, he became the youngest ever Dorset County Champion at the Swanage and Studland (IoP) course in 1931. Two years later, playing with his mentor, they won the Flag Foursomes at Broadstone, and a flashback to those years brings a reminder of a now defunct golf rule . . . "he laid three stymies against his Came Down opponents G Glass Hooper and W B Dunnett".

In the following year, playing on his home course of Parkstone, he won the 'Bystander Trophy' from Viscount Mandeville, and again in the following year, this time at Felixstowe, he won it from Sir Basil Eddes. Playing for the army in his first year as a commissioned officer in the RASC, he won the Army Championship in a gale at Royal Porthcawl, repeating the feat at Royal Lytham & St Annes the next year; but perhaps more surprisingly, twenty years later he tied for the same title, losing in a play-off to Walker Cup Captain Tony Duncan!

His greatest golfing achievement was winning the Egyptian Open in 1939, only two weeks after arriving in the country, and on a course he had never played before.

He joined the Yeovil Club in 1951 and was Handicap and Match Secretary for many years. During this time he served the County Union as Captain and as Deputy President; and he continued to be a staunch supporter of County events right up to the time of his death in 1972.

Golden Jubilee

Again, no mention was made of the county union's fiftieth birthday, but since the twenty-fifth anniversary in 1948, when the county championship meeting became a three-day event, the fixture list had grown from six to sixteen events, and the income-expenditure sheet had reached four-figure proportions.

The 1950s was a decade of achievement and innovation. The county teams won five SWCGA championships: entered the English county championships for the first time: introduced a juniors championship: designed a county badge: started the Union of Dorsetshire Golfers: and introduced the County 'Close' championship.

The fifties also saw the death of Reg Whitcombe; the emergence of Ernest Millward, Ray Lawford and Ken Longmore; and Lance Luffman completed twenty-five years service as the Honorary Secretary.

In 1963 Lyme Regis hosted the county championship event for the first time; coaching for boys was introduced; the Dorset Captains Golfing Society was formed; printed fixture lists were introduced; and Graham Butler won his seventh gold medal.

In 1972 the county entered the Channel League.

The county entered a team in the inaugural four-counties junior tournament in 1973. Winning the draw, the team played their first match at Parkstone in April, ending up second to Somerset, with Devon and Cornwall third and fourth.

Graham Butler's remarkable record of wins in the County Championship continued through to 1978, when he recorded his tenth win; a feat that will probably never be equalled, and incidentally, his ninth gold medal was the last to be awarded to the County Champion. By this time the cost of the gold medal had risen to £160, so it was decided to replace it with a silver salver.

At the 1979 AGM, the President (R G Peach) announced that another attempt would be made to form a *Dorset County Golf Association,* to be run on similar lines to that of the 'County Captains'. It was envisaged that two meetings a year would be held in mid-week, play to be foursomes, with both scratch and handicap sections, and possibly a division for the over-sixties.

The purpose of the new association was not to provide additional funds, but an attempt to involve 'the ordinary club member into the affairs of the county'.

A trial meeting was held at the Came Down Club in 1978, when over forty members attended, and was judged to have been a great success. It was proposed to charge an entrance fee of five pounds, with no annual subscription, but it was eventually decided not to include a separate section for seniors.

In Ken Longmore's report on the juniors at the 1981 AGM, he announced that the first winners of his Longmore Junior Shield were the Came Down team, who won five matches against Ferndown's four. He paid a glowing tribute to Gary Emerson, who at eighteen years of age and playing off a handicap of two, represented Great Britain in the De Vere tournament in Venezuela. Gary lost 2 and 1 in the four-ball event, and halved in the

D Sewell.
Ferndown 1963 –

foursomes and the singles. He also finished third in the am/am tournament and seventh in the 54-hole medal, with scores of 81, 71 and 75.

He won the 36-hole scratch medal at Parkstone; and as a schoolboy international reached the third round of the amateur championship at Burnham. He also played for Great Britain against Ireland in the junior PGA Cup; won the Dorset schoolboys championship for the second year running, and has won the Aer Lingus regional championship for the last four years.

Gary Emerson

County Cards

At the November 1988 meeting, which was held at the Ferndown club, the Isle of Purbeck representative questioned the desirability of continuing with the county card scheme.

The cost to members of the cards had increased yearly, and in 1989 stood at £25. The income from the cards had subsidised the county union since its inception, and this income had been used to minimise the *per capita* levy on members.

The most popular clubs had for some time resented the influx of members from the less popular courses, and claimed a lack of reciprocity because their own club members were not interested in playing on the other courses. In addition, it was argued that the card-holders imposed a strain on the already crowded popular courses and it was often difficult to fit them into a time slot between members' times and visiting golf societies.

It was suggested that the cards should no longer be used as a means of providing finance for the county, and that a better method would be to impose a levy on each of the eighteen clubs.

This motion was overwhelmingly rejected by the meeting and the representatives voted instead in favour of retaining the cards and increasing the annual subscription to 90p. The Isle of Purbeck representative then announced that her club would probably withdraw from the scheme, but would support the county's finances with a donation.

In order to safeguard the future of the cards the Executive Committee recommended an increase in the annual subscription from 90p to £1.80p, and to permit the participating clubs to retain the revenue raised from the sale of the cards.

This was agreed and it proved to be a very sensible decision, because Broadstone, Ferndown and Parkstone subsequently withdrew, leaving about sixteen participating clubs who have agreed that card holders should pay half the green fee at each visit.

Lakey Hill and Highcliffe Castle were welcomed into the county union in 1980, and in the following year the Christchurch club joined Dorset from Hampshire. The Minutes also recorded the formation in 1981 of the *Dorset County Golfers Association* with an initial membership of one hundred. It would be run on the same lines as the *County Captains,* and have three seasonal fixtures a year.

Within a year of its formation the association had a membership of 100. The President appealed to the club representatives to try to increase the figure to 200, and it was agreed to hold three seasonal meetings.

When, in 1992, the membership reached 300 the number of meetings was increased to four, and the entrance fee raised to £10. This enabled the County to give the host club a sizeable gratuity for providing the courtesy of the course, and after deducting the cost of prizes, the balance is used to help finance the cost of coaching promising young players.

In 1982, Richard Southcombe, who took over the Secretaryship from the ailing Lance Luffman in 1966, was elected to the office of President, but he retained his position as Secretary because of the decision to rotate the office of President around the member clubs and to limit the term to two years.

In this year two of the county's young players Jimmy Leggett and Gary Emerson left the amateur ranks, Leggett to be an Assistant with Doug Sewell at Ferndown, and Gary Emerson who went on to become the Professional at the West Wilts Golf Club.

The outstanding achievements of Stephen Edgley of Parkstone, and Robert

Mabb and Michael Watson, of Weymouth, were recorded in the minutes of the 1984 General meeting and they have since extended their experience and successes at county, national and international levels.

In 1985 Meyrick Park was represented at the Annual General Meeting for the first time, and Bournemouth Artisans affiliated two years later, in advance of the main Bournemouth club's decision to transfer from Hampshire.

Richard Southcombe announced at the 1985 meeting his intention to resign as Secretary, and in the following year Lt Col Maurice Hutchins, the Fixtures and Competition Secretary was voted into the office.

Richard's brother 'Bunny' served as Match Secretary for nineteen years and resigned in 1987 through ill-health. Both brothers enjoyed a wonderful record in sport: Dick played rugby at wing three-quarter for Sale;

Lt Col Maurice Hutchins

captained Yeovil cricket club from 1936-39 and played for the county; was captain of Yeovil golf club in 1964; county captain in 1981; played in the SWGA from 1956-63; was President of the Association in 1976; and President of his golf club in 1986.

'Bunny' also played cricket and rugby for Yeovil; was captain of his golf club in 1958; played in the SWGA from 1957-61 and was captain of Dorset in 1967. Sadly, he died in 1992.

Nigel Tokeley, the Broadstone professional was invited to become the 'County Pro' in 1987 to help and advise the county players during the winter months.

Ken Robshaw, the 1987 President had the dismal task of announcing that Graham Butler had died at the age of 47. He described him as 'probably the finest golfer who has ever represented Dorset and his death at such an early age is a severe blow to county golf'.

Nigel Tokeley

Graham Butler

The most consistently successful player in this recorded history of Dorset golf. He won his first gold medal in 1959 at the age of twenty-one, playing on his own course at Ferndown and went on to set an unassailable record of ten championship wins.

These successes were spread over six courses, and the only one which seemed to defeat him on these occasions was Broadstone, but it proved to be no obstacle in many other competitions, notably in the 1978 meeting when he won both the Parkstone and Weymouth Cups.

Unfortunately he was unable to collect a round figure of ten medals, because in 1977 the committee finally decided that the cost of the medal was too great and it was replaced by a silver salver.

After his untimely death at the age of forty-nine, his wife April presented the medals to his club Ferndown. She also donated the 'Graham Butler Trophy' which the County Champion would receive in addition to the salver; in her own words, she felt that trophy winners like to be able to see the names of previous champions ... something that was lacking with the medal and the salver.

Graham achieved over 100 wins for Dorset in inter-county matches between 1959 and 1983 and represented his county in the South Western Championships for twenty-four years, during which time he won the regional individual title. He also represented the South West region against the Midlands and captained the side in 1981.

His county contemporaries rated Graham as *the finest golfer Dorset had ever had ... a super sportsman and a perfect gentleman.*

On the lighter side, the President congratulated Michael (Tom) Watson who represented England in the European Boys championships and played for England in the Home championships. He also announced that Steve Edgley had won a scholarship to the North Western University in Illinois.

At the sixtieth AGM in 1988, the President was able to read out a string of successes for the county, and introduced a new county seniors championship, and county foursomes league, to be played during the winter months. This was sponsored by the Western Gazette newspaper and designed to raise the standard of the county's foursomes play.

Ken Shaw of Parkstone golf club tied for the individual title in the SW counties seniors championships, and won the inaugural SW counties strokeplay championship at Saunton.

Tony Lawrence, playing in the county championships at Broadstone, won the matchplay title and the salver for the leading qualifier for the third consecutive year. His prize for the matchplay event was the new Graham Butler trophy.

In 1989, the sixty-third year of the Union, Moors Valley golf club applied to be affiliated to the county and to the EGU, making a total of nineteen clubs. In the following year Canford school was represented, and Halstock was also added to the list, and for the first time, the name 'East Dorset' appeared, following the many changes which had taken place in the ownership and the layout of what used to be the Lakey Hill Golf Club.

Almost up-to-date: the 1990 President Ray Lawford announced that Ian Donnelly of Ferndown had won the SW counties colts championships at Newquay: that Lee James of Broadstone had been chosen to play for England

Tony Lawrence with the Graham Butler trophy

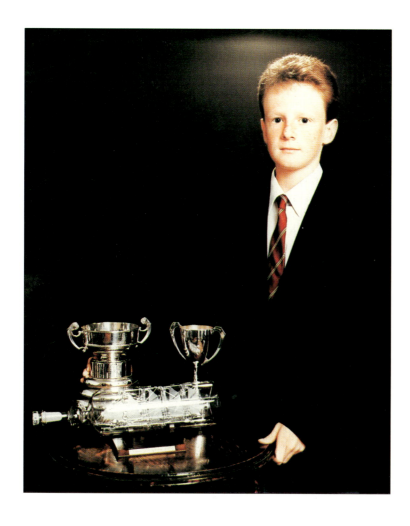

Paul Donnelly

Boys in the international match at Hunstanton; and that Peter McMullen of Ferndown, the County Champion had established a new course record of 64 at Lansdown.

The joy and satisfaction in the Donnelly household was tempered by the memory of the tragic death in the previous year of Ian's younger brother Paul. Sixteen year old Paul was one of the three-strong Ferndown side which won the Brokenhurst junior team open competition. He and Fergus Moore were killed when their car crashed into another car on their way back across the New Forest heathland road to the club to collect the trophy. Paul would have been making his debut for Dorset juniors in the annual four counties tournament. He was selected after finishing fifth in the Dorset Boys championship at Knighton Heath on the day before the Brokenhurst tournament.

Ray Donnelly presented a trophy to commemorate his son, to be played for annually between boys of Hampshire and Dorset.

New competitions and county matches were introduced; and Weymouth golf club formed the Dorset County Junior league, with twelve teams competing in two sections.

This expanded to twenty participating clubs, with four sections and play-offs for each winner; and in 1991 the county took over the administration.

Another new trophy was given by Mrs Mary Nash in memory of Cyril, who acted as the Starter in county events for a number of years, and who was a great supporter of the juniors. This is a competition for teams of four boys and is played on the Wareham course.

Two more clubs, Queens Park and the Mid-Dorset applied for affiliation in 1991, making a total of twenty-four clubs and about eleven thousand members in the county union.

This chapter, and the historical review of the county union ends with the 1992 Annual General Meeting, which was held at the Ferndown golf club on the 21st of November.

In his report, the President welcomed three new clubs: Dudsbury, Crane Valley, and Chedington Court, which made a new total of twenty-seven, and a membership of 12,000.

The winning Boys team in 1991
Back row: I Parsons   R Norris   A Elwick   D Miles   M Searle
             Yeovil   Yeovil   L Regis   Meyrick   L Regis
Front row: R Donnelly   M Higley   D Norris   S Meakins
             Asst Manager Yeovil   Manager   Broadstone

The winning Boys team in 1992
Left to right: R Norris   Ian Parsons   Paul Cooper   Jason Silk   Mike Whitlock
                Junior Sec   *Yeovil*   *B'mth & Meyrick*   *Ferndown*   *Yeovil*
                Trevor Ashworth Chris Brook   Sean McDonagh   Steve Meakin   Nick Rodgers
                (Capt) Torquay *Ferndown*   *Broadstone*   *Broadstone*   *Ashley Wood*

1992 saw the introduction of the South of England Boys open championship for boys under the age of seventeen. The prize is a gold putter donated by Tony Jacklin. It is a 72-hole competition played annually over the Sherborne and Yeovil courses in August, when the nearby Sherborne school is closed and therefore available to offer dormitory accommodation to the visiting competitors. The first winner of the event was Ben Sandry of the Exeter golf club.

The event attracted a huge response, undoubtedly helped by the publicity boost given by Peter Alliss, who referred to it during his commentary from the 'Open' at Muirfield.

County championships for Category 2, 3, and 4, sponsored by Bray & Sear (Suzuki UK), were introduced in 1992. Each club nominated either the May, June, or July monthly medal competition as the qualifying round, and the winners in each category played the finals at the East Dorset Golf Club in September.

Each qualifier received a medallion, and the winners the 'John Finding' trophies.

New competitions for 1993 will include a championship for boys under 16 and under 14; and further along the age spectrum, a mid-amateur 36-hole scratch competition for the over-35s.

In the front of this book is a list of 'Acknowledgements' . . . grateful thanks to the sponsors who have helped with the production and publications costs of this historical record, in addition to the numerous sources who have helped with research, advice, and information. Now, at the end of this (almost) seventy years record of the county union's activities, the author and compiler of this work would like to add a personal tribute and thanks to the officials and the players who together have contributed to producing a perfect end to this chapter. The success at Weston super Mare and the phenomenal performances at Kings Norton could not have been better orchestrated as a finale for this publication!.

On the first day of this historic English County Finals, Dorset beat the holders Middlesex. On the second day, Yorkshire were the victims, but torrential rain washed out the afternoon singles. On the morning of the third day, with the course dried out and in good weather, the team finally beat Staffordshire after a very tough battle, and went into the afternoon singles matches needing only two and a half points to win the title. Despite losing the top two matches, they halved the third and won the last three matches and clinched the title.

The last words are fittingly left to the happy team captain Doug Pratt in his report to the 1992 AGM.

'Trying to maintain the achievements of the previous captain, David Lock, was always going to be a hard act to follow; Dorset having won the Channel League for the first time, and winning both the team and individual strokeplay events at the SW championship in 1991 for the second time in four years.

'However, what was going to be just an ordinary captain's report has turned out to be the most rewarding that any captain has had the privilege to write . . . the team having made history for Dorset golf in 1992.

'The events which took place at Kings Norton between the 2nd and 4th of October during the English County Finals saw Dorset achieve the pinnacle of success when they won the title of *Champions of England* for the very first time, by beating the reigning champions Middlesex, followed by victories over Yorkshire and Staffordshire. Truly a memorable week-end for the team and all who were there to witness this emotional occasion.

'Obviously the foundations of this famous victory were laid some years ago, and I merely had the privilege of reaping the benefit of past years of effort. I thank the previous captains, and David Lock in particular, for selecting me to lead the players during this most successful year.

'For the record, the players who represented the county were:- Lee James *Broadstone,* Roger Hearn and Steve Edgley *Parkstone,* Peter McMullen and Martyn Thompson *Ferndown,* Tony Lawrence *Sherborne,* and Michael Watson *Weymouth.*

'The "team" of course not only includes the players, but officials, caddies, bag carriers and supporters, without whom none of this would have been possible. I know that the players would wish me to convey their sincere thanks to them all.

'Everything else that happened during the season now takes on a different perspective: Dorset repeated last year's achievements at the SW championship by successfully defending both the team and individual titles in the stroke-play event.

MAGNIFICENT SEVEN: back row (from left) Steve Edgley, Martyn Thompson, Peter McMullen, Lee James; front: Michael Watson, Rodger Hearn, Tony Lawrence.

Echo golf writer ANDY GOODALL reports from Birmingham on an historic victory for Dorset

UNDERDOGS Dorset sprang one of the biggest giant-killing feats in the amateur game to win the English County Finals for the first time in their 67-year history at Kings Norton yesterday.

The minnows brushed aside reigning champions Middlesex, Yorkshire and Staffordshire to win all three matches in the round robin competition.

Many of the game's pundits believed Dorset were merely there to make up the numbers after finishing with the wooden spoon on their two previous trips to the finals.

But Dorset upstaged their illustrious opponents with a display of supreme quality and team spirit to earn the right to wear the crown of English champions.

The experience gained at Hoylake last year, and the availability of American university graduates Steve Edgley and Michael 'Tom' Watson, provided the grit needed to win.

An emotional Dorset captain, Doug Pratt declared: "This is the proudest day in Dorset golf and one which will live on in the memories of those lucky enough to have been here to witness it."

The magnitude of Dorset's success is all the more remarkable when the number of clubs in the county is compared with those of their opponents.

Despite only having 27 clubs to choose from Dorset produced a team capable of toppling the likes of Yorkshire which can boast more than 160 clubs and a crop of international players.

Dorset's triumphant three days began with a 5-4 victory against Middlesex with county champion Lee James leading the charge with a 3 and 2 victory against England international Warren Bennett.

And to prove the result was no flash in the pan Dorset rode the storm to outwit a star-studded Yorkshire line-up in a match reduced to foursomes because of torrential rain.

The stage for a championship upset was set for the final day with a game against Staffordshire who had only their pride to fight for after losing both their previous matches.

After winning the foursomes 2-1 Dorset needed 2 1/2 points from the singles and Ferndown's Martyn Thompson quickly bagged the first one, demolishing his opponent Steve Perry 8 and 7.

Watson, who flys back to Nevada today, picked up a draw and Rodger Hearn and Tony Lawrence sealed the match with 3 and 2 wins for a famous 5 1/2 to 3 1/2 victory.

The scenes of joy on the 16th green were reminiscent of the Ryder Cup as players, officials, and supporters celebrated the historic occasion.

The championship title is just reward for county stalwarts Hearn, Lawrence and Peter McMullen who have provided the backbone of the team which has qualified for the finals three times in the past five years.

And the form of James, Thompson, Edgley and Watson must surely have impressed the England selectors and improved the prospects of a Dorset player representing England at senior level.

'What thrillers they both were: in the team event Dorset's performance over the closing holes left the rest of the counties standing... eventually winning by nine shots. The individual event was a nail-biting affair as Michael Watson, Steve Edgley and Mathew Stanford of Gloucester (an English International player) were all involved in a play-off over four holes of stroke-play, after the 36-hole tournament. The match went to the last green, with Watson and Edgley battling it out, but with victory going to Edgley by just one shot. The standard of golf was superb and a credit to the county.

'In the Channel League, an unfortunate defeat by Gloucester (8-7) in the first match at Sherborne, followed by a very difficult match at Perranporth against Cornwall, left Dorset with a tremendous task if they were to retain the title.

'We kept at least one hand on the title as we ran up good results against Wilts, Devon, and Somerset, before receiving a battering from Glamorgan in atrocious weather at Royal Porthcawl. Form, and honour were restored when we denied Gwent of any hopes they had of winning the title at Broadstone.

'Dorset's individual match results (Won 64 Lost 40) were bettered only by Cornwall, showing how very close we came to retaining the title, despite finishing four points behind the eventual winners, Gloucester.

'There have been several highlights during the year and I would like to mention some of them; they are an indication of the quality of play and the sportsmanship which has become an established tradition with Dorset for many years.

'Individual performances which need to be mentioned are:

Steve Edgley, SW champion and winner of the Dorset stroke-play title.

Lee James, Dorset champion, and for his many fine performances in county matches, in which he gained some notable scalps, including Gary Wolstenholme, Colin Edwards, Richard Dinsdale, Warren Bennett, and only losing to Matt McQuire by a fraction when Lee's ball completed a full circuit of the hole at Kings Norton, but failed to drop. He has also performed well in major events throughout the season.

Michael Watson for his performances in the 'Faldo Jug' and the East Sussex Open.

Tony Lawrence for beating English International Mathew Stanford, and recording a Hole-in-One at Perranporth.

Mike Searle of Lyme Regis for his fine performance in the English championships at Deal.

'I save the best until last... I know that everyone will agree that **Roger Hearn's** performance at the English Finals, where he was undefeated in five games, will have been the greatest in his long career with Dorset... Well done Roger!

'The sportsmanship, the humour, and the friendship which were so much in evidence in all the year's events are epitomised in just one amusing incident: those of you who were at the SW championships will remember Bill Raymond of Broadstone and Jez Tomlinson of Wilts. "hacking about" at the last hole of their match... much to the annoyance of both team captains who were monitoring the slow progress through binoculars. Both players made hard work of the hole, so much so that one team captain was heard to growl "for ***** sake why don't you agree to take a half in seven and finish with it"!

'When the players finally did putt-out they turned to the captains and amid much laughter informed them that the match had finished three holes back and they were just putting on a charade for the benefit of the onlookers!

'All in all it was a VERY SUCCESSFUL SEASON: we played 18, and won 12. In the foursomes, the matches won were 40, lost 32. In the singles, matches won 91, lost 66.

'Peter McMullen represented the county on every occasion and recorded 19 wins to 9 losses, with four halved. He continued this record through to the very end of the season, and he too was unbeaten in the English Finals . . . *thank you* Peter for your loyal support.

'One other fact became evident through the season: the standard of golf now being played in the South West is equal to that anywhere in the country. This was highlighted in the number of players who reached the last 32 of the English Championships when at least 12/15 came from among the Channel League counties. The achievement of Dorset in the English Finals confirms this fact.

'We may not have had a host of well-known players before, compared with the rest of the country, but we certainly do now. Dorset conquered a mountain in 1992, but there will be many more peaks to climb in '93. I know that the team will not rest on its laurels, but will treat each as a new challenge.

'Defence of the title *Champions of England* is the ultimate challenge but I am confident that the team will lead the way in 1993'.

Joy unconfined

The County Union Presidents and Captains

Presidents

1923	Capt. A V Hambro
1931	Major J Gundry
1932	O B P Burdon
1933	Major C E Morrison
1935	Capt. N H Carter RN. Retd.
1936	C C Roberts
1946	Major J S Ruttle
1958	G E Newton
1972	R G Peach
1982	R Southcombe
1984	K Longmore
1986	K V Robshaw
1988	Major J H Wyllie
1990	R Lawford
1992	Dr. D M Holmes

Captains

1923	Major J Gundry	1964	R G Peach
1925	Capt. E L James	1967	W Southcombe
1926	Major J Gundry	1969	G Butler
1928	E Hunter	1971	K Longmore
1929	O B P Burdon	1973	R Lawford
1930	C C Roberts	1975	T Jenkins
1936	G E Newton	1976	J Nash
1948	R E Garrett	1978	A Jones
1950	H C Neilson	1980	G Eley
1952	E J Nicholl	1982	J Calver
1954	R G Peach	1984	B Crutcher
1956	M R Gardner	1986	D Scholes
1958	P J Urlwin-Smith	1988	T Griffin
1960	R Southcombe	1990	D Lock
1962	E A Horsington	1992	D Pratt

The English Counties Championship Trophy. Tappit Hen — an ancient Scottish drinking vessel

4

The Honours Boards
Dorset County Golf Union
County Amateur Championship

Year	Venue	Winner	Runner-up
1923	Broadstone	Capt. A V Hambro (C)	Major Stephens (FGC)
1924	Came Down	Capt. A V Hambro (C)	V Weldon (FGC)
1925	Ferndown	Major Stephens	
1926	Parkstone	Major Stephens	E J Dobson
1927	Broadstone	E Hunter	T P Whitaker
1928	Ferndown	W R Wills-Sandford (B)	
1929	Came Down	Sqdn. Ldr. J P Shorten (C)	
1930	Ferndown	C L Gordon-Stewart (C)	
1931	Swanage	Col. M R Gardner (P)	
1932	Ferndown	C L Gordon-Stewart (C)	
1933	Came Down	G Glass-Hooper (Brid)	A Dore (BA)
1934	Parkstone	Col. M R Gardner (P)	A Dore
1935	Broadstone	A Dore	A J Webb (BGC)
1936	Ferndown	H E Botting (FGC)	J A Elliott (FGC)
1937	Came Down	R M Chadwick	C Mayo
1938	Broadstone	E J Nicholl (N)	G Glass-Hooper (Brid)
1939	Ferndown	G Glass-Hooper (Brid)	F F Laugher (FGC)
1946	Parkstone	K J Longmore (N)	E B Millward (PGC)
1947	Came Down	O Austreng (PGC)	K J Longmore (N)
1948	Parkstone	E B Millward (PGC)	K J Longmore (PGC)
1949	Ferndown	J F E Santall (PGC)	P J Urlwin-Smith (PGC)
1950	Broadstone	E B Millward (PGC)	K J Longmore (PGC)
1951	Parkstone	R E Garrett (PGC)	E B Millward (PGC)
1952	Came Down	E B Millward (PGC)	O Austreng (PGC)
1953	Northborne	K Clarke (N'borne)	R G Peach (PGC)
1954	Ferndown	R E Garrett (PGC)	K J Longmore (PGC)
1955	Broadstone	R Lawford (B)	R E Garrett (PGC)
1956	Yeovil	K J Longmore (PGC)	A Buchan (Y)
1957	Parkstone	K J Longmore (PGC)	R G Peach (PGC)
1958	Came Down	P Sanders (B)	K J Longmore (PGC)
1959	Ferndown	G J Butler (FGC)	K J Longmore (PGC)
1960	Broadstone	K J Longmore (PGC)	C T McInerney (FGC)
1961	Yeovil	G J Butler (FGC)	S Brewis (B)
1962	Parkstone	A J Richmond (PGC)	R G Peach (PGC)
1963	Lyme Regis	G J Butler (FGC)	D Cowan (KH)
1964	Came Down	A J Richmond (PGC)	G J Butler (FGC)
1965	Ferndown	G J Butler (FGC)	Dr. D M Holmes (PGC)
1966	Yeovil	R G Peach (PGC)	P Sanders (B)
1967	Parkstone	G J Butler (FGC)	Dr. D M Holmes (PGC)
1968	Broadstone	R G Peach (PGC)	A J Richmond (PGC)
1969	Came Down	G J Butler (FGC)	N Green (Came)
1970	Ferndown	R Lawford (B)	G J Butler (FGC)
1971	Yeovil	E J S Garrett (PGC)	R Lawford (B)
1972	Parkstone	G J Butler (FGC)	F K Shaw (PGC)
1973	Broadstone	A K Jones (B)	Dr. D M Holmes (PGC)

County Amateur Championship (continued)

Year	Venue	Winner	Runner-up
1974	Lyme Regis	J Lawrence (Y)	T Griffin (Y)
1975	Came Down	G J Butler (FGC)	J Calver (PGC)
1976	I.o.P.	G J Butler (FGC)	J Nash (B)
1977	Ferndown	D Scholes (B)	I Clarke (Came)
1978	Yeovil	G J Butler (FGC)	J Nash (B)
1979	Parkstone	M Farley (FGC)	J Calver (PGC)
1980	Broadstone	J Nash (B)	G J Butler (FGC)
1981	Lyme Regis	R Hearn (PGC)	J Leggett (PGC)
1982	Came Down	R Miles (Brid)	R Francis (PGC)
1983	I.o.P.	R Miles (Brid)	I Sparks (FGC)
1984	Ferndown	J Gordon (PGC)	A Lawrence (Sh)
1985	K. Heath	J Bloxham (Lyme)	R Hearn (PGC)
1986	Yeovil	A Lawrence (Sh)	R Hearn (PGC)
1987	Parkstone	A Lawrence (Sh)	A Hodgson (Sh)
1988	Broadstone	A Lawrence (Sh)	M Watson (Wey)
1989	Sherborne	A Lawrence (Sh)	R Hearn (PGC)
1990	Lyme Regis	P McMullen (FGC)	R Hearn (PGC)
1991	Came Down	A Lawrence (Sh)	M Thompson (FGC)
1992	I.o.P.	L James (B)	M Thompson (FGC)

(C) = Came Down   (B) = Broadstone   (BA) = Bournemouth Artisans
(N) = Northborne (now Knighton Heath)   (PGC) = Parkstone   (Y) = Yeovil
(FGC) = Ferndown   (KH) = Knighton Heath   (Sh) = Sherborne

County Handicap Medal
36-Hole Medal Play
Handicap Limit 18

Year	Venue	Winner	Year	Venue	Winner
1923	Broadstone	S Fletcher	1957	Parkstone	M R Thompson
1924	Came Down	C L Gordon-Stewart	1958	Came Down	H C Neilson
1925 - 1932		no results recorded	1959	Ferndown	M W Hillyer
1933	Came Down	H E Botting	1960	Broadstone	B H Longrigg
1934	Parkstone	(Tie) M R Gardner, J S C Walkington	1961	Yeovil	A J Richmond
			1962	Parkstone	B Raggett
1935	Broadstone	A Dore	1963	Lyme Regis	J C Lynham
1936	Ferndown	H E Botting	1964	Came Down	A J Richmond
1937	Came Down	J Powell	1965	Ferndown	R Lawford
1938	Broadstone	B Asker	1966	Yeovil	N Robbins
1939	Ferndown	P L Helm	1967	Parkstone	R M Drake
1946	Parkstone	B Asker	1968	Broadstone	S D Brewis
1947	Came Down	O Austreng	1969	Came Down	(Tie) R Biggs, D McWhinney
1948	Parkstone	E B Millward	1970	Ferndown	R Lawford
1949	Ferndown	E B Millward	1971	Yeovil	J Nash
1950	Broadstone	J H Trapnell	1972	Parkstone	D G Trickett
1951	Parkstone	R E Garrett	1973	Broadstone	K Clarke ('County' Prize)
1952	Came Down	E B Millward	1974	Lyme Regis	P J Cox ('County' Prize)
1953	Northborne	P Pelling	1975	Came Down	A Watts ('County' Prize)
1954	Ferndown	J B Bradford	1976	I.o.P.	S Buenfeld ('County' Prize)
1955	Broadstone	D Marriott	1977	Ferndown	(Tie) R Moses, E J Garrett
1956	Yeovil	K Richards	1978	Yeovil	D Barnes ('County' Prize)

Amateurs v Professionals

This was one of the three original annual competitions arranged by the first Executive Committee, and was first played at the Ferndown Golf Club on September 3rd 1923. No records of the results were kept until 1935, but the format was 12 amateurs versus 12 professionals, playing singles in the morning and foursomes in the afternoon. Amateur handicaps '2-up'; one professional to play the better ball of two amateurs. In 1958 the event was changed to a 36-hole medal competition, known as the County 'Close' Championship. The Weymouth Club presented money prizes for the professionals, and to celebrate the Club's Golden Jubilee the Weymouth Corporation donated a cup for the amateur winners. In 1973 the Parkstone Golf Club donated a cup for the overall winner, with the Weymouth Cup going to the best amateur, and in 1980 it became an amateur event…the Dorset Stroke-Play Championship.

Year	Venue	Result			
1933	Ferndown	Amateurs by	18½	to	13½
1934	Broadstone	Amateurs	22	to	14
1935	Parkstone	Amateurs	35	to	17
1936	Came Down	Amateurs	15	to	7
1937	Ferndown	Amateurs			
1938	Parkstone	Amateurs	11½	to	8½
1939	Northbourne	Professionals	13	to	9
1946	Ferndown	Amateurs	12½	to	11½
1947	Northbourne	Professionals	11½	to	8½
1948	Broadstone	Amateurs	10½	to	9½
1949	Parkstone	Amateurs			
1950	Lyme Regis	Amateurs			
1951	Northbourne	Amateurs	15½	to	4½
1952	Yeovil	Amateurs	16	to	8
1953	Parkstone	Amateurs	17	to	7
1954	Came Down	Amateurs	14½	to	7½
1955	Swanage	Amateurs	15	to	5
1956	Ferndown	Amateurs	17	to	7
1957	Yeovil	Amateurs	15	to	5
1958	Broadstone	Amateurs	22	to	5
1959	**Event changed to 36-hole medal, amateurs' handicap limited to 12. £5 to winning professional, Weymouth Cup to amateur. 'Close' Championship**				

Year	Venue	Professional	Amateur
1959	Weymouth	F H Beets	L G Emmett
1960	Lyme Regis	Alec Alliss	G J Butler
1961	Parkstone	E N Le Suer	K Longmore
1962	Yeovil	G Scobbing	R G Peach
1963	Ferndown	Alec Alliss	G E Butler **(£15 to Pro)**
1964	Sherborne	N Norris	T Durrant
1965	Came Down	N Stainer	S P Roberts
1966	Lyme Regis	P Bowditch	R A Budd
1967	Weymouth	D N Sewell	R A Budd
1968	Yeovil	N Stainer	R W Beckett
1969	Northbourne	R Smith	G J Butler
1970	Lyme Regis	P Bowditch	P G Holmes
1971	I.o.P.	B J Bamford	W G Peach
1972	Weymouth	B J Bamford	C J Knowles
1973	**Came Down (Parkstone Cup for overall winner, Weymouth Cup best amateur)**		
		B J Bamford (£40)	G Eley
1974	Parkstone	B J Bamford	J Calver
1975	Yeovil	B J Bamford	Dr. D M Holmes
1976	Ferndown		G J Butler **(67 Am. Course record)**
1977	Sherborne		G J Butler
1978	Broadstone		G J Butler
1979	I.o.P.		G Eley

Parkstone Cup

Year	Venue	Winner	
1959	Weymouth	L G Emmett	71 + 74 = 145
1960	Lyme Regis	G J Butler	73 + 70 = 143
1961	Parkstone	K Longmore	71 + 74 = 145
1962	Yeovil	R G Peach	70 + 74 = 144
1963	Ferndown	G J Butler	79 + 70 = 149
1964	Sherborne	T H Durrant	67 + 70 = 137
1965	Came Down	S R Roberts	77 + 68 = 145
1966	Ferndown	R A Budd	77 + 73 = 150
1967	Ferndown	R A Budd	72 + 69 = 141
1968	Parkstone	R W Beckett	73 + 69 = 142
1969	Northbourne	G J Butler	73 + 70 = 143
1970	Lyme Regis	P G Holmes	71 + 70 = 141
1971	I.o.P.	W G Peach	72 + 74 = 146
1972	Weymouth	C J Knowles	67 + 75 = 142
1973	Came Down	G Eley	77 + 74 = 151
1974	Parkstone	J Calver	72 + 73 = 145
1975	Yeovil	Dr. D M Holmes	70 + 71 = 141
1976	Ferndown	G J Butler	71 + 67 = 138
1977	Sherborne	G J Butler	70 + 69 = 139
1978	Broadstone	G J Butler	66 + 72 = 138
1979	I.o.P.	G Eley	77 + 75 = 152
1980	Lyme Regis	R Francis	71 + 69 = 140
1981	Weymouth	J M Tryor	71 + 78 = 149
1982	Yeovil	A Lawrence	69 + 68 = 137
1983	Broadstone	R Hearn	68 + 76 = 144
1984	Parkstone	R Hearn	72 + 72 = 144
1985	I.o.P.	A Lawrence	71 + 73 = 144
1986	Came Down	M Welch	69 + 74 = 143
1987	Sherborne	A Lawrence	68 + 70 = 138
1988	K. Heath	S Edgley	66 + 70 = 136
1989	Yeovil	R Mabb	69 + 73 = 142
1990	Ferndown	A Lawrence	68 + 72 = 142
1991	Lyme Regis	M Searle	71 + 71 = 142
1992	Weymouth	S Edgley	70 + 71 = 141

County Handicap Championship

Trophy presented by John Finding of the Came Down Golf Club in 1970.

Year	Winner
1970	J Smith (Broadstone)
1971	E Antell (Broadstone)
1972	R G Peach (Parkstone)
1973	P J Cox (Broadstone)
1974	S B Potter (Yeovil)
1975	P J Cox (Broadstone)
1976	G Eley (Came Down)
1977	D Barnes (I.o.P.)
1978	M H Fuller (Came Down)
1979	J H Leggett (Parkstone)
1980	P Holbert (Highcliffe)
1981	P L Southcombe (Yeovil)
1982	A Lawrence (Sherborne)

County Handicap Championship (continued)

Year	Winner
1983	M Churchill (I.o.P.)
1984	I Sparkes (Ferndown)
1985	R Hearn (Parkstone)
1986	J Roberts (Broadstone)
1987	N Cook (Parkstone)
1988	R Allen (Broadstone)
1989	A Lawrence (Sherborne)
1990	A Lawrence (Sherborne)
1991	Not Presented
1992	**Became the 'Category 2, 3 & 4 Championship Cups'**

Category 2, 3 & 4 Handicap Championships

This new competition was introduced in 1992 to provide the higher handicap club golfer with an opportunity to compete in county championship events.

Clubs nominate either of their May, June or July monthly medal competitions as the qualifying round, and the winners in each category go forward to compete for the title of County Champion.

The cup presented in 1970 by John Finding of the Came Down Golf Club for the County Handicap Championship became the trophy for the Category 2 winner, and he donated additional cups for the other two categories.

Every qualifier receives a commemorative medallion, thanks to sponsorship by Messrs Bray & Sear (Suzuki UK Ltd).

Year	Venue	Winner	
1992	East Dorset G C	Cat. 2. J Ruskin (I.o.P.)	86 - 11 = 75
		Cat. 3. D Gregory (Mid Dorset)	91 - 18 = 73
		Cat. 4. P Collins (Mid Dorset)	96 - 23 = 73

Colts Championship

The Luffman Cup was presented to the Under-23 winner at the County Championship meetings until 1987, after which it became the Colts Trophy for the Under-21 winner.

Year	Venue	Winner	
1979	Parkstone	D Rolls (Parkstone)	149
1980	Broadstone	D Jeffreys (K. Heath)	146
1981	K. Heath	M Haskell (Broadstone)	149
1982	Sherborne	A Lawrence (Sherborne)	138
1983	Came Down	J Leggett (Ferndown)	145
1984	Bridport	M Bennett (Came Down)	134
1985	Lakey Hill	R Ord-Smith (Ferndown)	156
1986	K. Heath	B Moncaster (K. Heath)	148
1987	Weymouth	S Edgley (Parkstone)	139
1988	Broadstone	R Mabb (Weymouth)	146
1989	Sherborne	R Davies (Weymouth)	147
1990	Lyme Regis	M Thompson (Ferndown)	145
1991	Came Down	L James (Broadstone)	143
1992	I.o.P.	L James (Broadstone)	149

Flag Foursomes

First suggested at an Executive Committee Meeting at Parkstone Golf Club December 18 1924 as an annual knock-out competition between all clubs: 1 amateur and 1 professional. 18-hole matches, final to be played over 36 holes. Major Stephens presented a flag trophy.

The competition ceased in 1988 because the number of entrants had fallen to such a degree that it was no longer a viable proposition.

It was decided to revise the format to amateur foursomes in an effort to improve the standard of County foursomes play.

Year	Venue	Winner	Players
1925		Came Down	A V Hambro, R Whitcombe
1926	Broadstone	Came Down	Major Gundry, R Whitcombe
1927	Ferndown		
1928	Parkstone		
1929	Swanage		
1930	Yeovil		
1931	Came Down		
1932			
1933	Broadstone	Parkstone	M R Gardner, R A Whitcombe
1934	Ferndown	Parkstone	F R Bacon, R A Whitcombe
1935	Yeovil	Broadstone	J S Ruttle, P Sanders
1936	Northborne	Northborne	E J Nicholl, E C Wren
1937	Parkstone	Crichel Park	J H Joham, A J Jolly
1938	Shaftesbury	Crichel Park	J H Joham, A J Jolly
1939	Scheduled for Crichel Park in September, but cancelled due to war		
1946	Yeovil	Parkstone	E B Millward, R A Whitcombe
1947	Crichel Park	Broadstone	S G Butt, K McIntyre
1948	Sherborne	Parkstone	E B Millward, R A Whitcombe
1949	Bridport	Ferndown	G E Newton, Percy Alliss
1950	Came Down	Parkstone	E B Millward, R A Whitcombe
1951	Weymouth	Parkstone	E J Nicholl, R A Whitcombe
1952	Ferndown	Ferndown	E B Millward, Peter Alliss
1953	Sherborne	Ferndown	T R Jenkins, Percy Alliss
1954	Broadstone	Came Down	J Dear, A T Bennett
1955	Yeovil	Ferndown	E B Millward, Percy Alliss
1956	Swanage	Broadstone	P Sanders, E N Le Seur
1957	Cancelled		
1958	Weymouth	Yeovil	M R Gardner, G Scobling
1959	Lyme Regis	Parkstone	R G Peach, Alec Alliss
1960	Yeovil	Parkstone	R G Peach, Alec Alliss
1961	Northborne	Northborne	B Thornton, K Bowring
1962	Sherborne	Yeovil	M R Gardner, G Scobling
1963	Weymouth	Yeovil	P Southcombe, M Neil
1964	Ferndown	Ferndown	G J Butler, N Stainer
1965	Broadstone	Yeovil	P Southcombe, Neil Morris
1966	Came Down	Yeovil	P Southcombe, Neil Morris
1967	Lyme Regis	Ferndown	G J Butler, D N Sewell
1968	Weymouth	Ferndown	G J Butler, N Stainer
1969	Yeovil	Parkstone	R Shakeshaft, A Jordan
1970	Northborne	Northborne	P Hayes, Roger Smith
1971	Came Down	Ferndown	G J Butler, Nigel Stainer
1972	Sherborne	Bridport	R C Miles, P Bowatch (Pro. £10)
1973	Lyme Regis	I.o.P.	D Scott, Brian Bamford
1974	I.o.P.	I.o.P.	Sherstone, Brian Bamford

Flag Foursomes (continued)

Year	Venue	Winner	Players
	Competition changed to 36-hole Scratch Medal		
1975	Ferndown	Tie between Ferndown and Northborne	
		Ferndown	M B Toosey, D Sewell
		Northborne	C S Carouth, N Stainer
1976	Sherborne	Broadstone	J Nash, Peter Ward
1977	Weymouth	Lyme Regis	D Lock, A Forrester
1978	K. Heath	Ferndown	G J Butler, D Sewell
1979	Lyme Regis	Ferndown	G J Butler, D Sewell
1980	Came Down	Ferndown	G J Butler, D Sewell
1981	Yeovil	Lyme Regis	S Priest, A Forrester
1982	Lyme Regis	Parkstone	R Hall, R Francis
1983	Weymouth	Parkstone	R Hall, R Francis
1984	Sherborne	K. Heath	D Jeffreys, Gary Smith
1985	Bridport	Came Down	M Stickley, R Preston
1986	Sherborne	K. Heath	D Jeffreys, Gary Smith

Scratch Foursomes Championship
President's Trophy

Competition initiated in 1988 to improve the standard of foursomes play at county level. Players do not have to be from the same Club.

Year	Venue	Winners	
1988	Ferndown	A Lawrence/A Hodgson (Sherborne)	78 + 71 = 149
1989	Broadstone	M Watson/R Davies (Weymouth)	71 + 73 = 144
1990	K. Heath	L James (Broadstone)/R Davies (Weymouth)	70 + 70 = 140
1991	Parkstone	J Gordon/D Cook (Parkstone)	71 + 71 = 142
1992	K. Heath	A Walker/M Welsh (Broadstone)	75 + 70 = 145

Secretary's Trophy

Year	Winner
1987	J Riley (Yeovil)
1988	J Cowan (Broadstone)
1989	R Bestwick (K. Heath)
1990	R Bestwick (K. Heath)
1991	J Holloway (Wareham)
1992	J Cowan (Broadstone)

County Team Championship

First proposed at the 1932 AGM, and held in conjunction with the county championship event. Best score of three out of four.

Year	Venue	Club	Team
1933	Came Down	Swanage	R M Chadwick, R Corbett, C L D Fawcus
1934	Parkstone	Tie { Parkstone	M R Gardner, F R Bacon, C Walker
		Broadstone 'B'	C Scott, H Clapham, H Stringer
1935	Broadstone	Broadstone	A V Hambro, C M Grant Goven, A J Webb
1936	Ferndown	Ferndown 'A'	J A Elliott, J S Ruttle, G E Newton
1937	Came Down	Ferndown	G E Newton, M R Gardner, J S Ruttle
1938	Broadstone	Northbourne	E J Nicholl, P Stuart-Smith, B Asker
1939	Ferndown	Ferndown 'B'	
1946	Parkstone	Parkstone 'A'	E B Millward, V Haggard, E J Nicholl
1947	Came Down	Parkstone 'A'	O Austreng, E B Millward, E J Nicholl
1948	Parkstone	Parkstone 'A'	O Austreng, E B Millward, E J Nicholl
1949	Ferndown	Parkstone	O Austreng, E B Millward, R G Peach
1950	Broadstone	Parkstone	E B Millward, K Longmore, E J Nicholl
1951	Parkstone	Parkstone 'A'	E B Millward, K Longmore, E J Nicholl
1952	Came Down	Parkstone 'A'	E B Millward, K Longmore, O Austreng
1953	Northborne	Parkstone 'A'	R G Peach, E J Nicholl, J D Crawford
1954	Ferndown	Ferndown 'A'	E B Millward, R E Garrett, W P Williams
1955	Broadstone	Ferndown	E B Millward, R E Garrett, A J D Gibbings
1956	Yeovil	Parkstone 'A'	K Longmore, R G Peach, F G R Vowles
1957	Parkstone	Parkstone 'A'	K Longmore, R G Peach, E B Millward
1958	Came Down	Yeovil 'A'	M R Gardner, W & R Southcombe
1959	Ferndown	Ferndown 'B'	G Butler, M R Thompson, C T McInerney
1960	Broadstone	Broadstone 'A'	B H Longrigg, D Marriott, H A Wilton
1961	Yeovil	Broadstone 'A'	S Brewis, R Lawford, H Wilton
1962	Parkstone	Parkstone 'A'	S Brewis, R G Peach, K Longmore
1963	Lyme Regis	Ferndown 'A'	G Butler, N L Cook, C McInerney
1964	Came Down	Ferndown	G Butler, H A Wilton C McInerney
1965	Ferndown	Broadstone 'A'	R Lawford, P Sanders, S Brewis
1966	Yeovil	Parkstone 'A'	A J Richmond, K Clarke, D M Holmes
1967	Parkstone	Parkstone 'A'	R G Peach, D M Holmes, A J Richmond
1968	Broadstone	Broadstone 'A'	R Lawford, P Shillington, R de Beauvais
1969	Came Down	Ferndown	
1970	Ferndown	Broadstone	
1971	Yeovil	Parkstone 'B'	B Crutcher, W Peach, E Garrett
1972	Parkstone	Parkstone 'B'	D M Holmes, F K Shaw, N Cook
1973	Broadstone	Broadstone 'A'	J Nash, A Page, A K Jones
1974	Lyme Regis	Broadstone 'A'	J Nash, A Page, E Antell
1975	Came Down	Broadstone 'A'	
1976	I.o.P.	Parkstone 'A'	
1977	Ferndown	Parkstone 'B'	
1978	Yeovil	Broadstone 'A'	J Nash, R Hearn D Scholes
1979	Parkstone	Ferndown 'A'	G Butler, P McMullen, W Raymond
1980	Broadstone	Broadstone 'A'	J Nash, A Jones, C Duffy, D Scholes
1981	Lyme Regis	Sherborne	A Lawrence, A Hodgson, A Mason, W Loader
1982	Came Down	Sherborne	A Lawrence, A Hodgson, A Mason, W Loader
1983	I.o.P.	Ferndown	P McMullen, W Raymond, I Sparkes
1984	Ferndown	Ferndown	I Sparkes, P McMullen, W Raymond, G Butler
1985	K. Heath	Parkstone	R Hearn, S Edgley, R Davies
1986	Yeovil	Parkstone	

County Team Championship (continued)

Year	Venue	Club	Team
1987	Parkstone	Parkstone	D M Holmes, N Cook, R Francis
1988	Broadstone	Broadstone	J Nash, D Scholes, G Archer, T Dobbs
1989	Sherborne	Sherborne	A Lawrence, P Lynch, T Prideaux-Bruce
1990	Lyme Regis	Ferndown	P McMullen, W Raymond, M Thompson
1991	Came Down	Broadstone	L James, J Nash, I Fullerton
1992	I.o.P.	Broadstone	L James, J Nash, G Archer

Garrett Salver

Presented by Maureen Garrett in 1958 to commemorate her husband R E Garrett. Awarded to the winner of the qualifying rounds in the County Championship.

Year	Venue	Winner/Score		Year	Venue	Winner/Score	
1959	Ferndown	K Longmore	74, 74 = 148	1977	Ferndown	G J Butler	71, 80 = 151
1960	Broadstone	B H Longrigg	76, 72 = 148	1978	Yeovil	D Barnes	73, 69 = 142
1961	Yeovil	G J Butler	145 gross	1979	Parkstone	A K Jones	78, 71 = 149
1962	Parkstone	S D Brewis	149 gross	1980	Broadstone	D Jeffreys	70, 76 = 146
1963	Lyme Regis	G J Butler	74, 81 = 155	1981	Lyme Regis	A Hodgson	71, 72 = 143
1964	Came Down	A J Richmond	80, 78 = 158	1982	Came Down	A Lawrence	39, 71 = 110
1965	Ferndown	G J Butler	150 gross		(Fog reduced morning round to 10 holes)		
1966	Yeovil	A J Richmond	150 gross	1983	I.o.P.	A Lawrence	74, 72 = 146
1967	Parkstone	R Lawford	145 gross	1984	Ferndown	I Sparkes	70, 73 = 143
1968	Broadstone	W G Peach	149 gross	1985	K. Heath	R Hearn	71, 72 = 143
1969	Came Down	R Biggs	74, 72 = 146	1986	Yeovil	A Lawrence	74, 67 = 141
1970	Ferndown	A K Jones	72, 73 = 145	1987	Parkstone	A Lawrence	75, 69 = 144
1971	Yeovil	J Nash	69, 68 = 137	1988	Broadstone	A Lawrence	
1972	Parkstone	Dr. D M Holmes	74, 72 = 146	1989	Sherborne	A Lawrence	72, 66 = 138
1973	Broadstone	J Nash	72, 67 = 139	1990	Lyme Regis	A Lawrence	69, 69 = 138
1974	Lyme Regis	G J Butler	68, 72 = 140	1991	Came Down	P McMullen	71, 70 = 141
1975	Came Down	T Griffin	78, 74 = 152	1992	I.o.P.	A Hodgson	72, 73 = 145
1976	I.o.P.	B Crutcher	72, 80 = 152				

Inter-Club Foursomes

No records kept until 1933

Year	Venue	Result
1933	Parkstone	R Close, G Newton bt Capt. F Bacon, M R Gardner
1934	Ferndown	N H Carter, K Suttill bt R M Chadwick, R Corbett
1935	Bridport	G E Newton, J A Elliott bt G Glass-Hooper, F R Ferris
1936	Crichel Park	E J Nicholl, B Asker bt G Glass-Hooper, F R Ferris
1937	Broadstone	G Glass-Hooper, C L Gordon-Stewart bt B Asker, P McCaull
1938	Swanage	M R Gardner, G L Newton bt J T Clegg, L H Joham
1939	Sherborne	Cancelled
1946	Bridport	K J Longmore, B Asker bt D A Ibbetson, W G Scott
1947	Lyme Regis	G E Newton, R E Garrett bt O Austreng, E B Millward
1948	Yeovil	E B Millward, O Austreng bt G E Newton, R E Garrett
1949	Weymouth	R E Garrett, G E Newton bt H Wyllie, W K Price
1950	Yeovil	C R Carter, H L Luffman bt H Wilkinson, R W Baker
1951	Swanage	H C Neilson, H E Scott bt F G R Vowles, L G Tarver
1952	Lyme Regis	J D Dear, H D Jordan bt G Cosby, J Sear

Became a Scratch plus Handicap event

Year	Venue	Result
1953	Weymouth	(S) R Southcombe, W H Southcombe (H) A Fletcher, A Coombs
1954	Bridport	(S) R Southcombe, W H Southcombe (H) J B Bradford, J Morton
1955	Came Down	(S) E B Millward, B Elliott (H) G L Tarver, G H Kendall
1956	Parkstone	(S) R G Peach, E J Nicholl (H) G H Kendall, L Vowles
1957	Swanage	(S) M R Gardner, R Southcombe (H) W N Southcombe, N Lock
1958	Yeovil	(S) B H Longrigg, C Cave (H) T Clark, L Vowles
1959	Weymouth	(S) D Bassett, L Vowles (H) J Powell, J Rose
1960	Sherborne	(S) D Bassett, L Vowles (H) A K Weston, R Greenwood
1961	Lyme Regis	(S) R Southcombe, M R Gardner (H) L H Mileham, J D Wright
1962	Came Down	(S) D Bassett, D Richmond (H) L H Mileham, J D Wright
1963	Sherborne	(S) R & P Southcombe (Father & Son)
1964	Parkstone	(S) G Wiley, J Lynham (H) D Cowan, P Pelling
1965	Yeovil	(S) G J Butler, H A Wilton (H) R Barber, D Solomon
1966	N Northborne	(S) L Lawford, C Cave (H) R Barber, D Solomons
1967	Ferndown	(S) G J Butler, R A Budd (H) R H Kendall, E J Garrett
1968	Came Down	(S) R Lawford, C Cave (H) R H Kendall, E J Garrett
1969	Sherborne	(S) R Lawford, C Cave (H) H Hawkins, A W Briddle
1970	Weymouth	(S) T Griffin, H Robbins (H) L Vowles, R Wright

Inter-Club Foursomes (continued)

1971	Lyme Regis	(S) N D Owers, R Wright
		(H) R Owen, R Wright
1972	Northborne	(S) T Griffin, J Lawrence
		(H) R Diamond, M Birchenough
1973	Yeovil	(S) D Lock, R Robbins
		(H) C Neale, D Thorn
1974	Sherborne	(S) D Hope, D Bennett
		(H) J Finding, P Thorpe
1975	Weymouth	(S) S Priest, C R Neale
		(H) K Grout, N Florey
1976	Came Down	(S) D M Holmes, R A H Kendall
	(36 hole Medal)	(H) K Grout, N Florey
1977	I.o.P.	(S) D Barnes, N Coombs
		(H) R Hearn, B Pavitt
1978	Sherborne	(S) R Francis, A Hodgson
		(H) J S Magee, D W Rogers
1979	K. Heath	(S) R G Peach, N Cook
		(H) J Nash, R Hearn
1980	I.o.P.	(S) A P R Eden, G Lovelady
		(H) M Haskell, J Tryor
1981	Broadstone	(S) A Hodgson, D Hill (Bennett Cup)
		(H) T Mathews, M J Walker
1982	H. Castle	(S) A Hodgson, D Hill (2 scratch + 2h/cap pairs from each Club)
		(H) G Drage, M Page
1983	K. Heath	(S) P McMullen, I Sparkes
		(H) D Proctor, G Taylor
1984	K. Heath	(S) D Jeffreys, H McCann
		(H) J Farrer, J Turner
1985	H. Castle	(S) R Hearn, S Edgley
		(S) S Gibson, N Cook
1986	I.o.P.	(S) D Sullivan, M Thompson
		(H) K Robinson, C Bradford (Sherborne Cup)
1987	Sherborne	(S) A Lawrence, A Hodgson
		(H) S Hector, D Talbot
1988		(S) A Lawrence, A Hodgson
		(H) P Addis, A Pedrick
1989	Ferndown	(S) P McMullen, S Allen
		(H) D Mathews, T Dobbs
1990	Bridport	(S) C Tozer, A Nicholl
		(H) R Wright, S Burke
1991	Broadstone	(S) M Wiggett, R Thomson
		(H) A Jones, B Pavitt
1992	Yeovil	(S) J Pounder, D Chant
		(H) P Allen, R Emerson

Inter-Club Mixed Foursomes

One couple from each Club

No results were recorded between 1923 and 1932

1933	Lyme Regis	Mr & Mrs H L Luffman bt G Newton, Miss Beard
1934	Ashley	W. Cdr. Hunt, Mrs Graham Jones bt F Laugher, Miss Courage
1935	Came Down	G E Newton, Miss Morant bt A W Hunt, Mrs Graham-Jones
1936	Weymouth	G L Gordon Stewart, Mrs Gr-Jones bt C E Jennings, Miss D Clarke
1937	Sherborne	C Mayo, Miss M Gliddon bt F R Lindsay, Miss Cunningham
1938	Weymouth	C Mayo, Miss Sliddon bt S Marshall, Miss M Johnstone
1939	Ashley Wd.	E G Waldy, Miss J Johnstone bt F F Laugher, Miss Graham-Jones
1946	Sherborne	E B Millward, Mrs Hill bt G E Newton, Mrs Beard
1947	Weymouth	G E Newton, Miss C Bannister bt Mr & Mrs Stuart-Smith
1948	Came Down	E B Millward, Mrs Bond bt S Trethaway, Miss Martin
1949	Lyme Regis	G E Newton, Mrs Milligan bt O Austreng, Mrs McPherson
1950	Parkstone	G E Newton, Mrs Milligan bt T A Guest, Mrs Everett
1951	Sherborne	O Austreng, Mrs Milligan bt W N Southcombe, Mrs Lock
1952	Broadstone	T A Guest, St. Leger-Carter bt R E Garrett, Miss C Bannister
1953	Bridport	R G Peach, Mrs P Crow bt M R Gardner, Mrs R Lock

Became a Scratch plus Handicap event

1954	Yeovil	(S) R G Peach, Mrs P Crow bt R E Garrett, Miss Bannister
		(H) W N Southcombe, Mrs Lock bt J W Birch, Mrs N Warry
1955	Weymouth	(S) F G R Vowles, Mrs P Crow bt Mr & Mrs R Southcombe
1956	Came Down	(S) J Dear, Miss Alexander bt R G Peach, Mrs P Crow
1957	Lyme	(S) J Dear, Miss Alexander bt R G Peach, Mrs P Crow
		(H) Mr & Mrs Clarke bt Mr & Mrs Stainforth
1958	Sherborne	(S) J D Dear, Miss Alexander bt J A Clegg, Mrs J Cooper
		(H) S C Cook, Mrs M Wenzel bt A T Fletcher, Miss T Coombs
1959	Swanage	(S) R G Peach, Mrs Cooper bt C J Butler, Miss M Bannister
		(H) J W Bird, Miss M Lock bt C T McInerney, Mrs B Meyer
1960	Parkstone	(S) R G Peach, Mrs P Crow bt G Butler, Miss Buchanan
		(H) J W Birch, Miss M Lock bt S C Cook, Mrs Wenzel
1961	Weymouth	(S) J W Birch, Miss T Ross Steen bt H A Wilton, Mrs J Cooper
		(H) G Eley, Mrs Thompson bt M R Gardner, Mrs Lock
1962	Lyme	(S) R G Peach, Mrs P Crow bt A E J Horsington, Mrs Sugden
		(H) R W Bolton, Mrs Cooper bt D Cowan, Mrs Doig
1963	Yeovil	(S) R Clarke, Mrs Wilson bt G E Newton, Miss Bannister
1964	B'stone	(S) P Southcombe, Mrs Southcombe (Mother & Son) bt G E Newton, Miss Bannister
		(H) T Clark, Mrs Clark bt G C Unwin, Mrs Hamer
1965	N'bourne	(S) K Clarke, Mrs L Wilson bt J Lynham, Mrs P Thompson
1966	Sherborne	(S) R G Peach, Miss B Dixon bt C J Cave, St. Leger-Carter
		(H) P Pelling, Mrs Drew bt K Watson, Mrs R Lock
1967	Came Down	(S) G C Eley, Miss Alexander bt R Lawford, Mrs L Wilson
		(H) J L Williams, Miss Bannister bt T J Davies, Mrs E Stuart-Smith

1968	I.o.P.	(S) D Bennett, Mrs P Goss bt R G Peach, Miss B Dixon
		(H) V Morley, Mrs C J Elliott bt L Watson, Mrs R Locke
1969	Weymouth	(S) R G Peach, Miss B Dixon bt R Lawford, Mrs A Humphreys
		(H) G H P Thomas, Mrs J Lewis bt Mr & Mrs R Southcombe
1970	Sherborne	(S) K J Longmore, Miss B Dixon bt M Swift, Mrs Swift
		(H) Mr & Mrs R Southcombe bt G H P Thomas, Mrs J Lewis
1971	Ferndown	(S) M Toosey, Miss J Bowden bt T Griffin, Mrs Cross
		(H) Mr & Mrs R Owen bt J Smith, Mrs N Elliott
1972	Lyme Regis	(S) T Griffin, Mrs B Gross bt R G Peach, Miss D Chalkley
		(H) R M Sutton, Miss L Getliffe bt J Smith, Mrs N Elliott
1973	N'bourne	(S) R Lawford, Miss P Flay bt M B Toosey, Miss J Bowden
		(H) S Priest, Miss D Gibbs bt Mr & Mrs Morris
1974	Came Down	(S) M Fuller, Mrs Hussey bt J Lawrence, Mrs Gardner
		(H) B J White, Mrs Walker bt Mr & Mrs Finding

1975 changed to (S) P Urlwin-Smith Cup (H) Elliott Cup

1975	Bridport	(S) D J Lock, Mrs Fox bt M B Toosey, L J Newman
		(H) S V C Nicholson, Miss D Gibbs bt Mr & Mrs Briteman
1976	Lyme Regis	(S) Mr & Mrs J Sugden bt Mr & Mrs R Sutton
		(H) Mr & Mrs Kershaw bt S Priest, Miss D J Gibbs
1977	K. Heath	(S) D Jeffreys, Miss J Miles
		(H) S Priest, Mrs Cruikshank
1978	Came Down	(S) D Jeffreys, Miss J Miles
		(H) R Slee, Miss J Hussey
1979	Sherborne	(S) D Jeffreys, Miss J Miles
		(H) Mr & Mrs R Walkington
1980	Bridport	(S) R Slee, Mrs R Page
		(H) Mr & Mrs Walkington
1981	Lakey Hill	(S) J Leggett, Mrs B Langley
		(H) P Pelling, Mrs J Jones
1982	Weymouth	(S) L Peters, Mrs R Page bt P McMullen, Miss F Eden
		(H) Mr & Mrs P Love bt P Pelling, Mrs Jones
1983	Lyme Regis	(S) H McCann, Miss A Monk bt A K Jones, Miss S Lowe
		(H) Mr & Mrs Cox bt P Amery, Mrs Stephenson
1984	Weymouth	(S) R Slee, Mrs Kelly bt N Snadden, Mrs H Davidson
		(H) J Smith, Mrs P Flay bt D Pidgeley, Mrs D Joyce
1985	Yeovil	(S) G L Hannam, Miss A Monk bt N Harvey, Mrs H Davidson
		(H) N B Pratt, Mrs A de Cruchy bt D Gardner, Miss J Calam
1986		(S) G Hannan, Miss H Delew bt J Pounder, Mrs H Davidson
		(H) J Farrar, Miss S Way bt Mr & Mrs J Stewart
1987	K. Heath	(S) R Mabb, Miss T Loveys bt R Walkington, Mrs H Davidson
		(H) Mr & Mrs J Stewart bt Mr & Mrs M Martin
1988	Parkstone	(S) R Hearn, Mrs J Sugden bt J Pounder, Mrs H Davidson
		(H) D Talbot, Mrs A Dean bt Mr & Mrs P Cox
1989	Came Down	(S) L Thompson, Miss K Northcott bt J Carpenter, Mrs Brown
		(H) V Wakely, Mrs L Garrett bt M Hammerton, A de Cruchy
1990	Sherborne	(S) J Nash, Mrs P Flay bt P Holbrook, Mrs H Davidson
		(H) J Farrar, Miss S Way bt C Duffy, Miss S Phillips
1991	Lyme Regis	(S) M Searle, Mrs Culpin bt D Toms, Miss T Loveys
		(H) Joint winners: { Mr & Mrs D Hill / Mr & Mrs R Walkington
1992	Bridport	(S) R Clapp, Miss Culpin bt I Parsons, Mrs H Davidson
		(H) Mr & Mrs A Severn bt P Widger, Miss C Biggs

Wimborne Cup
Inaugurated in 1911 and played at Parkstone

Year	Winner		Year	Winner	
1911	E P Sugden	157	1959	C McInerney	144
1912	J J Lane	160	1960	C W Cole	140
1913	F W Beckford	147	1961	Dr. D M Holmes	147
1919	W E Johnson	165	1962	C W Cole	145
1920	T Homer	153	1963	K Longmore	151
1921	C H Armstrong	155	1964	K Longmore	141
1922	C H Armstrong	152	1965	J B Airth	147
1923	E F Rees-Mogg	156	1966	R Lawford	140
1924	V Weldon	147	1967	R Lawford	146
1925	D A Turpin	154	1968	R E Searle	145
1926	Major C E M Morrison	154	1969	J C Davies	140
1927	E J Dobson	153	1970	J C Davies	141
1928	N G Holt	148	1971	N L R Cook	139
1929	N G Holt	148	1972	J Nash	138
1930	N G Holt	139	1973	N L R Cook	139
1931	S H Vine	152	1974	Dr. D M Holmes	143
1932	S H Vine	151	1975	P Edgington	139
1933	S H Vine	153	1976	B Crutcher	141
1934	S H Vine	154	1977	B Winteridge	147
1935	S H Vine	151	1978	R E Searle	143
1936	S H Vine	148	1979	R E Searle	139
1937	R Williams-Freeman	148	1980	B Townsend	146
1938-45	not played		1981	R E Searle	146
1946	K Longmore	153	1982	K Weeks	142
1947	E B Millward	137	1983	R Hearn	142
1948	E B Millward	149	1984	R A Latham	139
1949	H C Neilson	149	1985	I Jones	141
1950	K Longmore	144	1986	R Guy	142
1951	E B Millward	137	1987	A Raitt	142
1952	E B Millward	140	1988	T Spence	132
1953	K Longmore	146	1989	J Nash	142
1954	J H Wyllie	145	1990	A Mew	135
1955	S J Fox	146	1991	K Weeks	142
1958	K V Robshaw	158	1992	K Weeks	141

Purbeck Swords
Inaugurated in 1977 and played at the Isle of Purbeck

Year	Winner	Year	Winner	Year	Winner	Year	Winner
1977	D Barnes	1981	K Weeks	1985	N Howie	1989	M Pooley
1978	D Barnes	1982	T Wenham	1986	K Weeks	1990	S Amor
1979	N D Owers	1983	K Weeks	1987	K Weeks	1991	S Amor
1980	K Weeks	1984	K Weeks	1988	S Amor	1992	M Watson

The South West Four Counties
Junior Championship

Trophy presented by J E Beakes, President of the Somerset GU 1975

Dorset Winners

		1981	G P Emerson	1986	G Archer	1991	M Higley
1978	J M Tryor	1984	R Mabb	1987	M J Watson	1992	S Meakin
1979	A J Parish	1985	S Edgley	1990	L Thompson		

Boys' Championship

Initiated at the 1953 AGM at Came Down. The competition of 18 holes medal play, open to all boys under the age of 18 on the day of the championship, with a handicap of 24 or less. The President (J S Ruttle) presented a Challenge Trophy, and in addition the winner would receive an inscribed silver medal. Prizes also awarded to the runner-up; the best nett score; and the best gross score for a boy under the age of 15.

Year	Venue	Results
1954	Parkstone	(1) D Marriott (Broadstone) (2) J R Morton (Yeovil) h/c J Bolton (Parkstone) Best gross under 15 I G Birch (Came Down)
1955	Ferndown	(1) M C Winn
1956	Broadstone	(1) D Marriott (Broadstone) (2) G A C Pope (Lyme) h/c I G Birch (Came Down) Best under 15 A C Brown (Parkstone) Youngest competitor R Thompson (Ferndown)
1957	Came Down	(1) I G Birch (Came Down) (2) A C Brown (Parkstone) h/c S D R Brewis (Broadstone) Best under 15 M R Thompson (Ferndown) Youngest R Bolton (Parkstone)
1958	Parkstone	(1) G A C Pope (Axe Cliffe) (2) S D R Brewis (Broadstone) h/c D Bolton (Parkstone) Best under 15 R Birch (Came Down) Youngest M R Thompson (Ferndown)
1959	Broadstone	(1) M R Thompson (Ferndown) (2) R W Birch (Came Down) h/c D K Geddes (Northborne) Best under 15 J H Nash (Wareham) Youngest R C Windebank (15 yrs) (Parkstone)
1960	Ferndown	(1) R J Thompson (Ferndown) (2) R Hill (Parkstone) h/c D Beck (Ferndown) Best under 15 J H Nash (Wareham) Youngest C Clement Brown (Parkstone)
1961	Came Down	(1) R Howlett (2) R W Birch h/c Ian Clark Best under 15 R A H Kendall (Parkstone) Youngest J R Windebank (15 yrs) (Parkstone)
1962	Northborne	(1) R Chapman (2) R A H Kendall (Parkstone) h/c J Nash (Wareham) Best under 15 A Medcroft Youngest D Scholes
1963	Parkstone	(1) J H Nash (Wareham) (2) R A H Kendall (Parkstone) h/c A P Medcroft Best under 15 W G Peach (Parkstone) Youngest A Mileham
1964	Broadstone	(1) R A H Kendall (Parkstone) (2) J Nash (Wareham) h/c O W Pawle Best under 15 W G Peach (Parkstone) Youngest C Price
1965	Yeovil	(1) N Robbins (Yeovil) (2) R A H Kendall (Parkstone) h/c N Green (Came Down) Best under 15 G Marshall (Wareham) Youngest P Wintle (12 yrs) (Parkstone)

Boys' Championship (continued)

1966 Broadstone (1) W G Peach (Parkstone) (2) N J Robbins (Yeovil)
h/c S Leach
Best under 15 P Wintle (Parkstone)
Youngest N B Joslin

1967 Came Down (1) W G Peach (Parkstone) (2) N Green (Came Down)
h/c M Swift (Sherborne)
Best under 15 M Taylor (Parkstone)
Youngest J B Cooper (Came Down)

1968 Northbourne (1) Graham Pound (2) F Wood
h/c J Bridle
Best under 15 D Gardner

1969 Ferndown (1) N B Josling (2) P Bridle
h/c G Simons
Best under 15 D F Hawkins
Youngest D Hope (12 yrs)

1970 I.o.P. (1) M V Piper (Northborne) (2) M Vaudin (Parkstone)
h/c S Jenner (I.o.P.)
Best under 15 D Rolls & N K Whalley (Parkstone)
Youngest S F Bishop (11 yrs) (Bridport)

1971 Parkstone (1) M McKenna (Northborne) (2) B Emberly (Broadstone)
h/c M Gale (Yeovil)
Best under 15 M Birchenough (Came Down)
Youngest S F Bishop (Bridport)

1972 Broadstone (1) Adrian Page (2) S Jenner
h/c M W Farley
Best under 15 N K Whalley (Parkstone)
Youngest S F Bishop (Bridport)

1973 Ferndown (1) S Potter (Yeovil) (2) G Kerley (Northbourne)
h/c J E Thornton (Broadstone)
Best under 15 M K Whalley (Parkstone)
Youngest Godfrey Abel (12 yrs)

1974 Yeovil (1) M G Williams (I.o.P.) (2) Andy Watts (Yeovil)
h/c M Watts (Yeovil)
Best under 15 D Barnes (I.o.P.)
Youngest G Whale (Came Down)

1975 Northbourne (1) R Moses (Sherborne) (2) P Hare (Northbourne)
h/c J Leggett (Ferndown)
Best under 15 T Saunders (I.o.P.)
Youngest J Russell (9 yrs) (Ferndown)

1976 Bridport (1) P McMullen (Ferndown) (2) S Lee (Bridport)
h/c M Wilkes (Lyme Regis)
Best under 15 G Whale (Came Down)
Youngest J Russell (10 yrs) (Ferndown)

1977 Yeovil (1) G Whale (Came Down) (2) J Tryor (Broadstone)
h/c M Churchill (I.o.P.)
Best under 15 M Stupple (Broadstone)
Youngest P Norris (11 yrs) (Ferndown)

1978 Came Down (1) M Stupple (Parkstone) (2) A Stupple (Parkstone)
h/c J Sewell (Ferndown)
Best under 15 G Emerson (Parkstone)
Youngest W J Russell (12 yrs) (Ferndown)

Boys' Championship (continued)

1979 Parkstone — (1) J Coles (K. Heath) (2) T Sharpley (Parkstone)
h/c I Birch (I.o.P.)
Best under 15 A Smith (Came Down)
Youngest…No prize given

1980 Sherborne — (1) D Jeffreys (K. Heath) (2) A Pakes (Ferndown)
h/c W Dean (K. Heath)
Best under 15 T Sharpley (Parkstone)
Youngest S Edgley (11 yrs) (Highcliffe)

1981 Bridport — (1) G Emerson (Parkstone) (2) N Aubin (Ferndown)
h/c S Horne (Broadstone)
Best under 15 M Collins (Broadstone)
Youngest S Edgley (12 yrs) (Highcliffe)

1982 K. Heath — (1) S Edgeley (Highcliffe) (2) S Taylor (Broadstone)
h/c K Jackson (Yeovil)
Best under 15 M Watson (Weymouth)

1983 Sherborne — (1) J Unthank (Sherborne) (2) A Greig (K. Heath)
h/c N Thompson (Broadstone)
Best under 15 S Edgley (Highcliffe)

1984 Lakey Hill — (1) S Burke (L. Hill) (2) S S Stevens (Broadstone)
h/c J R Page (Weymouth)
Best under 15 L Malpass (11 yrs) (Came Down)

1985 Came Down — (1) J Page (Weymouth) (2) T Hill (Parkstone)
h/c C Beats (Weymouth)

1986 Parkstone — (1) S Edgley (Parkstone) (2) M Thompson (K. Heath)
h/c S Walker (Meyrick Park)

1987 Broadstone — (1) M Hewitson (L. Hill) (2) M Watson (Weymouth)
h/c A Frew (Broadstone)

(Rule Change: A.M. 18 holes h/c and players with handicaps of 12 and under to play for 36-hole scratch title)

1988 I.o.P. — (1) T Hill (Parkstone) (2) M Cummins (Ashley Wood)
h/c P Tapper (Broadstone)

1989 K. Heath — (1) L James (Broadstone) (2) A Walker (Broadstone)
h/c P Donnelly (Ferndown)

1990 Weymouth — (1) A Horne (Broadstone) (2) M Foster (Came Down)
h/c P Brine (Sherborne)

1991 Sherborne — (1) L James (Broadstone) (2) M Searle (Lyme Regis)
h/c N Rogers (Ashley Wood)

1992 Ferndown — (1) S Meakin (Broadstone) (2) P Northway (Q Park)
h/c A Beck (Knighton Heath)

Bournemouth & District Professional & Amateur Golfers' Alliance

Data supplied by J H H Burdett   Hon Secretary.

The Alliance was formed in January 1931 by the local professionals and some invited amateur golfers, known as 'Vice Presidents'.

The records for the years 1931 to 1946 are missing, but the senior officers of the Alliance from 1947 are listed below. It is interesting to note that a foursome matchplay tournament was held annually, limited to thirty-two couples. Intermediate rounds were played on neutral courses, with the final played over thirty-six holes. For reasons which cannot be ascertained the event ceased in January 1966.

Annual matches used to be played against the South Wales Alliance and the Hampshire Alliance, but again these ceased for reasons not recorded.

Officials

Year	President	Captain	Secretary	Year	President	Captain	Secretary
1947	Dr. D Arnott		D Gow	1970	H Baker	G W Dean	G M Hughes
1948	Dr. D Arnott		D Gow	1971	E A Manson	J Stirling	G M Hughes
1949	Dr. D Arnott		D Gow	1972	D T Dunlop	C G Baggs	G M Hughes
1950	E T Green		D Gow	1973	P Swann	R K Freeman	G M Hughes
1951	E T Green		D Gow	1974	E Hooker	P Osmond	G M Hughes
1952	E Law		D Gow	1975	H A Sales	J Sharkey	G M Hughes
1953	E Law		D Gow	1976	A S Butt	K Hockey	G M Hughes
1954	T R Jenkins		D Gow	1977	E J Chubb	M G Curtis	G M Hughes
1955	T R Jenkins		D Gow	1978	R Baker	P Ward	G M Hughes
1956	P Evans		D Gow	1979	J Baker	B Crutcher	F J Meddings
1957	P Evans		D Gow	1980	J Stirling	W Lander	J H H Burdett
1958	D Gow		D Gow	1981	W Shankland	A P R Eden	J H H Burdett
1959	D Gow		D Gow	1982	P Osmond	P Coombs	J H H Burdett
1960	F W Prentice		D Gow	1983	J Sharkey	C J Astin	J H H Burdett
1961	F W Prentice		D Gow	1984	J Sharkey	G Smith	J H H Burdett
1962	G K Speake		W A Sutton	1985	J Sharkey	D C Vatcher	J H H Burdett
1963	G K Speake		W A Sutton	1986	J Sharkey	R Hill	J H H Burdett
1964	W A Sutton		L E Bickell	1987	J Sharkey	A Cristofoli	J H H Burdett
1965	W A Sutton		L E Bickell	1988	J Sharkey	B J Wells	J H H Burdett
1966	Percy Alliss	F J Meddings	L E Bickell	1989	J Sharkey	G Packer	J H H Burdett
1967	F J Meddings	E N Le Sueur	G M Hughes	1990	J Sharkey	C N Middleton	J H H Burdett
1968	E N Le Sueur	E W Timson	G M Hughes	1991	J Sharkey	N Tokely	J H H Burdett
1969	E W Timson	P Swann	G M Hughes	1992	J Sharkey	K Wilson	J H H Burdett

The Championship Cup

Awarded to the Alliance winner (professional or amateur) returning the lowest gross score over 36 holes of stroke play.

Year	Winner	Venue	Year	Winner	Venue
1947	Percy Alliss		1970	N Stainer	Broadstone
1948	J A Patterson		1971	J Sharkey	Sherborne
1949	R A Whitcombe		1972	D N Sewell	Broadstone
1950	R A Whitcombe		1973	D N Sewell	Broadstone
1951	R A Whitcombe	Barton-on-Sea	1974	P Coombs	
1952	Peter Alliss			N Stainer	Brokenhurst Manor
1953	E B Millward*		1975	M McKenna	Came Down
1954	Percy Alliss		1976	J Sharkey	Sherborne
	Peter Alliss		1977	J Sharkey	Brokenhurst Manor
1955	K Longmore*		1978	D N Sewell	Broadstone
1956	Peter Alliss		1979	G Smith	Brokenhurst Manor
1957	K Longmore*		1980	N Coombs	Knighton Heath
1958	E N Le Sueur		1981	D Allen	Sherborne
1959	Percy Alliss		1982	N Blenkarne	Brokenhurst Manor
1960	Percy Alliss		1983	N Blenkarne	
	Alec Alliss			G Smith	Sherborne
1961	J Stirling	Barton-on-Sea	1984	G Smith	Brokenhurst Manor
1962	J Stirling		1985	G Emerson	Sherborne
1963	C L Cargill	Barton-on-Sea	1986	G Smith	Isle of Purbeck
1964	J Stirling	Barton-on-Sea	1987	G Emerson	Sherborne
1965	Dr. D M Holmes*	Broadstone	1988	N Tokely	Sherborne
1966	J Stirling	Brokenhurst Manor	1989	G Emerson	Sherborne
1967	J Stirling	Came Down	1990	N Tokely	Sherborne
1968	P Coombs		1991	N Tokely	Sherborne
1969	J Sharkey	Sherborne	1992	M Wiggett	Sherborne

* Amateur

Winning SWCGA Team at Burnham & Berrow 1954

Back row: R E Garrett   H C Neilson   E Nicholl   W P Williams   I Campbell-Gray
Front row: R G Peach   J Crawford   E B Millward   A J Horsington

Winning SWCGA Team at Broadstone 1955

Back row: R Lawford   I Campbell-Gray   R de Beauvais   J S Ruttle   K Longmore   L Luffman   P Sanders
Front row: E Nicholl   R E Garrett   R G Peach   P Urlwin-Smith   H C Neilson

Winning SWCGA Team at Ferndown 1966

Back row: A J Richmond D M Holmes K Longmore N L R Cook P Sanders
Seated: R Lawford G J Butler R G Peach H A Wilton R Budd

SWCGA Team at Burnham & Berrow 1968

Back row: A J Richmond D M Holmes K Longmore P G Shillington S D R Brewis G Eley
Seated: N L R Cook R G Peach W N Southcombe G J Butler R Lawford

Winning SWCGA Team at Saunton 1972

Back row: F K Shaw   W G Peach   T Griffin   A Jones   J Nash
Seated: D Owers   R G Peach   K Longmore R Lawford G J Butler

SWCGA Team at Saunton 1978
This was not a winning team but the long hair and flared trousers are worth recording.

Back row: R Francis   D Barnes   J Calver   N L R Cook   J Nash   J Leggett   R Hearn
Front row: D Scholes   G J Butler A K Jones D M Holmes   K Longmore G Eley

Winning Seniors Team at Broadstone 1992

Left to right: D M Holmes   F K Shaw   E Antell   A Dutton   A Hodgson D Mathews   R Lawford

Major J S Ruttle, President of the EGU, presenting the English Amateur Trophy to Doug Sewell at Walton Heath in 1958

The South Western Counties Golf Association

This annual meeting is acknowledged to have been the premier inter-counties meeting before the official inter-county championships were inaugurated, and it is still regarded by many to be the finest week of competitive amateur golf in England.

The format is unique, involving the six south western counties of Wiltshire, Gloucester, Somerset, Devon, Dorset and Cornwall, each playing the other in a series of matches over five days, with a 36-hole medal on the remaining day to decide the individual South Western championship.

The medal competition also decides which county shall represent the south western area in the English county championship finals. This is determined by the aggregate scores of six players from each of the six counties whose names are nominated prior to the commencement of play. This qualification was introduced in 1955 and, in recent years, its outcome has tended to overshadow the result of the South Western *team* championship, which is decided by matchplay, and has always been regarded as the *raison d'être* of the meeting.

Each match of the team championship consists of eight singles played in the mornings for one point (halved games ½) followed in the afternoons by four foursomes matches, each valued at one and a half points (¾ for halved matches). It is believed that this order of play, with foursomes worth higher points value than singles, is unique in team golf and places great emphasis on successful foursomes play. There are instances on record where a team has led by seven matches to one after the morning singles, only to lose all the afternoon foursome games and finish with the most disappointing result of seven points each.

The Ryder Cup is the only event in which top-class professional golfers play the foursomes format, but even at this level, where the degree of skill between the players is marginal, in addition to a thorough understanding of individual ability, the captain must have an intimate knowledge of his players' personalities to arrive at the most effective pairings.

Consider then how much more difficult is the captain's task in amateur golf, where even at county level the playing standards can vary widely. To add to his problems the captain in the south west team championship is allowed only two substitutes from the eight players nominated for the morning singles, and these two cannot be paired together. With 1½ points at stake in each match, he would like to field at least three of the most successful pairings each day, but this cannot be done if players are to be allowed at least a half-day's rest in the week. Consequently he is faced with the dilemma of either overplaying his best players, or deciding which of the opposing counties will provide the weakest opposition to allow him to field less successful partnerships on that day. Luck, allied to good judgement, plays an important role in these circumstances.

It is very rare to win a match overall without at least sharing the foursomes. On the five occasions in the last forty years when Dorset won the team championship, the results of the foursomes matches in each year were: (Dorset points first)

1954	3-3:	3¾-2¼:	3-3:	3-3:	3-3:
1955	6-0:	3¾-2¼:	3¾-2¼:	5¼-¾:	4½-½
1956	4½-1½:	3¾-2¼:	3¾-2¼:	3-3:	5¼-¾
1966	3-3:	4½-1½:	3-3	5¼-¾:	3¾-2¼
1972	3¾-2¼:	3-3:	2¼-3¾:	3-3:	6-0:

Thus on only one occasion out of the twenty-five matches has the foursomes match been lost, with nine tied matches, illustrating the importance of foursomes play in the overall result. In the 1956 meeting at St Enodoc, Dorset played Somerset in the last match on the final day; each had won four matches so the destiny of the team championship rested on the result. The weather during the week had been ideal, but the final day dawned with a high wind and driving rain. At lunch Somerset led by six matches to two and were confident of winning because in the afternoon foursomes they had to win only one or halve two matches for victory, whereas Dorset was faced with the task of winning three of the four matches and at least halving the other as a minimum to avoid defeat.

In the top match Mike Gardner and Dick Peach, who had won all of their foursomes up to this point, arrived at the ninth green four down, needing to hole out from fifteen yards to avoid going five down. Peach, who by his own admission had played badly in the morning and had continued in similar vein up to that point, holed out for the half and promptly forgot how miserably wet he was and remembered instead his responsibilities as team captain. Such are the vagaries of golf that six holes later the match was all square. The wind was so strong that Mike Gardner, a player of considerable physical substance and commensurate power, used a Brassie from the elevated fifteenth tee and found the narrow green one hundred and sixty yards away. Two holes later the Dorset pair were Dormy one, only to have the prize snatched from them when Jack Poole holed out from at least twenty-five yards on the eighteenth green to win the hole and to halve the match for Somerset.

Everything depended upon the outcome of the other three matches. Two were safely won, but there was a nail-biting finish in the remaining match in which Richard Southcombe, the oldest player in the Dorset side and playing in his first SW championship, was paired with Ray Lawford, the youngest member. They had to get down in two from just over the back of the eighteenth green to win their match . . . and the team championship. Ray Lawford was left with a four foot putt, which he calmly sank, as he was to do so many times in his career as a county player.

Thus the overall match was won by the narrow margin of 7¼ to 6¾, despite losing the singles by two matches to six.

The records show that the county does not perform well in foursomes play, and in spite of providing more experience by including foursomes events into the fixture lists, and arranging more informal matches throughout the year, it is still the county's *Achilles heel*. In addition, Somerset appears to have become the main stumbling block to success, and in the years where Dorset has been successful, the highlight has been the win over Somerset.

During the last fifteen years most of the county teams have been composed mainly of younger men who have had the benefit of professional coaching and the time to play frequently. But prior to the explosion in the popularity of the game, county players tended to be mature business or professional people aged between thirty and the late forties and essentially week-end golfers. Players younger than thirty were rare, whereas today, most county teams include very few players over twenty-five. In those earlier years, whilst the commitment was the same, the atmosphere was less intense, with a wonderful atmosphere of good natured rivalry. Most of the players were in full-time employment, the majority had families and they had very few opportunities for mid-week play; so the physical and mental strain of playing thirty-six holes of competitive golf every day for a week took its toll, with the result that by the final day these fatigued fathers were prone to become involved in some bizarre incidents, especially in the foursomes matches. Fortunately these retired warriors have good memories and some of the more notable incidents can be recorded.

(The majority of the anecdotes have been supplied by Dick Peach, so presumably he has the best memory or was involved in the most incidents!)

There was the occasion when a very good Devon player, now a well-known golf historian, having hit two excellent shots to the par 5 seventeenth at Westward Ho! to within thirty yards of the green, proceeded to shank a series of pitch shots, circumnavigating the green in the process before finally getting the ball on to the putting surface.

Also at Westward Ho! in 1963 in a final day's foursome match against Somerset, Dr Donald Holmes, partnering Dick Peach, rifled their second shot to within eight yards of the pin at the eighteenth. Kinnersley for Somerset dragged his second into a dry stony ditch, pin high but about fifteen yards off the green. As the Dorset pair were one up at the time, the outcome seemed a foregone conclusion. The Somerset pair were about to concede the match when George Irlam decided to play the shot. He clambered into the ditch, and amid a hail of dirt and stones, blasted the ball out and across the green to an equal distance on the other side, from where his partner played a desultory chip to about ten yards short of the hole. By this time the ball was egg-shaped and covered in dried mud, but Irlam signalled to the caddie to remove the pin, and barely pausing in his stride, hit the ball, mud and all, straight into the hole for a five.

With three shots for a win, Peach, who had been battling with the dreaded 'Yips' all the week, was about to strike the ball when a stage-whispered admonition (the exact words cannot be printed) from Aubrey (Paddy) Horsington from just off the green caused him to 'fluff' the putt just half-way to the hole. Holmes, in characteristic fashion, attacked the hole, but the ball lipped the hole and finished two feet away. Peach duly missed the return and the match was halved, with the result that the team halved the match instead of winning it. Fortunately the incident did not affect the Dorset position in the final table.

Departing the green in high glee, the Somerset pair bequeathed to the Dorset captain the sobriquet *putt putt Peach*, which remained with him to the end of his playing days. However an opportunity for revenge presented itself a couple of years later at St Enodoc, again on the final day. Dorset was drawn to play Somerset and Peach drew Kinnersley in the singles. The Somerset team was staying in the same hotel and lost no time in reminding the Dorset player of the Westward Ho! incident, but in the event Peach had the last laugh; this time he was on a purple streak and putting everything, so he was able to thoroughly relish his opponent's discomfort. Dorset won the foursomes 4½ to 1½ and the overall match by eight points to three. There was less reference to *putt putt* after that!

In the 1956 individual championship event at St Enodoc, Dick Peach was paired with Dr Dennis Maunsell of Gloucester. At the notorious sixth Maunsell was two under par. He played his tee shot sensibly short of the dreaded Himalaya bunker, then he carefully lined up his shot, but the ball just failed to clear the hill and rolled back into the bunker. Showing no emotion he elected to play it out backwards, and hit the ball back almost to where he had played it from. Again, and with extreme care, he proceeded to repeat the horror . . . the ball rolling back to rest four inches below the surface of the sand . . . which he had forgotten to rake! This time he decided to go for it, but failed to get it out, and he eventually took eleven, so after a morning round of 74 and in eleventh place, he notched up 81 in the afternoon's disastrous round.

The two protagonists met again a few years later when they were drawn together in the British amateur championship's SW region qualifying round at Burnham & Berrow.

At the tenth Maunsell carved his tee shot into deep rough. Declaring it unplayable he tee'd up a second ball . . . and repeated the shot; reloading he did it yet again, but this time he decided he would have to play it. However, when he got to the ball it was resting under a bush in an unplayable position. Taking a drop and lining it up very carefully, he proceeded to drive the ball straight back into the bush . . . and finally holed out in fourteen!

Muttering something about a malign influence, he played the rest of the game in silence . . . and shortly afterwards emigrated to Australia!

Ken Longmore shared a room with Ernest Millward one year, and vows that throughout the night Millward would reach out to the bedside table in his sleep, pick up a sweet, unwrap it and pop it into his mouth.

Brian Barnes was initiated into County golf at Westward Ho! in 1963. He was an unconventional dresser and on this occasion turned up in short shorts, much to the concern of the others who had experienced painful encounters with the spiky rushes. These wicked hazards are reputed to be responsible for Westward Ho! having the highest percentage of one-eyed golfers in the country, the result of having to bend down to retrieve wayward golf balls!

Barnes played again in 1964 at Burnham & Berrow, when he won the SW counties title. He was due to play Tony Richmond in the morning singles, but on the previous evening, en route to a dance at the Weston super Mare Golf Club the Dorset player became involved in a car accident, and Paddy Horsington, the non-playing captain, had to take his place. Horsington was a governor of Millfield School where Barnes was a pupil, and he must have exerted an intimidating influence because in spite of just having won the championship, Barnes lost the match by one hole.

Richmond seriously injured his arm in the crash and needed an extensive skin graft, which team member Donald Holmes performed at the local cottage hospital . . . proof of the wisdom of including a doctor in the team.

Another amusing story, again involving Horsington concerned an embarrassing fall from grace at St Enodoc in 1965. In the morning round of the 36-hole strokeplay competition he drove his ball into an impossible lie in the notorious Himalaya bunker (The illustration from an old book gives some idea of its size). Instead of doing the sensible thing and declaring it unplayable, he climbed to the top amid a great deal of barracking from his 'friends', including shouts of *you should have brought a Sherpa* and other unprintable advice, and attempted to play it out, finally extracting his ball and himself after ten shots.

The bunker seemed to hold a magnetic attraction for him because he was in it again in the afternoon. This time he tried to drag his trolley to the top . . . with the inevitable consequence . . . much to the delight of the onlookers, he overbalanced and tumbled to the bottom, trolley and all. After this performance he was always called *Hilary*!

In 1991 Roger Hearn holed a most unlikely pitch at the eighteenth hole at Saunton to win a foursomes match which was 'lost' against Gloucester, but resulted in victory by a quarter of a point.

Presidents of the Association

1924	A V Hambro
1925	L C H Palairet (Devon)
1926	F Temple Cole (Somerset)
1927	J Gundry
1928	G Field (Wilts)
1929	F N Cowling (Glos)
1930	T Corbett (Cornwall)
1931	Hon. Denys Scott (Devon)
1932	E J B Akerman (Somerset)
1933	N H Carter
1934	W M B Burridge (Wilts)
1935	E F T Fowler (Glos)
1936	F H Wills (Cornwall)
1937	H C Bennett (Devon)
1938	W L Bate (Somerset)
1939	J S Ruttle
1947	L H D Thornton (Wilts)
1948	A D Murray (Glos)
1949	F H Wills (Cornwall)
1950	W J Brockman (Devon)
1951	C H Young (Somerset)
1952	G E Newton
1953	J Polehampton (Wilts)
1954	W H J Watson (Glos)
1955	E Foster-Mitchell (Cornwall)
1956	W J Brockman (Devon)
1957	A T Laws (Somerset)
1958	H C Neilson
1959	G F MacPherson (Wilts)
1960	J J Cole (Glos)
1961	W H Wearne (Cornwall)
1962	W J Brockman (Devon)
1963	S H Newman (Somerset)
1964	R G Peach
1965	A J Combes (Wilts)
1966	E Scott-Cooper (Glos)
1967	W O Meade-King (Cornwall)
1968	L C Lake (Devon)
1969	J W R Swayne (Somerset)
1970	M R Gardner
1971	K A Swift (Wilts)
1972	D H Davis (Glos)
1973	T A B Mason (Cornwall)
1974	J P Phillips (Devon)
1975	R N Jutsum (Somerset)
1976	R Southcombe
1978	W B Mann (Glos)
1979	G H Rouse (Cornwall)
1980	D I Stirk (Devon)
1981	K Longmore
1982	J A Pakeman (Wilts)
1983	J M M Richardson (Somerset)
1984	J Baker (Glos)
1985	G R D A Nadin (Cornwall)
1986	J W D Goodban (Devon)
1987	R F Buthlay (Wilts)
1988	R Lawford
1989	G T Irlam (Somerset)
1990	R J Gardiner (Glos)
1991	R O Gilbert (Cornwall)
1992	B G Steer (Devon)

Amateur Champions

At the outset the winner received a gold medal; the runner-up a silver medal; and the third received the captain's prize for the best 36 holes under handicap.
In 1948 the winner received a silver cup; the second a silver medal; and the third a bronze medal.
In 1951 the winner received a silver cup; the runner-up a pint tankard and the third a half-pint tankard.

Year	Winner	Score	Club	Venue	Year	Winner	Score	Club	Venue
1924	A V Hambro	158	Came Down	R.N.D.	1962	G N Bicknell	151	Newquay	Trevose
1925	R A Riddell	156	Weston super Mare	Long Ashton	1963	R N Jutsum	143	Weston super Mare	R.N.D.
1926	C H Young	154	Bristol & Clifton	Broadstone	1964	B W Barnes	145	Burnham & Berrow	Burnham & Berrow
1927	J A Pierson	158	Burnham & Berrow	Burnham & Berrow	1965	J A Bloxham	141	Cotswold Hills	St. Enodoc
1928	E Hunter	154	Broadstone	Broadstone	1966	R Lawford	143	Broadstone	Ferndown
1929	C L Chard	152	Yelverton	St. Enodoc	1967	P Y Yeo	144	Bude & N Cornwall	Saunton
1930	R D Howard	155	Bristol & Clifton	Saunton	1968	B G Steer	145	Tavistock	Burnham & Berrow
1931	F Smith	152	Burnham & Berrow	Burnham & Berrow	1969	D J Carroll	141	Cirencester	Trevose
1932	G C Brooks	145	Bristol & Clifton	Broadstone	1970	P J Yeo	145	Bude & N Cornwall	R.N.D.
1933	S H R Hornby	147	Burnham & Berrow	St. Enodoc	1971	J A Bloxham	142	Cotswold Hills	St. Enodoc
1934	P B M Wallace	150	Newquay	R.N.D.	1972	J H Davis	150	Cotswold Hills	Saunton
1935	S H R Hornby	153	Burnham & Berrow	Burnham & Berrow	1973	R W Tugwell	143	Knowle	Ferndown
1936	G E Newton	146	Ferndown	Broadstone	1974	C S Mitchell	151	Bristol & Clifton	Burnham & Berrow
1937	E J Poole	142	Weston super Mare	St. Enodoc	1975	R Abbot	141	Shirehampton Park	Trevose
1938	L C Lake	151	Saunton	Saunton	1976	G T Irlam	148	Weston super Mare	R.N.D.
1947	L F Brown	146	Lilley Brook	Ferndown	1977	G Brand	135	Knowle	St. Enodoc
1948	E B Millward	147	Parkstone	Trevose	1978	G Brand	143	Knowle	Saunton
1949	J Payne	151	Weston super Mare	R.N.D.	1979	S C Davidson	142	Knowle	Ferndown
1950	J Payne	149	Weston super Mare	Burnham & Berrow	1980	C S Mitchell	150	Bristol & Clifton	Burnham & Berrow
1951	E B Millward	144	Parkstone	Ferndown	1981	P Newcombe	143	East Devon	St. Mellion
1952	E B Millward	149	Parkstone	Trevose	1982	D Ray	140	Long Ashton	R.N.D.
1953	E D Trapnell	153	R.N.D.	R.N.D.	1983	C S Edwards	140	Bath	St. Enodoc
1954	E B Millward	146	Parkstone	Burnham & Berrow	1984	M Blaber	146	Yelverton	Saunton
1955	R Lawford	147	Broadstone	Broadstone	1985	C Phillips	70★	Newquay	Ferndown
	(after a tie with R G Peach)				1986	C Phillips	141	Newquay	Trevose
1956	R G Peach	144	Parkstone	St. Enodoc	1987	P Newcome	152	East Devon	Burnham & Berrow
1957	E D Trapnell	148	R.N.D.	Saunton	1988	J P Langmead	142	Newton Abbott	R.N.D.
1958	R C Champion	148	Burnham & Berrow	Burnham & Berrow	1989	K Jones	139	Lansdown	St. Enodoc
1959	G J Butler	151	Ferndown	St. Enodoc	1990	S Amor	140	Marlborough	Saunton
1960	E D Trapnell	147	R.N.D.	R.N.D.	1991	P McMullen	137	Ferndown	Ferndown
1961	R N Jutsum	152	Weston super Mare	Saunton	1992	S Edgley	140	Weston super Mare	Parkstone
						(inc. play-off between M Watson and M Stanford)			

★ Rain stopped play

Team Championship

Year	Venue	Winners	Dorset Team
1933	St. Enodoc	Devon	Major Ruttle. Capt. N H Carter. R L Close. G E Newton. M R Gardner. A J Webb. J A Elliott. W M Samson. H L Luffman. Capt. F R Bacon. C C Roberts. G Glass-Hooper.
1934	R N Devon	Somerset	Major Ruttle. Capt. N H Carter. M R Gardner. W M Samson. R L Close. J A Elliott. A J Webb. H L Luffman. F F Laugher. F R Bacon. C G Simmons.
1935	Burnham	Devon	Major Ruttle. Capt. N H Carter. M R Gardner. W M Samson. R L Close J A Elliott. C Mayo. A J Webb. H L Luffman. C G Simmons. F R Bacon. D Arnott.
1936	Broadstone	Somerset	Major Ruttle. C W Scott. J A Elliott. G E Newton. D Arnott. W M Samson. R L Close. A J Webb. F R Bacon. G F Morgan. A V Hambro. H L Luffman.
1937	St. Enodoc	Somerset	M R Gardner. C Mayo. G Glass-Hooper. J S Ruttle. G E Newton. J A Elliott. R L Close. D Arnott. F F Laugher. H L Luffman.
1938	Saunton	Devon	G E Newton. G Glass-Hooper. C Mayo. J S Ruttle. F F Laugher. J A Elliott. R L Close. D Arnott. F W Prentice. J F Lewis. R A Rapp. H L Luffman. J F E Santall.
1947	Ferndown	Devon	G E Newton. O Austreng. K Longmore. E B Millward. R E Garrett. P Urlwin-Smith. E J Nicholl. R G Peach. R L Close. H L Luffman. C R Carter. J J McInnes. B Elliott. A J D Gibbins.
1948	Trevose	Glos	E B Millward. R E Garrett. G E Newton. E J Nicholl. B Elliott. P Urlwin-Smith. T R Jenkins. J J McInnes. H L Luffman. R L Close.
1949	R N Devon	Somerset	R E Garrett. H C Neilson. V Haggard. E J Nicholl. P Urlwin-Smith. J Dear. G E Newton. B Elliott. H L Luffman. E R James.
1950	Burnham	Somerset	R E Garrett. H C Neilson. E Millward. E J Nicholl. J Dear. G E Newton. B Elliott. P Urlwin-Smith. A Gibbins. T R Jenkins.
1951	Ferndown	Dorset	H C Neilson. E Millward. R E Garrett. O Austreng. T R Jenkins. J H Wyllie. E J Nicholl. B E Elliott. G E Newton. P Urlwin-Smith. J G Tice. K Longmore.
1952	Trevose	Dorset	H C Neilson. E Millward. O Austreng. M R Gardner. R E Garrett. E J Nicholl. F K Allen. G E Newton. I Campbell-Gray. T R Jenkins. B Elliott. P Urlwin-Smith. J G Tice.
1953	R N Devon	Devon	E J Nicholl. M R Gardner. H C Neilson. R E Garrett. R G Peach. J H Wolfson. B Elliott. J D Crawford. G E Newton. F G R Vowles.
1954	Burnham	Dorset	E J Nicholl. E Millward. R E Garrett. I Campbell-Gray. K Longmore. P Sanders. H C Neilson. R G Peach. E A J Horsington. W P Williams. J D Crawford.
1955	Broadstone	Dorset	R G Peach. R Lawford. R E Garrett. I Campbell-Gray. P Sanders. K Longmore. H C Neilson. R de Beauvais. E J Nicholl. P Urlwin-Smith. T R Jenkins.

Dorset qualified for the English County Finals at Formby

Year	Venue	Winners	Dorset Team
1956	St. Enodoc	Dorset	R G Peach. M R Gardner. R Lawford. R E Garrett. D R Otway. T R Jenkins. R Southcombe. E Horsington. P Urlwin-Smith. B Elliott. A Buchan.
1957	Saunton	Devon	M R Gardner. K Longmore. P Sanders. R G Peach. T R Jenkins. T Deighton. R Southcombe. B Longrigg. W N Southcombe. R E Garrett. P Urlwin-Smith. A J Horsington.

Team Championship (continued)

Year	Venue	Winners	Dorset Team
1958	Burnham	Somerset	M R Gardner. K Longmore. R G Peach. R Lawford. R Southcombe. T R Deighton. H C Neilson. F G R Vowles. T R Jenkins. W Southcombe. H Wilton. A J Horsington.
1959	St. Enodoc	Somerset	P Urlwin-Smith. G Butler. R G Peach. R Lawford. A Horsington. M R Gardner. B Longrigg. C Cave. T R Jenkins. R Southcombe.
1960	R.N.D.	Devon	G Butler. K Longmore. R G Peach. P Urlwin-Smith. R Lawford. B Longrigg. H A Wilton. C T McInerney.
1961	Saunton	Devon	R Southcombe. K Longmore. G Butler. H A Wilton. B Longrigg. M R Gardner. S Brewis, C Cave. W. Southcombe. A Horsington. P Urlwin-Smith.
1962	Trevose	Somerset	R Southcombe. K Longmore. N Cook. C Cave. G Butler. A J Richmond. R Lawford. H A Wilton. S Brewis. E J Smith. B H Longrigg. M R Gardner.
1963	R.N.D.	Devon	A J Horsington. G Butler. K Longmore. R G Peach. D M Holmes. R Lawford. N Cook. D Bassett. A J Richmond. C T McInerney. M R Gardner. R Southcombe.
1964	Burnham	Somerset	A J Horsington. A J Richmond. G Butler. K Longmore. D M Holmes. R G Peach. R Lawford. M R Gardner. H A Wilton. N Cook. C T McInerney.
1965	St. Enodoc	Cornwall	R G Peach. G Butler. D M Holmes. K Longmore. R Lawford. A J Richmond. C Cave. H A Wilton. A J Horsington. M R Gardner.
1966	Ferndown	Dorset	R G Peach. G Butler. D M Holmes. R Lawford. A J Richmond. H A Wilton. N Cook. R A Budd, P Sanders. K Longmore.
1967	Saunton	Devon	G Butler. R Budd. K Longmore. R Lawford R G Peach. C Cave. N Cook. W G Peach. E J Smith. A J Richmond.
1968	Burnham	Glos	R Lawford. K Longmore. G Butler. R G Peach. A Richmond. N Cook. D Brewis. G Eley. D M Holmes. P Shillington.

Dorset qualified for the English County Finals at Copt Heath

Year	Venue	Winners	Dorset Team
1969	Trevose	Cornwall	G Butler. R Lawford. J Nash. P Shillington. N Cook. K Longmore. W G Peach. A J Richmond. R G Peach. N Green.
1970	R.N.D.	Glos	G Butler. A K Jones. R Lawford. K Longmore. S Brewis. A J Richmond. R G Peach. D M Holmes. J Nash.
1971	St. Enodoc	Glos	K Longmore. J Nash. T Griffin. A K Jones. G Butler. E J S Garrett. D Owers. N L R Cook. J Lawrence. B Crutcher.
1972	Saunton	Dorset	G Butler. T Griffin. A K Jones. W G Peach. R G Peach. D Owers. R Lawford. J Nash. F K Shaw. K Longmore.
1973	Ferndown	Glos	G Butler. T Griffin. D M Holmes. E Antell. S Potter. N Cook. A K Jones. R Lawford. J Nash.
1974	Burnham	Devon	G Butler. T Griffin. D M Holmes. R Lawford. S Potter. B Crutcher. J Lawrence. J Nash. A Page.
1975	Trevose	Devon	D M Holmes. E Antell. N Cook. J Calver. C R Neale. S Potter. G Butler. B Crutcher. W G Peach. R Lawford.
1976	R.N.D.	Glos	G Butler. J Calver. R Lawford. D Barnes. D Scholes. S Beunfeld. I Clark. D M Holmes. J Nash. W G Peach. S Potter.
1977	St. Enodoc	Glos	J Calver. I Clark. J Nash. S Beunfeld. A Jones. D Barnes. S Potter. D Scholes. G Butler. R Hearn.

Team Championship (continued)

Year	Venue	Winners	Dorset Team
1978	Saunton	Glos	A K Jones. N Cook. R Hearn. G Eley. D M Holmes. N Fuller. R Francis. J Nash. J Leggett. D Barnes. N Cook. S Potter.
1979	Ferndown	Devon	G Butler. N Cook. M Farley. R Francis. J Nash. W Raymond. A K Jones.
1980	Burnham	Wilts	G Eley. G Butler. R Francis. A K Jones. J Leggett. J Nash. W Raymond.
1981	St. Mellion	Glos	G Eley. R Hearn. D Jeffreys. A Lawrence. J Leggett. J Nash. W Raymond.
1982	R.N.D.	Devon	J Calver. G Butler. R Hearn. A Lawrence. P McMullen. J Nash. W Raymond.
1983	St. Enodoc	Glos	J Calver. W Raymond. M Savage. I Sparkes. P McMullen. J Nash. G Butler. R Francis.
1984	R.N.D.	Glos	A Lawrence. I Sparkes. M McKenna. J Gordon. R Hearn. J Nash.
1985	Ferndown	Glos	J Bloxham. R Hearn. A Lawrence. S Allen. S Hector. M McKenna. J Gordon. J Nash. P McMullen. (Thunderstorm stopped play)
1986	Trevose	Devon	M Welch. D Jeffreys. W Raymond. S Edgley. R Davis. J Nash. R Hearn S Allen. P McMullen.
1987	Burnham	Glos	D Scholes. J Gordon. R Hearn M Welch. M Watson. P McMullen. A Lawrence. S Allen. W Raymond.
1988	R.N.D.	Dorset	T Griffin. J Pounder. P McMullen. D Barnes. R Mabb. A Lawrence. R Hearn. J Nash. S Edgley. M Watson.

Dorset qualified for the English County Finals at Seacroft

Year	Venue	Winners	Dorset Team
1989	St. Enodoc	Glos	T Griffin. L Thompson. R Hearn. P McMullen. J Nash. R Davies. A Lawrence. D Barnes. J Pounder. I Donnelly.
1990	Saunton	Glos	L Thompson. J Nash. D Talbot. S Hector. I Donnelly. A Lawrence. M Thompson. R Davies. W Raymond. R Hearn. P McMullen.
1991	Ferndown	Middx	R Hearn. R Davies. L James. J Nash. M Thompson. P McMullen. W Raymond. M Watson. I Donnelly.

Dorset qualified for the English County Finals at Hoylake

Year	Venue	Winners	Dorset Team
1992	W s Mare	Dorset	S Edgley. M Watson. P McMullen. A Lawrence. L James. I Donnelly. M Thompson. G Archer. R Hearn W Raymond.

Dorset qualified for the English County Finals at Kings Norton (and won)

Inter-Counties Team Championship

In 1924 the competition was played as 36 holes of strokeplay, with teams of four between the counties of Devon, Dorset, Gloucester and Somerset.
In 1925 only Devon, Gloucester and Somerset competed.
In 1926 Dorset and Wiltshire rejoined the above three, but no Wiltshire scores were returned.
All six counties competed for the first time in 1927 and a matchplay format was introduced with teams of ten; foursomes in the morning and singles in the afternoon.
In 1928 this was reversed, with the singles being played in the morning.
In 1929 1½ points for a foursomes win was instituted.
1931 Devon did not take part.
1932 Singles only, with teams of eight.
Prior to 1933 all matches had been played to a result, but halved matches were recorded for the first time and they reverted to teams of ten.
The championship resumed in 1947 with teams of eight.

Year	Winner	Year	Winner	Year	Winner	Year	Winner
1924	Devon	1949	Somerset	1967	Devon	1985	Gloucestershire
1925	Gloucestershire	1950	Somerset	1968	Gloucestershire	1986	Devon
1926	Somerset	1951	Dorset	1969	Cornwall	1987	Gloucestershire
1927	Gloucestershire	1952	Dorset	1970	Gloucestershire	1988	Devon
1928	Somerset	1953	Devon	1971	Gloucestershire	1989	Gloucestershire
1929	Devon	1954	Dorset	1972	Dorset	1990	Gloucestershire
1930	Devon	1955	Dorset	1973	Gloucestershire	1991	Gloucestershire
1931	Somerset	1956	Dorset	1974	Devon	1992	Gloucestershire
1932	Dorset	1957	Devon	1975	Devon		
1933	Devon	1958	Somerset	1976	Gloucestershire	*Wins To Date*	
1934	Somerset	1959	Somerset	1977	Gloucestershire	Devon	17
1935	Devon	1960	Devon	1978	Gloucestershire	Gloucester	15
1936	Somerset	1961	Devon	1979	Devon	Somerset	12
1937	Somerset	1962	Somerset	1980	Wiltshire	Dorset	8
1938	Devon	1963	Devon	1981	Gloucestershire	Cornwall	2
1939	Gloucestershire	1964	Somerset	1982	Devon	Wiltshire	1
1947	Devon	1965	Cornwall	1983	Gloucestershire		
1948	Gloucestershire	1966	Dorset	1984	Gloucestershire		

The counties have been represented by the following number of players between 1927 and 1992

Cornwall	186	Dorset	151	Somerset	148
Devon	151	Gloucester	157	Wilts	171

Personal Achievements

Ten victories in one year

This has been recorded three times:
1933   L C Lake (Devon)   1933   H C Neilson (Devon)   1982   D Ray (Gloucester)
NB: The achievement of Lake and Neilson is interesting because not only did they win all their singles matches, but they partnered each other in the foursomes. Further, it was Neilson's first appearance in the S W Championships.

Unbeaten in ten matches in one year

Year	Player	County	Won	Halved	Year	Player	County	Won	Halved
1934	F F Laugher	(Dorset)	9	1	1962	P O Green	(Somerset)	9	1
1934	H J Colmer	(Somerset)	9	1	1971	D J Carroll	(Gloucester)	9	1
1949	F Smith	(Somerset)	8	2	1980	J N Fleming	(Wiltshire)	9	1
1951	R N Jutsum	(Somerset)	9	1	1981	M C Edmunds	(Cornwall)	7	3
1953	G T Irlam	(Somerset)	8	2	1984	M C Edmunds	(Cornwall)	7	3
1955	P Sanders	(Dorset)	9	1	1992	M McEwan	(Somerset)	9	1
1961	J W D Goodban	(Devon)	9	1					

NB: No player has lost 10 matches in any one year, but some famous names have come perilously close.

Personal Achievements (continued)

Centurions
100 or more victories have been recorded by the following:

1930/62	L C Lake	(Devon)	120	out of 224	matches
1935/71	D I Stirk	(Devon)	101	172	
1937/72	R N Jutsum	(Somerset)	117	203	
1948/80	G T Irlam	(Somerset)	138	238	
1959/83	G J Butler	(Dorset)	109	254	
1964/91	R E Searle	(Wilts)	111	263	
1955/70	R B Redfern	(Devon)	69	142	
1957/78	R P F Brown	(Devon)	75	132	
1958/73	R J Gardiner	(Glos)	68	142	
1959/78	G K Baker	(Som)	73	164	
1962/79	P Edgington	(Wilts)	65	163	
1962/80	N L R Cook	(Dorset)	52	108	
1963/82	B G Steer	(Devon)	88	178	
1964/79	R J Radway	(Devon)	55	125	
1965/86	J W Bradley	(Cornwall)	63	140	
1966/85	D J Carroll	(Glos)	90	179	
1968/85	L F Millar	(Som)	64	131	
1969/89	R Abbott	(Glos)	93	143	
1969/92	J Nash	(Dorset)	60	178	
1972/86	M R Lovett	(Wilts)	52	116	
1973/87	C S Mitchell	(Glos)	54	78	
1973/91	M G Symons	(Devon)	83	152	
1974/92	R H P Knott	(Devon)	60	108	
1981/92	P H Newcombe	(Devon)	64	115	
1982/92	D M Powell	(Glos)	59	102	
1982/92	C S Edwards	(Som)	57	98	

50 or more victories have been recorded by the following:

1928/39	A J T Rees	(Devon)	50	out of 77	matches
1930/39	P McAllister	(Somerset)	55	85	
1931/65	M R Gardner	(Dorset)	65	134	
1933/36	E J Poole	(Somerset)	97	190	
1935/65	J W D Goodban	(Devon)	67	125	
1947/64	G N Bicknell	(Cornwall)	81	176	
1947/81	E D Trapnell	(Devon)	81	161	
1947/72	R G Peach	(Dorset)	75	149	
1947/72	K Longmore	(Dorset)	73	141	
1948/61	G C Griffiths	(Glos)	50	107	
1948/67	E Bennett	(Cornwall)	68	162	
1955/76	R Lawford	(Dorset)	86	191	

Inter-Counties Matchplay Championship
1927 – 1992
Dorset county players personal achievements

		Won	Halved	Lost			Won	Halved	Lost
Archer G	1992	4	1	4	Crawford J D	1953/54	3	1	7
Allen S	1985/87	5	3	18	Close R L	1929/48	30	6	52
Antell E	1975	3	1	3	Carter C R	1947	0	0	2
Austreng O	1947/52	16	2	11	Carter N H	1928/35	25	1	22
Allin F K	1952	0	0	1	Carter J N	1931	3	0	5
Arnott D D	1929/39	14	6	26	Cotton C K	1929/32	15	0	6
Archer G D	1928	3	0	1	Courtney P D A	1927/31	7	0	13
Bloxham J	1985	3	0	7	Chadwick R H	1932	1	0	1
Barnes D	1977/89	11	4	15	Carey-Wood C	1928	2	0	0
Buenfeld S	1977	2	0	1	Davies M	1991	0	1	1
Budd R A	1966/67	11	1	6	Davies R	1989/91	3	2	9
Bassett D	1963	1	1	3	Davis R	1986	2	4	4
Brewis S D R W	1961/68	8	4	11	Donnelly I	1989/92	8	7	11
Butler G J	1959/83	109	50	115	Deighton T R	1957/58	10	0	7
Buchan A	1956	0	0	3	de Beauvais R E	1955	1	1	2
Bacon F R	1932/39	29	7	16	Dear J	1949/50	7	3	2
Burden O P B	1928/31	3	0	1	Dobson E J	1928	4	0	2
Calver J	1975/80	18	7	22	Edgley S	1986/92	18	5	15
Cook N L R	1962/80	52	8	48	Eley G	1968/70	0	1	9
Crutcher B	1971/75	3	2	6	Elliott B	1947/56	21	4	19
Clark I	1976/77	6	1	9	Elliott J A	1933/38	24	9	23
Cave C J	1959/67	16	4	15	Edmonstone C G	1928/32	26	0	13
Campbell-Gray I	1952/55	14	3	12	Francis R A R	1978/83	18	5	19

Dorset county players personal achievements (continued)

		Won	Halved	Lost			Won	Halved	Lost
Farley M	1979/80	6	2	9	Otway D R	1956	3	1	2
Gordon J	1984/87	12	3	15	Page A	1973/74	9	4	5
Griffin T	1971/74	11	8	19	Pavitt B A	1979	5	1	1
Green N	1969/70	0	2	5	Peach R G	1947/72	75	26	48
Garrett E J S	1971	4	1	4	Peach W G	1967/76	24	8	23
Garrett R E	1947/57	44	13	39	Poore R M	1927/31	7	0	3
Gardner M R	1931/65	65	20	49	Potter S	1975/77	15	2	11
Gibbings A J D	1939/50	6	0	8	Pounder J	1988/92	8	3	13
Gow D J	1939	4	1	4	Prentice F W	1938	4	1	5
Glass-Hooper G	1933/38	12	1	8	Rapp R A	1938/39	5	4	7
Gundry J	1927/28	0	0	6	Rainey H	1927/28	4	0	2
Hector S	1981/90	9	6	14	Raymond W	1979/92	31	11	56
Hodgson A	1981/84	9	2	13	Richmond A J	1962/70	23	7	37
Hearn R	1977/92	39	13	39	Richards E H	1929	0	0	2
Holmes D M	1963/78	32	9	37	Roberts A H	1932	0	0	1
Horsington A J	1954/65	16	4	16	Roberts C C	1929/33	6	1	5
Helm P L	1939	2	1	7	Ruttle J S	1928/39	40	12	54
Haggard V E D	1949	0	0	8	Samson W M	1930/36	20	7	20
Hambro A V	1928/36	7	0	7	Sanders P	1954/66	19	1	6
Hunter E	1927/28	8	0	6	Santall J F E	1938/39	2	1	3
James L	1991/92	10	3	5	Savage M	1982/83	5	1	9
James E R	1949	2	0	2	Scholes D	1973/86	8	2	17
James E J S	1930	4	0	6	Scott C W	1928/39	10	1	14
Jones A K	1970/81	33	7	44	Shaw F K	1972	3	0	3
Jeffreys D	1979/86	10	3	13	Shillington P	1968	2	0	3
Jenkins T R	1948/59	23	9	27	Simmons C G	1934/35	11	0	7
Lawrence A	1981/92	35	11	28	Smith E J	1962/67	6	0	10
Lawrence J C	1971/74	9	4	7	Southcombe R	1956/63	21	3	20
Lawford R	1955/76	86	20	85	Southcombe W N	1957/61	5	1	7
Laugher F F	1934/38	20	3	6	Sparkes I	1983/84	8	2	10
Leggett J H A	1978/81	7	3	14	Stephens F A	1927/28	8	0	5
Longmore K J	1947/72	73	17	51	Stringer H S	1927/29	4	0	6
Longrigg B H H	1957/62	16	6	10	Struyer H S	1929	1	0	1
Luffman H L	1927/49	44	8	40	Stubbs P S F	1928/32	11	0	7
Lewis J F	1938	2	2	3	Talbot D	1990	1	1	5
Mabb R	1988	3	2	2	Taylor E	1927	3	0	2
McKenna M	1984/85	5	0	11	Thompson L	1989/90	3	0	4
McInnes J J	1947/48	4	1	11	Thompson M	1988/92	14	6	16
McInerney C T	1960/64	8	1	10	Thompson M R	1959	4	0	4
McMullen P	1982/92	38	13	43	Tice J G	1951/52	1	0	1
Marriott D	1960	3	3	2	Urlwin-Smith P	1947/61	30	8	30
Mayo C	1935/39	11	8	10	Vowles F G R	1953/58	3	1	8
Millward E B	1947/54	33	3	11	Watson M	1987/92	18	4	21
Morgan G F	1936/37	10	2	4	Webb A J	1929/36	26	6	30
Moore R B	1928	4	0	5	Welch M	1986/88	6	2	13
Morrison C E F	1927/31	6	0	3	Whittingham A E	1928/32	20	0	11
Nash J	1969/92	60	26	92	Wills-Sandford	1928	1	0	0
Neale C R	1975	1	1	3	Wilton H A	1958/66	18	10	23
Neilson H C	1949/58	42	8	24	Williams W P	1954	4	0	3
Nicholl E J	1947/55	46	8	24	Wolfson J H	1953	2	0	5
Newton G E	1933/53	42	12	47	Wyllie J H	1951	6	0	1
Olson J	1991	4	4	2	Young F H	1928	1	0	1
Owers D	1971/72	5	3	6					

Inter-Counties Matchplay Championship

Dorset -v -

Year	Cornwall	Devon	Gloucester	Somerset	Wiltshire
1934	10-7	7¾-9¾	8-9½	8-9½	11½-6½
1935	14½-3	7½-10	6¾-10¼	4-13½	16¼-1¼
1936	8¼-9¼	6¼-11¼	11-6½	6-11½	11-6½
1937	10¾-6¾	6¼-11¼	11¾-5¾	5¼-12¼	13-4½
1938	9¾-7¾	5½-12	6¼-11¼	7½-10	10-7½
1939	11½-6	6½-11	4¼-13¼	3-14½	6¾-10¾
1947	12½-1½	8-6	3½-10½	7¾-6¼	10-4
1948	5-9	4½-9¾	4¾-9¼	7-7	9½-4½
1949	4¾-9¼	9-5	3¾-10¼	3¾-10¼	8-6
1950	8¾-5¼	6½-7½	6-8	7½-6½	12½-1½
1951	10½-3½	10-4	11-3	9¾-4¼	5½-8½
1952	9¼-4¾	10¼-3¾	6¼-7¾	9-5	7½-6½
1953	6½-7½	4¼-9¾	5-9	5¼-8¾	5½-8½
1954	10-4	9¼-4¾	7½-6½	9-5	8½-5½
1955	12½-1½	8¼-5¾	8¼-5¾	12¼-1¾	9½-4½
1956	8½-5½	7¾-6¼	7½-6½	7¼-6¾	8¾-5¼
1957	9-5	5½-8½	8½-5½	6½-7½	8½-5½
1958	6¾-7¼	7¾-6¼	3½-10½	5½-8½	10¼-3¾
1959	9-5	7¼-6¾	4½-9½	6½-7½	9-5
1960	10½-3½	3-11	9-5	8-6	9¼-4¾
1961	9¾-4¼	5-9	7½-6½	4-10	9-5
1962	3¾-10¼	5¼-8¾	7½-6½	3¼-10¾	8½-5½
1963	11-3	6-8	4¾-9¼	6¼-7¾	10¼-3¾
1964	8½-5½	7-7	7½-6½	5-9	7¾-6¼
1965	6½-7½	5-9	11-3	8-6	7½-6½
1966	10½-3½	8¼-5¾	9¼-4¾	6½-7½	8-6
1967	6½-7½	4-10	6¼-7¾	6½-7½	9½-4½
1968	9-5	6-8	3¾-10¼	4-10	6½-7½
1969	7½-6½	4½-9½	9-5	7½-6½	5¾-8¼
1970	10½-3½	4¾-9¼	6-8	2-12	6¼-7¾
1971	7½-6½	7½-6½	7-7	6½-7½	7-7
1972	11-3	7½-6½	7¼-6¾	7-7	7¼-6¾
1973	8½-5½	5-9	3½-10½	6-8	7½-6½
1974	9-5	3¼-10¾	6¾-7¼	6½-7½	7-7
1975	7¼-6¾	7¾-6¼	8-6	6¾-7¼	5-9
1976	7-7	7½-6½	5½-8½	6½-7½	9¾-4¼
1977	7¼-6¾	4½-9½	4-10	5½-8½	7¼-6¾
1978	7¼-6¾	4-10	1-13	3¼-10¾	2½-11½
1979	9¾-4¼	6¼-7¾	5-9	8-6	6½-7½
1980	7½-6½	5¾-8¼	6-8	3-11	7-7
1981	6½-7½	4¾-9¼	4¾-9¼	4½-9½	6-8
1982	9¼-4¾	3½-10½	2½-11½	5-9	7½-6½
1983	8½-5½	4½-9½	6¼-7¾	10½-3½	6-8
1984	8¾-5¼	3¾-10¼	6¾-7¼	4¾-9¼	9½-4½
1985	7¼-6¾	3½-10½	7½-6½	2¾-11¼	8-6
1986	6½-7½	4½-9½	3½-10½	7-7	6¼-7¾
1987	7-7	1½-12½	5-9	5-9	1½-12½
1988	10-4	5½-8½	5¾-8¼	5½-8½	6¾-7¼
1989	8-6	10-4	5¾-8¼	4½-9½	7¼-6¾
1990	5½-8½	7½-6½	7¼-6¾	6-8	5½-8½
1991	6¾-7¼	8¼-5¾	5¼-8¾	3½-10½	7¾-6¼
1992	8-6	8-6	5¾-8¼	4½-9½	9-5

	Won	Halved	Lost		Won	Halved	Lost		Won	Halved	Lost
v Cornwall	38	2	12	*v* Gloucester	17	1	34	*v* Wiltshire	34	3	15
v Devon	18	1	33	*v* Somerset	12	3	37				

The English County Championship
Kings Norton Golf Club
2 – 4 October 1992

Reprinted from the 1993 edition of the EGU Year Book.

Dorset's success in the English County Finals at Kings Norton was one of the romantic stories of the summer. On paper they had no chance. A small county of 24 affiliated clubs pitched into head-to-head combat with the mighty Yorkshire (155 clubs), Staffordshire (44) and Middlesex (37). In the event they emerged from three days of tough competition and even tougher weather at the top of the pile... with three victories. It was a tremendous performance by non-playing captain Doug Pratt and his doughty band of fighters from Thomas Hardy country.

Dorset have waited 60 years to claim this glittering prize, and they did it in style with a 100% record, although on a miserably wet Saturday their singles against Yorkshire had to be cancelled because of waterlogged greens and sodden fairways.

At that stage Dorset had taken the foursomes 2-1, and that result stood, as did Middlesex's similar lead over Staffordshire.

The foundations of a memorable victory were laid on the first day when Martyn Thompson's putt on the 18th green gave him a half against Graham Homewood. That meant Dorset had beaten the defending champions Middlesex 5-4, and the impossible dream was taking shape. Middlesex had led 2-1 in the foursomes, but Dorset took four out of six points from the singles, with Lee James, playing top, in splendid form against the redoubtable Warren Bennett, who had just returned from the Home Internationals in Scotland, where he was unbeaten.

James won 3 and 2 to add Bennett's scalp to those of other England players, Gary Wolstenholme and Colin Edwards, in matchplay this season.

Stephen Edgley was in top form too, casting aside the challenge of another England man, Andy Rogers, by 6 and 4, while Michael Watson, who had flown back from his American university especially for the event, squeezed home at the last against Tim Greenwood.

A half by that marvellous character Roger Hearn, 20 years a county player and still going strong, against young Stuart Goode, coupled with that share of the spoils by Thompson, sealed it for Dorset.

Yorkshire had little trouble in beating a disappointing Staffordshire, and on Friday evening, most of the talk was of how difficult it was going to be to beat Yorkshire.

The rain was beating down on the Saturday, and Dorset approached their tricky task against the 'Tykes' in waterproofs and umbrellas. Every green needed a squeegy, and luckily Kings Norton had borrowed five from the nearby Belfry.

Conditions made things as difficult for the referees as for the players. They had to give a decision on pretty well every hole where relief from water could be taken. But good sense and good humour prevailed, and there was some fine golf played in almost impossible conditions.

It was that man Hearn, playing with Peter McMullen, who eventually steered Dorset in front. They were three up after nine against Philip Wood and John Dockar, but had let it slip to one up by the 15th. However, a determined finish gave them victory on the 17th green. With Thompson and Edgley beating Ian Pyman and Stephen Pullan by 2 and 1 in the top match, it balanced out the 2 and 1 defeat of Watson and Tony Lawrence against Mark Pullan and Roger Roper.

Middlesex ran out 2-1 winners in the other match, to keep alive their hopes of retaining the title, but now Dorset only needed to draw with Staffordshire to win the crown, and they took a 2-1 foursomes lead on the final day, which although dry, was decidedly cold at times, with a north-easterly wind stalking the wide fairways.

For a time in the afternoon it looked as though Dorset might falter at the final hurdle. James, in a tense struggle with McGuire in the top singles, went down by one hole, and Edgley gave best to Poxon the Staffordshire captain, on the 15th hole. Then Watson, two up with two to play, saw Randle poach two birdies on the 16th and 17th to scramble a half. But Thompson had already taken an early shower after beating Steve Parry 8 and 7, and Hearn and Lawrence underlined Dorset's supremacy with 3 and 2 wins over Beech and Rob Maxfield respectively.

It was an emotional moment as Hearn and Lawrence walked in to applause from spectators around the 18th green and heart-felt congratulations from captain Doug Pratt and the rest of the team.

Bill Meredith

Match Results

2nd October		Dorset v Middlesex			3rd October		Dorset v Yorkshire	
Foursomes					*Foursomes*			
Edgley/Thompson	0	Bennett/Rogers	1		Thompson/Edgley	1	Pyman/S Pullan	0 (2/1)
Lawrence/Watson	0	Homewood/O'Shea	1		Watson/Lawrence	0	M Pullan/Roper	1 (2/1)
McMullen/Hearn	1	Goode/Greenwood	0		McMullen/Hearn	1	Wood/Dockar	0 (2/1)
Total	**1**		**2**		**Total**	**2**		**1**

Singles				
James	1	Bennett	0 (3/2)	
Edgley	1	Rogers	0 (5/4)	
Watson	1	Greenwood	0 (1 hole)	
Hearn	½	Goode	½	
Lawrence	0	O'Shea	1 (4/3)	
Thompson	½	Homewood	½	
Total	**4**		**2**	

Singles
Abandoned due to bad weather: all matches deemed to have been halved.
Result
Dorset beat Yorks 5 pts to 4.

4th October		Dorset v Staffordshire	
Foursomes			
Edgley/Thompson	½	McGuire/Poxon	½
James/Watson	1	Randle/Beech	0 (3/2)
McMullen/Hearn	½	Wild/Perry	½
Total	**2**		**1**
Singles			
James	0	McGuire	1 (1 hole)
Edgley	0	Poxon	1 (4/3)
Watson	½	Randle	½
Thompson	1	Perry	0 (8/7)
Hearn	1	Beech	0 (3/2)
Lawrence	1	Maxfield	0 (3/2)
Total	**3½**		**2½**

English County Finals

Year	Venue	Winning County	Dorset Team
1955	Formby	Yorkshire	E B Millward. P Sanders. R Lawford. R E Garrett. I Campbell-Gray. R G Peach.
1968	Copt Heath	Surrey Led by Peter Oosterhuis	R G Peach. G J Butler. A J Richmond. W G Peach. R Lawford. K Longmore
1988	Seacroft	Warwick	J Pounder. P McMullen. D Barnes. R Mabb. A Lawrence. S Edgley. R Hearn.
1991	Hoylake	Middlesex	P McMullen. L James. J Olsen. R Hearn. M Thompson. I Donnelly.
1992	Kings Norton	Dorset	L James. R Hearn. S Edgley. P McMullen. M Watson. M Thompson. A Lawrence.

South Western Counties v Midlands Counties

	Venue	SW	Midlands		Venue	SW	Midlands
1925	Burnham & Berrow	9½	5½	1971	Burnham & Berrow	11	7
1926	Little Aston	3	12	1972	Olton	4	14
1950	Burnham & Berrow	13	5	1973	Burnham & Berrow	8	10
1951	Blackwell	8	10	1974	Olton	7	11
1952	Burnham & Berrow	9½	8½	1975	Burnham & Berrow	6½	11½
1953	Beau Desert	2	16	1976	Blackwell	3½	11½
1954	Ferndown	7½	10½	1977	Burnham & Berrow	9½	5½
1955	Little Aston	4	14	1978	Copt Heath	3	12
1956	Burnham & Berrow	11	7	1979	Burnham & Berrow	5½	9½
1957	Copt Heath	3½	14½	1980	Worcestershire	8½	6½
1958	No Match			1981	Burnham & Berrow	9	6
1959	Burnham & Berrow	7½	10½	1982	Kings Norton	5	10
1960	Worcestershire	5	13	1983	Burnham & Berrow	8½	6½
1961	Burnham & Berrow	14	4	1984	Redditch	6½	8½
1962	Olton	5	13	1985	Parkstone	9½	5½
1963	Burnham & Berrow	7	11	1986	Little Aston	9	6
1964	Blackwell	4	14	1987	Saunton	8½	6½
1965	Burnham & Berrow	7	11	1988	Nottinghamshire	6	9
1966	Olton	7½	10½	1989	Broadstone	5½	9½
1967	Burnham & Berrow	6½	11½	1990	Kings Norton	4	11
1968	Harborne	3½	14½	1991	Burnham & Berrow	8	7
1969	Burnham & Berrow	9½	8½	1992	Northants County	6½	8½
1970	Blackwell	11	7	Results to date		16	28

Records of the Dorset Players
(Dorset represented in 26 of the 44 matches played)

		Played	Won	Halved	Lost			Played	Won	Halved	Lost
G J Butler	(59-72)	20	6	1	13	J Leggett	(1981)	2	1	0	1
R A Budd	(1966)	2	1	1	0	E Millward	(50-54)	6	2	2	2
J Calver	(75/76)	4	0	1	3	P McMullen	(1988)	2	0	0	2
S Edgley	(86)	2	1	1	0	H Neilson	(1953)	2	0	0	2
R Francis	(78/80)	4	0	2	2	J Nash	(72-89)	6	4	0	2
R E Garrett	(50-54)	6	1	1	4	R G Peach	(55-63)	10	4	2	4
M R Gardner	(52-62)	8	3	2	3	W G Peach	(72-74)	4	0	2	2
J Gordon	(1984)	2	0	0	2	W Raymond	(1980)	2	1	0	1
D M Holmes	(63-64)	4	0	0	4	F Smith	(1950)	2	1	1	0
R Hearn	(1984)	2	1	0	1	P Sanders	(1955)	2	0	0	2
D Jeffreys	(1981)	2	0	1	1	P Shillington	(1969)	2	2	0	0
R Lawford	(55-72)	10	2	1	7	I Sparkes	(1983)	2	0	0	2
K Longmore	(60-65)	6	1	2	3	V Weldon	(1925)	2	1	0	1

Burnham & Berrow
7th September 1925

C L Chard & Hon. D. Scott		½	v	C Bretherton & A D Williams		½
J H Baker & V Weldon	5/4	1	v	R P Humphries & J P Humphries		0
S L Dickinson & R G Cleveland	1/0	1	v	S C Craven & Rev. Foster Pegg		0
V K Whetstone & R A Riddell	5/3	1	v	J A Morton & F A Byrne		0
G C Brooks & C H Young	8/6	1	v	D Clayton & J Stockwin		0
		4½				½
Chard		0	v	Bretherton	1/0	1
Dickinson		0	v	R Humphries	8/7	1
Baker	8/7	1	v	Craven		0
Scott		0	v	Foster Pegg	2/1	1
Weldon		0	v	Williams	3/2	1
Whetstone		0	v	J Humphries	3/2	1
Brooks	6/5	1	v	Morton		0
Young	5/4	1	v	Stockwin		0
Cleveland	5/4	1	v	Clayton		0
Riddell	2/1	1	v	Byrne		0
		5				5
Grand Total		9½				5½

Burnham & Berrow
9th July 1950

(Captain: J S Ruttle)				(Captain: H J Roberts)		
J Payne & E J Poole	3/2	1	v	H J Roberts & J H Mitchley		0
E B Millward & R E Garrett		½	v	E W Fiddian & N A Seers		½
W S Wise & J W Harrison	7/6	1	v	S Lunt & W M Robb		0
R N Jutsum & G T Irlam		½	v	J M Urry & D M G Sutherland		½
J W D Goodban & E D Trapnell		0	v	C H Beamish & R Storey	4/3	1
D I Stirk & F Smith	2/1	1	v	P Squire & G B Wolstenholme		0
		4				2
Payne	2/0	1	v	Beamish		0
Millward		½	v	Fiddian		½
Wise		½	v	Lunt		½
Jutsum	2/1	1	v	Mitchley		0
Harrison	1/0	1	v	Roberts		0
Garrett		0	v	Sutherland	4/2	1
Poole	3/2	1	v	Urry		0
Stirk	1/0	1	v	Robb		0
Irlam	4/3	1	v	Wolstenholme		0
Goodban	4/3	1	v	Storey		0
Trapnell		½	v	Squire		½
Smith		½	v	Seers		½
		9				3
Grand Total		13				5

Little Aston
9th October 1926

S L Dickinson & C L Gordon Steward		0	v	C Bretherton & R W Lavi	4/3	1
J H Baker & G C Brooks		0	v	S L Lunt & T P Perkins	3/1	1
C H Young & R D Howard		0	v	C S Buckley & C J Reece	2/1	1
R G Cleveland & H C Hull		0	v	A E Mainwaring & H Arnold	1/0	1
R A Riddell & W H Anderson		0	v	F Scarf & W Archdale	4/2	1
		0				5
Dickinson	3/2	1	v	Bretherton		0
Brooks		0	v	Lunt	6/5	1
Gordon Steward		0	v	Perkins	2/1	1
Young		0	v	Lavi	2/1	1
Baker		0	v	Buckley	4/3	1
Cleveland		0	v	Reece	6/5	1
Howard	3/2	1	v	Arnold		0
Hull		0	v	Scarf	3/2	1
Riddell	6/4	1	v	Archdale		0
Anderson		0	v	Mainwaring	5/4	1
		3				7
Grand Total		3				12

Blackwell
15th April 1951

(Captain: J S Ruttle)				(Captain: H J Roberts)		
J Payne & E J Poole		0	v	H J Roberts & J S Mitchley	1/0	1
E B Millward & R E Garrett		0	v	E W Fiddian & N A Seers	2/1	1
W S Wise & J W Harrison	4/3	1	v	D M G Sutherland & J M Urry		0
R N Jutsum & G T Irlam		0	v	W M Robb & S L Elliott	4/3	1
D I Stirk & E D Trapnell		0	v	W L Smart & M B Morgan	2/1	1
L C Lake & J W R Swayne		0	v	G Mills & R Storey	1/0	1
		1				5
Payne	1/0	1	v	Fiddian		0
Millward		0	v	Roberts	5/4	1
Wise	1/0	1	v	Sutherland		0
Jutsum		0	v	Mitchley	7/5	1
Harrison	5/4	1	v	Robb		0
Garrett	3/1	1	v	Urry		0
Poole		0	v	Seers	2/1	1
Stirk		0	v	Smart	3/2	1
Irlam	2/1	1	v	Elliott		0
Trapnell	3/2	1	v	Morgan		0
Lake	1/0	1	v	Mills		0
Swayne		0	v	Storey	3/2	1
		7				5
Grand Total		8				10

Burnham & Berrow
28th September 1952

(Captain: J S Ruttle)				(Captain: H J Roberts)		
J O M Hill & G T Irlam	2/1	1	v	H J Roberts & W M Robb		0
J Payne & E J Poole	3/2	1	v	J R Butterworth & K R Frazier		0
W S Wise & M Swanston		0	v	M B Morgan & J B Fisher	2/0	1
M C Swift & G Platts		0	v	A Pullar & D M G Sutherland	7/6	1
D I Stirk & E D Trapnell		0	v	E W Fiddian & N A Seers	2/1	1
M R Gardner & W P Williams	5/3	1	v	W E Scott & C V Grafton		0
		3				3
Hill	5/4	1	v	Roberts		0
Payne	1/0	1	v	Morgan		0
Wise		0	v	Butterworth	2/1	1
Platts	1/0	1	v	Frazier		0
Irlam	2/0	1	v	Robb		0
Poole		0	v	Pullar	3/1	1
Swift		½	v	Sutherland		½
Stirk	1/0	1	v	Seers		0
Gardner		½	v	Fiddian		½
Swanston		0	v	Fisher	3/2	1
Williams		½	v	Scott		½
Trapnell		0	v	Grafton	1/0	1
		6½				5½
Grand Total		**9½**				**8½**

Ferndown
18th July 1954

(Captain: J S Ruttle)				(Captain: J L Morgan)		
E B Millward & R C Champion	2/1	1	v	J L Morgan & G B Wolstenholme		0
G C Griffiths & W S Wise		0	v	C Stowe & J Bailey	7/6	1
R E Garrett & G F Macpherson		0	v	J R Butterworth & K R Frazier	5/4	1
M C Swift & M Swanston		0	v	R Pattinson & R Hobbis	2/1	1
G T Irlam & E J Poole		0	v	J M Urry & A E Shepperson	2/1	1
L C Lake & E D Trapnell	3/2	1	v	P Skerritt & G G Gibberson		0
		2				4
Millward	1/0	1	v	C Stowe		0
Griffiths		0	v	Morgan	2/1	1
Wise		0	v	Butterworth	2/1	1
Swift	1/0	1	v	Skerritt		0
Champion		0	v	Pattinson	3/2	1
Garrett		0	v	Wolstenholme	2/1	1
Irlam		0	v	Urry	3/1	1
Poole	1/0	1	v	Frazier		0
Swanston	2/1	1	v	Bailey		0
Lake		0	v	Shepperson	2/1	1
Macpherson		½	v	Hobbis		½
Trapnell	2/0	1	v	Gibberson		0
		5½				6½
Grand Total		**7½**				**10½**

Beau Desert
19th July 1953

(Captain: J S Ruttle)				(Captain: H J Roberts)		
H C Neilson & W P Williams		0	v	C Stowe & H J Roberts	5/4	1
G T Irlam & E J Poole		0	v	J L Morgan & F W G Church	3/2	1
E D Trapnell & D I Stirk		0	v	J R Butterworth & E Walton	2/1	1
M Swanston & R A Black		0	v	J M Urry & D M G Sutherland	3/2	1
M C Swift & G Platts		0	v	L R Gracey & C H V Elliott	3/1	1
G F Macpherson & W Meredith		0	v	J B Fisher & J Bailey	2/1	1
		0				6
Neilson		0	v	Morgan	5/4	1
Irlam		0	v	Stowe	4/3	1
Williams		0	v	Roberts	5/3	1
Poole		0	v	Butterworth	4/3	1
Trapnell		0	v	Walton	4/3	1
Stirk	2/1	1	v	Sutherland		0
Swanston		0	v	Urry	2/0	1
Black		0	v	Fisher	6/5	1
Swift		0	v	Gracey	3/2	1
Platts	4/3	1	v	Elliott		0
Macpherson		0	v	Church	1/0	1
Meredith		0	v	Bailey	6/5	1
		2				10
Grand Total		**2**				**16**

Little Aston
17th July 1955

(Captain: W S J Watson)				(Captain: J L Morgan)		
R Lawford & P Sanders		0	v	R Bayliss & J L Morgan	3/2	1
M C Swift & A J Combes		0	v	J H Butterworth & R Hobbis	2/1	1
W S Wise & G T Irlam	1/0	1	v	D E Gardner & D Dailey		0
R C Champion & E D Trapnell		0	v	J B Fisher & G B Wolstenholme	2/1	1
G C Griffiths & D S Maunsell		½	v	H J Roberts & A E Shepperson		½
R G Peach & G Platts		0	v	P Skerritt & E Walton	6/5	1
		1½				4½
Lawford		0	v	Morgan	3/2	1
Swift		0	v	Roberts	1/0	1
Wise		0	v	Wolstenholme	1/0	1
Champion		0	v	Butterworth	1/0	1
Sanders		0	v	Shepperson	2/1	1
Maunsell	1/0	1	v	Gardner		0
Combes		0	v	Dailey	6/5	1
Trapnell		0	v	Bayliss	1/0	1
Griffiths		0	v	Fisher	2/1	1
Platts	2/1	1	v	Hobbis		0
Peach		½	v	Skerritt		½
Irlam		0	v	Walton	2/1	1
		2½				9½
Grand Total		**4**				**14**

Burnham & Berrow
15th July 1956

(Captain: C H Young)				(Captain: J M Urry)		
E J Poole & R C Champion		0	v	H J Roberts & J R Butterworth	3/2	1
R G Peach & R N Jutsum	4/2	1	v	J C Beharrell & R B Bayliss		0
E D Trapnell & M C Swift		½	v	M R S Lunt & F L Wilkinson		½
M R Gardner & R Lawford		½	v	C H Beamish & R P Yates		½
G T Irlam & G N Casson	2/1	1	v	K R Frazier & R J Brereton		0
G Platts & D S Maunsell		0	v	J M Urry & M Edwards	5/3	1
		3				3
Peach	2/1	1	v	Beharrell		0
Poole		0	v	Roberts	2/0	1
Lawford	4/3	1	v	Butterworth		0
Trapnell	1/0	1	v	Bayliss		0
Jutsum	1/0	1	v	Wilkinson		0
Gardner		0	v	Lunt	5/4	1
Champion	1/0	1	v	Beamish		0
Swift		½	v	Frazier		½
Irlam	2/1	1	v	Urry		0
Platts	4/2	1	v	Edwards		0
Maunsell		½	v	Yates		½
Casson		0	v	Brereton	6/5	1
		8				4
Grand Total		**11**				**7**

Burnham & Berrow
12th July 1959

(Captain: R G Peach)				(Captain: F W G Church)		
R N Jutsum & E D Trapnell		0	v	A E Shepperson & A F Bussell	3/2	1
R C Champion & E N Davies		0	v	M S R Lunt & H J Roberts	4/3	1
R G Peach & G Butler		0	v	M H Edwards & J C Beharrell	1/0	1
K P Harris & R J Gardiner	2/1	1	v	J R Butterworth & F W G Church		0
G T Irlam & D M Payne	1/0	1	v	D M G Sutherland & G C Marks		0
W G Meredith & J M Clarke		0	v	R W Sandilands & R A Jowle	3/2	1
		2				4
Jutsum		½	v	Lunt		½
Champion		½	v	Shepperson		½
Trapnell		0	v	Bussell	7/6	1
Irlam		0	v	Roberts	2/0	1
Butler	2/1	1	v	Marks		0
Gardiner	6/5	1	v	Beharrell		0
Davies	1/0	1	v	Butterworth		0
Peach	1/0	1	v	Sutherland		0
Meredith		0	v	Edwards	3/2	1
Harris		0	v	Jowle	5/4	1
Payne		½	v	Sandilands		½
Clarke		0	v	Church	5/4	1
		5½				6½
Grand Total		**7½**				**10½**

Copt Heath
14th July 1957

(Captain: G F Macpherson)				(Captain: J M Urry)		
W S Wise & M R Gardner		0	v	G B Wolstenholme & M S R Lunt	3/1	1
R G Peach & R N Jutsum		0	v	E Walton & H J Roberts	3/2	1
G C Griffiths & D Gould		0	v	S L Elliott & G G Gibberson	4/3	1
L C Lake & G T Irlam		½	v	E W Fiddian & M Edwards		½
G N Casson & R Lawford		0	v	D Gardner & J M Urry	3/2	1
G Platts & D S Maunsell		½	v	A W Pullar & A W Holmes		½
		1				5
Wise		0	v	Walton	4/3	1
Peach		½	v	Wolstenholme		½
Jutsum		½	v	Roberts		½
Irlam		0	v	Lunt	4/3	1
Lake	3/2	1	v	Elliott		0
Lawford		½	v	Gardner		½
Gardner		0	v	Fiddian	1/0	1
Griffiths		0	v	Gibberson	4/3	1
Platts		0	v	Pullar	4/3	1
Casson		0	v	Urry	2/1	1
Gould		0	v	Edwards	2/1	1
Maunsell		0	v	Holmes	4/3	1
		2½				9½
Grand Total		**3½**				**14½**

Worcester
3rd July 1960

(Captain: L C Lake)				(Captain: H J Roberts)		
K Longmore & G J Butler		½	v	H J Roberts & J R Butterworth		½
R C Champion & T Griffin		0	v	R W Sandilands & A Sheppard	1/0	1
R N Jutsum & P O Green	2/1	1	v	G C Marks & J B Fisher		0
D I Stirk & R J Kelley		½	v	R A Jowle & P D Kelley		½
R P F Brown & J M Clarke	4/3	1	v	K R Frazier & A D Crafts		0
I R Patey & D M Payne		0	v	M B Morgan & J M Leach	2/1	1
		3				3
Butler		0	v	Roberts	2/0	1
Champion		0	v	Sheppard	2/1	1
Stirk		0	v	Butterworth	4/3	1
Longmore		0	v	Sandilands	4/3	1
Jutsum		0	v	Fisher	3/2	1
Kelley		0	v	Marks	2/1	1
Green	6/5	1	v	Jowle		0
Griffin		0	v	Crafts	6/5	1
Clarke	3/2	1	v	Kelley		0
Patey		0	v	Frazier	3/1	1
Payne		0	v	Morgan	1/0	1
Brown		0	v	Leach	1/0	1
		2				10
Grand Total		**5**				**13**

Burnham & Berrow
14th May 1961

(Captain: L C Lake)				(Captain: A W Pullar)		
R C Champion & G T Irlam	2/1	1	v	M S R Lunt & A W Holmes		0
R N Jutsum & E D Trapnell	2/0	1	v	A W Pullar & H J Roberts		0
G J Butler & K Longmore	3/2	1	v	M H Edwards & A D Crafts		0
P O Green & J J Spencer	3/2	1	v	A Sheppard & J R Butterworth		0
R P F Brown & D M Brown	4/2	1	v	R W Sandilands & G C Marks		0
R J Gardiner & L C Lake	1/0	1	v	J B Fisher & R A Jowle		0
		6				0
Trapnell	1/0	1	v	Lunt		0
Irlam	2/1	1	v	Roberts		0
Champion		0	v	Pullar	3/1	1
Jutsum		0	v	Holmes	2/0	1
Green	2/1	1	v	Edwards		0
Butler	2/1	1	v	Sheppard		0
Longmore		0	v	Crafts	4/3	1
Spencer	1/0	1	v	Sandilands		0
Brown, R		½	v	Marks		½
Gardiner		½	v	Butterworth		½
Lake	1/0	1	v	Fisher		0
Brown, D	3/2	1	v	Jowle		0
		8				4
Grand Total		**14**				**4**

Olton
1st July 1962

(Captain: G C Griffiths)				(Captain: A W Pullar)		
P O Green & J W D Goodban		0	v	M S R Lunt & A W Holmes	2/0	1
G N Bicknell & D M Payne		0	v	H J Roberts & R A Jowle	5/4	1
G T Irlam & W G Meredith		0	v	A W Pullar & I R Fernyhough	5/4	1
D I Stirk & R B Redfern		0	v	G G Gibberson & J C Beharrell	2/0	1
I R Patey & G C Griffiths		0	v	P D Kelley & J R Butterworth	1/0	1
M R Gardner & J M Clarke	1/0	1	v	R D Christian & J B Flanders		0
		1				5
Bicknell		0	v	Lunt	1/0	1
Green	1/0	1	v	Holmes		0
Griffiths		0	v	Gibberson	2/1	1
Irlam		0	v	Fernyhough	3/2	1
Stirk		0	v	Jowle	4/3	1
Redfern	2/0	1	v	Pullar		0
Goodban	1/0	1	v	Roberts		0
Payne		0	v	Butterworth	2/1	1
Meredith		0	v	Beharrell	4/2	1
Patey		0	v	Kelley	1/0	1
Clarke		0	v	Christian	2/0	1
Gardner	1/0	1	v	Flanders		0
		4				8
Grand Total		**5**				**13**

Burnham & Berrow
30th June 1963

(Captain: M R Gardner)				(Captain: R P Yates)		
R N Jutsum & R J Gardiner	2/1	1	v	J R Butterworth & R A Jowle		0
G N Bicknell & I R Patey	4/3	1	v	A W Holmes & G G Gibberson		0
R B Redfern & G J Butler		0	v	G C Marks & I Wheater	6/5	1
D I Stirk & E D Trapnell	2/0	1	v	MD Tweddell & P D Kelley		0
R G Peach & D M Holmes		0	v	D P Cross & R P Yates	3/2	1
J N Littler & D M Brown		0	v	M J Skerritt & I Fernyhough	2/0	1
		3				3
Jutsum	3/2	1	v	Butterworth		0
Gardiner	3/2	1	v	Jowle		0
Butler		0	v	Holmes	2/0	1
Bicknell		0	v	Gibberson	1/0	1
Trapnell		0	v	Marks	5/3	1
Redfern		0	v	Tweddell	2/1	1
Littler	1/0	1	v	Wheater		0
Patey		0	v	Kelley	1/0	1
Peach	4/3	1	v	Skerritt		0
Holmes		0	v	Cross	1/0	1
Stirk		0	v	Fernyhough	1/0	1
Brown		0	v	Yates	2/0	1
		4				8
Grand Total		**7**				**11**

Blackwell
28th June 1964

(Captain: R N Jutsum)				(Captain: R P Yates)		
G T Irlam & B W Barnes		0	v	M S R Lunt & P D Kelley	4/3	1
R N Jutsum & R J Gardiner		0	v	G C Marks & I Fernyhough	1/0	1
J W D Goodban & B G Steer	2/1	1	v	N A Newbitt & R Hobbis		0
R B Redfern & D I Stirk		0	v	R P Yates & A Thomson	2/1	1
G J Butler & D E Jones	3/2	1	v	A W Holmes & J Leach		0
D M Holmes & A J Combes		0	v	R G Aitken & R W Sandilands	5/4	1
		2				4
Barnes		0	v	Newbitt	7/5	1
Irlam		0	v	Lunt	2/1	1
Gardiner		0	v	Kelley	2/1	1
Jutsum		0	v	Yates	3/2	1
Butler		0	v	Marks	4/3	1
Redfern		0	v	Fernyhough	2/1	1
Stirk	4/3	1	v	Hobbis		0
Goodban		0	v	Holmes	7/6	1
Holmes		0	v	Sandilands	2/1	1
Steer		0	v	Leach	3/2	1
Jones	3/1	1	v	Aitken		0
Combes		0	v	Thomson	4/3	1
		2				10
Grand Total		**4**				**14**

Burnham & Berrow
18th July 1965

(Captain: J W D Goodban)				(Captain: R P Yates)		
R N Jutsum & B G Steer	2/1	1	v	P D Kelley & A Smith		0
R J Gardiner & J A Bloxham	2/1	1	v	T R Shingler & R G Aitken		0
G T Irlam & T Griffin	4/3	1	v	R P Yates & H J Roberts		0
G J Butler & K Longmore		0	v	R D James & M G Lee	2/1	1
R B Redfern & E T Jackson		0	v	J A Fisher & N A Newbitt	5/4	1
P Edgington & R E Searle	4/2	1	v	D P Cross & R G Hiatt		0
		4				2
Bloxham		0	v	Kelley	1/0	1
Gardiner	1/0	1	v	Shingler		0
Jutsum		0	v	Smith	1/0	1
Steer		0	v	Roberts	3/2	1
Butler		0	v	Aitken	2/1	1
Redfern	3/2	1	v	Yates		0
Irlam		0	v	James	5/4	1
Edgington		0	v	Lee	2/1	1
Longmore		½	v	Newbitt		½
Griffin		½	v	Fisher		½
Jackson		0	v	Cross	1/0	1
Searle		0	v	Hiatt	4/2	1
		3				9
Grand Total		**7**				**11**

Burnham & Berrow
16th July 1967

(Captain: A J Combes)				(Captain: P Squire)		
P J Yeo & R J Radway		0	v	M S R Lunt & P D Kelley	4/3	1
R J Gardiner & G T Irlam		0	v	G C Marks & R D James	4/3	1
J A Bloxham & D J Carroll	1/0	1	v	M A Payne & R G Hiatt		0
T B Jones & J N May		0	v	R G Aitken & W Ridgeway	2/1	1
G K Baker & E T Jackson		0	v	M D Tweddell & A N Forrester	1/0	1
P Edgington & R A Combes	7/6	1	v	T M Estrop & J Chaplain		0
		2				4
Yeo	4/3	1	v	Marks		0
Radway	4/3	1	v	Lunt		0
Bloxham		0	v	Kelley	3/2	1
Gardiner	5/4	1	v	Payne		0
Irlam		0	v	James	1/0	1
Baker		0	v	Forrester	1/0	1
Jones		0	v	Aitken	5/4	1
May		0	v	Hiatt	5/4	1
Edgington	2/1	1	v	Estrop		0
Carroll		½	v	Ridgeway		½
Combes		0	v	Chaplain	3/2	1
Jackson		0	v	Tweddell	3/2	1
		4½				7½
Grand Total		**6½**				**11½**

Olton
17th July 1966

(Captain: G T Irlam)				(Captain: P Squire)		
G T Irlam & D E Jones		0	v	M S R Lunt & P D Kelley	7/6	1
R B Redfern & B G Steer		0	v	M G Lee & G C Marks	4/3	1
G J Butler & R A Combes	3/2	1	v	M A Payne & J B Fisher		0
J A Bloxham & D J Carroll		0	v	T R Shingler & A Forrester	5/3	1
P Edgington & J W Bradley	1/0	1	v	R G Hiatt & P R Batchelor		0
D R Hemming & R A Budd	1/0	1	v	R L Mansell & R G Aitken		0
		3				3
Jones		0	v	Lunt	8/7	1
Redfern		0	v	Lee	1/0	1
Bloxham	1/0	1	v	Kelley		0
Steer		0	v	Payne	2/1	1
Irlam		0	v	Marks	4/3	1
Butler		0	v	Shingler	3/2	1
Carroll		½	v	Forrester		½
Edgington	5/4	1	v	Hiatt		0
Budd		½	v	Batchelor		½
Hemming		½	v	Fisher		½
Bradley	3/2	1	v	Mansell		0
Combes		0	v	Aitken	1/0	1
		4½				7½
Grand Total		**7½**				**10½**

Harborne
14th July 1968

(Captain: A C Morgan)				(Captain: R J W Baldwin)		
R Lawford & P J Yeo		0	v	G C Marks & C R J Ibbotson	6/5	1
B G Steer & R J Radway		0	v	A J Thomson & P D Kelley	4/3	1
G M Brand & D J Carroll		½	v	A N Forrester & M S R Lunt		½
A J Hill & R B Williams		0	v	A Bussell & A Smith	2/1	1
R A Combes & R E Searle		0	v	R G Hiatt & J A Fisher	5/4	1
R J Gardiner & J Long		0	v	T R Shingler & M A Payne	2/0	1
		½				5½
Steer		0	v	Marks	4/3	1
Yeo		0	v	Forrester	2/1	1
Brand		0	v	Thomson	4/3	1
Lawford	2/1	1	v	Bussell		0
Williams		0	v	Kelley	1/0	1
Radway		0	v	Lunt	1/0	1
Gardiner		0	v	Ibbotson	4/3	1
Carroll		0	v	Hiatt	3/2	1
Searle	5/4	1	v	Smith		0
Combes	2/1	1	v	Fisher		0
Long		0	v	Payne	5/4	1
Hill		0	v	Shingler	1/0	1
		3				9
Grand Total		**3½**				**14½**

Burnham & Berrow
(No record of date)

(Captain: E D Trapnell)				(Captain: R J W Baldwin)		
D J Carroll & L F Millar		0	v	P D Kelley & A N Forrester	3/2	1
D W Frame & P J Yeo		0	v	J A Fisher & R G Hiatt	1/0	1
R B Williams & B G Steer	3/2	1	v	K Hodgkinson & R D James		0
G J Butler & P G Shillington	1/0	1	v	R Naylor & R A Jowle		0
B F McCallum & R E Searle	2/1	1	v	C R J Ibbotson & P M Baxter		0
R J Gardiner & A G Clay		0	v	R Aitken & T R Shingler	2/1	1
		3				3
Carroll		½	v	Forrester		½
Williams	5/3	1	v	Fisher		0
Millar		0	v	Kelley	3/2	1
Yeo		0	v	James	3/2	1
Frame	2/1	1	v	Hiatt		0
Steer		½	v	Hodgkinson		½
Butler		0	v	Naylor	2/1	1
Shillington	4/3	1	v	Shingler		0
McCallum	3/2	1	v	Ibbotson		0
Searle	1/0	1	v	Aitken		0
Clay		½	v	Baxter		½
Gardiner		0	v	Jowle	3/2	1
		6½				5½
Grand Total		**9½**				**8½**

Burnham & Berrow
11th July 1971

(Captain: D I Stirk)				(Captain: A F Bussell)		
J A Bloxham & D J Carroll	2/1	1	v	G C Marks & P D Kelley		0
R Abbott & P J Yeo	7/6	1	v	P H Moody & E W Hammond		0
P Berry & R E Searle	1/0	1	v	T R Shingler & J Toddington		0
L F Millar & B G Steer		0	v	J A Fisher & J F Graham	4/3	1
P Edgington & B F McCallum	2/1	1	v	A F Bussell & R D James		0
R J Gardiner & G J Butler		0	v	T W B Homer & A N Dathan	1/0	1
		4				2
Bloxham		0	v	Marks	1/0	1
Berry	6/5	1	v	Fisher		0
Yeo	1/0	1	v	Moody		0
Abbott		0	v	Kelley	1/0	1
Millar	6/5	1	v	Toddington		0
Searle	1/0	1	v	Shingler		0
Steer	3/2	1	v	James		0
Carroll		0	v	Homer	1/0	1
Edgington	2/1	1	v	Dathan		0
Gardiner		0	v	Bussell	2/1	1
McCallum	6/4	1	v	Graham		0
Butler		0	v	Hammond	2/1	1
		7				5
Grand Total		**11**				**7**

Blackwell
12th July 1970

(Captain: R J Gardiner)				(Captain: A F Bussell)		
P Edgington & B F McCallum	2/1	1	v	G C Marks & M A Payne		0
D J Carroll & P Berry	1/0	1	v	P D Kelley & K H Hodgkinson		0
A G Clay & R J Gardiner		0	v	A F Bussell & R D James	5/4	1
R B Williams & G K Baker		0	v	M W L Hampton & T R Shingler	3/1	1
B G Steer & R Lawford		0	v	J Mayell & R Hobbis	4/3	1
A J Hill & J K Graveney	1/0	1	v	J A Fisher & P Dawson		0
		3				3
Carroll		0	v	Kelley	3/2	1
McCallum		0	v	Marks	6/4	1
Clay		½	v	Hampton		½
Berry	4/2	1	v	James		0
Edgington	4/3	1	v	Payne		0
Williams		½	v	Bussell		½
Gardiner	2/1	1	v	Hodgkinson		0
Baker	5/4	1	v	Dawson		0
Steer	5/4	1	v	Mayell		0
Lawford		0	v	Shingler	3/2	1
Hill	2/1	1	v	Fisher		0
Graveney	2/1	1	v	Hobbis		0
		8				4
Grand Total		**11**				**7**

Olton
9th July 1972

(Captain: K Longmore)				(Captain: T R Shingler)		
D J Carrol & R J Gardiner		0	v	G C Marks & A Smith	4/3	1
B G Steer & W P Hucker		0	v	R D James & T R Shingler	1/0	1
R Lawford & G J Butler		0	v	J A Fisher & P H Hinton	5/4	1
L F Millar & P A Gilbert	1/0	1	v	C Ciesielski & R Larratt		0
J Nash & J H Davis	4/3	1	v	D J Russell & M Hopkinson		0
W G Peach & P J Lowe		0	v	D Humphries & M A Smith	7/5	1
		2				4
Carroll		0	v	Marks	6/5	1
Steer		0	v	James	2/1	1
Lawford		0	v	Fisher	4/3	1
Gardiner		0	v	Shingler	3/2	1
Millar		½	v	Smith		½
Butler		0	v	Hinton	1/0	1
Nash		0	v	Larratt	5/4	1
Hucker		0	v	Humphries	4/3	1
Lowe		0	v	Ciesielski	4/3	1
Davis		0	v	Smith	1/0	1
Peach		½	v	Russell		½
Gilbert	2/1	1	v	Hopkinson		0
		2				10
Grand Total		**4**				**14**

Burnham & Berrow
15th July 1973

(Captain: J K R Graveney)				(Captain: T R Shingler)		
L F Millar & W P Hucker		0	v	G C Marks & K H Hodgkinson	3/2	1
J A Bloxham & D J Carroll	½		v	D J Russell & R Larratt		½
R E Searle & R J Radway		0	v	J Mayell & T R Shingler	1/0	1
R Abbott & B G Steer	3/2	1	v	J A Fisher & P H Hinton		0
J J Ward & P Edgington		0	v	D Humphries & P J Holt	2/1	1
R Tugwell & J H Davis		0	v	P M Baxter & F W Wood	1/0	1
		1½				4½
Bloxham	1/0	1	v	Marks		0
Millar		½	v	Russell		½
Carroll		½	v	Hodgkinson		½
Searle		0	v	Fisher	3/1	1
Radway		0	v	Larratt	2/1	1
Abbott		½	v	Mayell		½
Steer		0	v	Shingler	7/6	1
Edgington		0	v	Hinton	3/2	1
Davis	1/0	1	v	Baxter		0
Tugwell	1/0	1	v	Holt		0
Ward	5/4	1	v	Humphries		0
Hucker	2/0	1	v	Wood		0
		6½				5½
Grand Total		**8**				**10**

Burnham & Berrow
13th July 1975

(Captain: G K Baker)				(Captain: R D James)		
R Abbott & C S Mitchell	1/0	1	v	G C Marks & A W B Lyle		0
G T Irlam & L F Millar		0	v	M A Poxon & P McEvoy	1/0	1
B G Steer & J W Bradley	2/1	1	v	A N Dathan & R D James		0
S R Butler & P A Gilbert	½		v	P D Kelley & K H Hodgkinson		½
S Potter & J Calver	½		v	T J Giles & A Carman		½
A P Vicary & J S Bridge		0	v	P M Baxter & M A Smith	3/2	1
		3				3
Abbott		0	v	Poxon	3/2	1
Steer		0	v	Marks	5/4	1
Mitchell	4/3	1	v	Lyle		0
Irlam		0	v	James	1/0	1
Bradley		½	v	McEvoy		½
Butler		0	v	Kelley	4/3	1
Millar		0	v	Dathan	1/0	1
Bridge	3/2	1	v	Hodgkinson		0
Gilbert		0	v	Giles	2/1	1
Potter	3/2	1	v	Carman		0
Calver		0	v	Baxter	2/1	1
Vicary		0	v	Smith	2/1	1
		3½				8½
Grand Total		**6½**				**11½**

Olton
14th July 1974

(Captain: G N Bicknell)				(Captain: T R Shingler)		
B G Steer & R Abbott		0	v	R D James & M Poxon	1/0	1
D J Carroll & C S Mitchell		0	v	M James & B Jones	1/0	1
P A Gilbert & J W Bradley		0	v	K H Hodgkinson & P Hinton	1/0	1
L F Millar & M Bagg		0	v	J Langridge & T R Shingler	3/2	1
B M Townsend & W G Peach		0	v	A W B Lyle & P M Baxter	4/3	1
S R Davidson & A P Vicary	4/3	1	v	P Holt & R Hiatt		0
		1				5
Mitchell		½	v	Hodgkinson		½
Abbott	4/3	1	v	Poxon		0
Carroll		½	v	Lyle		½
Steer		0	v	James, M	5/4	1
Gilbert	2/0	1	v	James, R		0
Bradley		0	v	Jones	2/0	1
Millar		0	v	Langridge	4/2	1
Bagg		0	v	Shingler	2/1	1
Townsend	2/1	1	v	Hinton		0
Peach		½	v	Baxter		½
Vicary	1/0	1	v	Holt		0
Davidson		½	v	Hiatt		½
		6				6
Grand Total		**7**				**11**

Blackwell
11th July 1976

(Captain: R Lawford)				(Captain: R D James)		
G T Irlam & G K Baker		0	v	P Downes & A W B Lyle	4/3	1
R Abbott & R H P Knott	½		v	P McEvoy & T Giles		½
S Dunlop & J W Bradley		0	v	M A Payne & I T Simpson	3/2	1
B G Steer & R J Ibbetson		0	v	R D James & R D Christian	4/3	1
S Potter & J Calver		0	v	R R W Davenport & P G Shillington	1/0	1
		½				4½
Irlam		½	v	Downes		½
Dunlop		0	v	Lyle	4/3	1
Abbott	2/0	1	v	McEvoy		0
Knot		0	v	Giles	2/1	1
Steer		0	v	Davenport	5/4	1
Baker		0	v	Payne	6/4	1
Potter		0	v	Simpson	5/4	1
Bradley		½	v	Shillington		½
Ibbetson	2/1	1	v	Christian		0
Calver		0	v	James	2/1	1
		3				7
Grand Total		**3½**				**11½**

Burnham & Berrow
10th July 1977

(Captain: R B Robertson)				(Captain: R D James)		
J W Bradley & B G Steer		0	v	P Downes & G C Marks	2/1	1
M E Lewis & S Dunlop	2/1	1	v	R D James & T Shingler		0
R Abbott & G Brand		0	v	A Smith & C Banks	1/0	1
D J Carroll & J Calver	3/2	1	v	M Biddle & E Hammond		0
B M Townsend & R E Searle	5/4	1	v	J Mayell & C Poxon		0
		3				2
Brand	4/3	1	v	Downes		0
Dunlop	4/3	1	v	Marks		0
Steer		½	v	Smith		½
Bradley		0	v	Shingler	3/1	1
Lewis	1/0	1	v	Banks		0
Abbott		0	v	James	3/2	1
Searle	2/0	1	v	Biddle		0
Carroll	1/0	1	v	Poxon		0
Townsend		0	v	Hammond	2/1	1
Calver	4/3	1	v	Mayell		0
		6½				3½
Grand Total		**9½**				**5½**

Burnham & Berrow
22nd July 1979

(Captain: P A Gilbert)				(Captain: J M H Mayell)		
S R Davidson & R D Broad		0	v	P Downes & A D Carman	2/1	1
B G Steer & N J Gunn		0	v	F Fernyhough & D Blakeman	5/4	1
R H P Knott & M E Jewell		0	v	J M H Mayell & T R Shingler	2/1	1
M R Lovett & P A Gilbert		0	v	C A Banks & I T Simpson	4/3	1
S Butler & C R Phillips		0	v	M A Smith & B Wheatley	3/2	1
		0				5
Davidson	5/4	1	v	Downes		0
Jewell		0	v	Carman	1/0	1
Broad	3/2	1	v	Shingler		0
Steer		½	v	Mayell		½
Knott	5/3	1	v	Simpson		0
Gilbert	2/1	1	v	Banks		0
Phillips		0	v	Fernyhough	2/1	1
Gunn		0	v	Blakeman	2/1	1
Butler	4/3	1	v	Smith		0
Lovett		0	v	Wheatley	4/3	1
		5½				4½
Grand Total		**5½**				**9½**

Copt Heath
2nd September 1978

(Captain: R Abbott)				(Captain: J Mayell)		
G Brand & C S Mitchell		0	v	P McEvoy & A Carman	4/3	1
R Abbott & S R Davidson		0	v	S Bennett & K Walters	1/0	1
P A Gilbert & A Lyddon	4/2	1	v	P Downes & T Allen		0
R A R Francis & R M W Drake		0	v	J Mayell & A Dathan	1/0	1
M E Jewell & R H P Knott		0	v	D Blakeman & M A Smith	1/0	1
		1				4
Brand		½	v	McEvoy		½
Mitchell		½	v	Downes		½
Abbott		½	v	Bennett		½
Francis		½	v	Waters		½
Lyddon		0	v	Allen	6/5	1
Jewell		0	v	Carman	3/1	1
Knott		0	v	Mayell	6/4	1
Drake		0	v	Blakeman	2/1	1
Davidson		0	v	Smith	3/2	1
Gilbert		0	v	Dathan	6/5	1
		2				8
Grand Total		**3**				**12**

Worcestershire
30th August 1980

(Captain: B G Steer)				(Captain: M A Smith)		
C S Mitchell & S R Davidson		0	v	E W Hammond & T M Allen	2/1	1
M G Symons & R H P Knott		0	v	S Gough & M A Smith	3/2	1
S Butler & J N Fleming	4/3	1	v	G R Krause & R J Hall		0
A Lyddon & M Boggia		½	v	R A Jowle & R A Lane		½
J Nash & W Raymond	2/1	1	v	G Broadbent & M Hassall		0
		2½				2½
Mitchell		½	v	Allen		½
Fleming	2/1	1	v	Hammond		0
Davidson	1/0	1	v	Gough		0
Symons	2/1	1	v	Smith		0
Butler	5/4	1	v	Jowle		0
Knott		½	v	Krause		½
Boggia	1/0	1	v	Hall		0
Nash		0	v	Broadbent	3/2	1
Lyddon		0	v	Lane	3/2	1
Raymond		0	v	Hassall	2/1	1
		6				4
Grand Total		**8½**				**6½**

Burnham & Berrow
29th August 1981

(Captain: G J Butler)				(Captain: M A Smith)		
M E Lewis & C S Mitchell	1/0	1	v	P M Baxter & R W Guy		0
A Sherborne & D Ray		½	v	A K Stubbs & D Boughey		½
A Lyddon & J R Hirst		½	v	R J Hall & G R Krause		½
M E Jewell & P Newcombe		½	v	M A Smith & D Gilford		½
J H A Leggett & D Jeffreys		0	v	N Stewart & N Tarratt	2/1	1
		2½				2½
Newcombe		0	v	Baxter	2/1	1
Mitchell	3/2	1	v	Stubbs		0
Sherborne		0	v	Guy	1/0	1
Lyddon	2/0	1	v	Stewart		0
Lewis	2/1	1	v	Boughey		0
Ray	4/3	1	v	Hall		0
Hirst		0	v	Krause	3/2	1
Leggett	2/1	1	v	Smith		0
Jewell	2/1	1	v	Gilford		0
Jeffreys		½	v	Tarratt		½
		6½				3½
Grand Total		**9**				**6**

Burnham & Berrow
20th August 1983

(Captain: D J Carroll)				(Captain: P M Baxter)		
A Sherborne & C S Mitchell	2/1	1	v	P Downes & G Krause		0
R E Searle & C S Edwards		0	v	C Poxon & D Boughey	4/3	1
M Bessell & A Lyddon		0	v	A Martinez & G Wolstenholme	2/1	1
P Newcombe & M G Symons	3/1	1	v	P M Baxter & T Leigh		0
M Edmunds & I Sparkes		0	v	P Benson & S Briddick	1/0	1
		2				3
Sherborne	2/1	1	v	Downes		0
Edwards		½	v	Poxon		½
Mitchell		0	v	Krause	2/1	1
Searle		½	v	Martinez		½
Lyddon	1/0	1	v	Baxter		0
Symons		½	v	Boughey		½
Bessell	4/3	1	v	Benson		0
Newcombe	2/1	1	v	Leigh		0
Sparkes		0	v	Wolstenholme	6/5	1
Edmunds	1/0	1	v	Briddick		0
		6½				3½
Grand Total		**8½**				**6½**

Kings Norton
28th August 1982

(Captain: A J Hill)				(Captain: P M Baxter)		
M Grieve & I Hewson		0	v	E Hammond & T Allen	4/2	1
P Newcombe & M G Symons		0	v	A Stubbs & D Blakeman	4/2	1
M Bessell & A J Hill	4/3	1	v	P Shaw & D Gilford		0
M E Jewell & K A Clark		0	v	G Broadbent & M Higgins	2/1	1
P Howlett & G Hedley		0	v	R Guy & R Lane	1/0	1
		1				4
Newcombe		0	v	Stubbs	3/2	1
Symons	4/2	1	v	Blakeman		0
Jewell		0	v	Allen	1/0	1
Hill		0	v	Broadbent	2/1	1
Clark		0	v	Gilford	4/3	1
Grieve		½	v	Higgins		½
Bessell		½	v	Hammond		½
Howlett	3/2	1	v	Guy		0
Hedley		0	v	Lane	2/1	1
Hewson	3/2	1	v	Shaw		0
		4				6
Grand Total		**5**				**10**

Redditch
11th August 1984

(Captain: J Calver)				(Captain: P M Baxter)		
A Sherborne & R Searle		½	v	D Eddiford & M Reynard		½
M Symons & C Edwards		½	v	G Wolstenholme & A Martinez		½
M Edmunds & M Blaber		0	v	K Valentine & J Vaughan	2/1	1
J Gordon & D Carroll		0	v	D McCart & S Riley	3/2	1
R Hearn & D Powell		0	v	D Boughey & C Radford	1/0	1
		1				4
Sherborne	3/2	1	v	Valentine		0
Blaber		0	v	Eddiford	5/4	1
Searle	3/2	1	v	Wolstenholme		0
Edwards	5/4	1	v	Martinez		0
Symons	2/1	1	v	McCart		0
Edmunds		½	v	Reynard		½
Gordon		0	v	Riley	2/1	1
Hearn	2/1	1	v	Boughey		0
Powell		0	v	Vaughan	2/1	1
Carroll		0	v	Radford	2/1	1
		5½				4½
Grand Total		**6½**				**8½**

Parkstone

5th October 1985

(Captain: J Bradley)				(Captain: J Bramley)		
D Powell & A Lyddon		0	v	G Wolstenhome & C Williamson	4/3	1
R Searle & J Langmead	3/2	1	v	D Eddiford & R Larwood		0
A Lawrence & C Phillips	3/2	1	v	P Sweetsur & I Baxter		0
C Edwards & N Holman	4/3	1	v	K Diss & D Beech		0
M Symons & P Newcombe	6/5	1	v	B Griffiths & W Painter		0
		4				1
Phillips	1/0	1	v	Wolstenholme		0
Lyddon		½	v	Williamson		½
Edwards		0	v	Eddiford	2/1	1
Powell		½	v	Sweetsur		½
Langmead	1/0	1	v	Griffiths		0
Searle		0	v	Diss	1/0	1
Symons	3/1	1	v	Beech		0
Newcombe		½	v	Larwood		½
Holman	2/0	1	v	Baxter		0
Lawrence		0	v	Painter	6/5	1
		5½				4½
Grand Total		**9½**				**5½**

Saunton

10th October 1987

(Captain: R H P Knott)				(Captain: R W Guy)		
P Newcombe & J Langmead	1/0	1	v	P Broadhurst & J Cook		0
A Nash & C Phillips		½	v	G Wolstenholme & P Sweetsur		½
G Clough & S Amor		0	v	K Diss & R Claydon	3/2	1
R White & R Broad		0	v	D Prosser & M Houghton	3/2	1
C Edwards & N Holman	2/1	1	v	T Seaton & J Feeney		0
		2½				2½
Newcombe		½	v	Broadhurst		½
Nash		0	v	Wolstenholme	3/2	1
Langmead		0	v	Cook	3/2	1
Edwards	1/0	1	v	Claydon		0
Phillips		0	v	Houghton	5/3	1
Clough	6/5	1	v	Sweetsur		0
Amor		½	v	Prosser		½
Holman	4/3	1	v	Diss		0
Broad	5/4	1	v	Feeney		0
Knott	4/3	1	v	Seaton		0
		6				4
Grand Total		**8½**				**6½**

Little Aston

11th October 1986

(Captain: B F McCallum)				(Captain: J F Bramley)		
J Langmead & M Symons		0	v	P Broadhurst & J Cook	4/3	1
C Phillips & P Clayton	1/0	1	v	C Poxon & D Eddiford		0
P Newcombe & C Edwards		0	v	G Wolstenholme & T Clarke	5/4	1
G Clough & S Amor		½	v	P Sweetsur & A Hare		½
S Edgley & G Thomas	2/0	1	v	R Guy & B Griffiths		0
		2½				2½
Phillips		0	v	Broadhurst	3/2	1
Langmead		0	v	Wolstenholme	4/3	1
Newcombe	2/1	1	v	Poxon		0
Clough		0	v	Cook	3/2	1
Symons	2/1	1	v	Eddiford		0
Edwards	2/1	1	v	Clarke		0
Clayton	4/2	1	v	Hare		0
Thomas	2/1	1	v	Sweetsur		0
Edgley		½	v	Guy		½
Amor	5/4	1	v	Griffiths		0
		6½				3½
Grand Total		**9**				**6**

Notts (Hollinwell)

8th October 1988

(Captain: R Hare)				(Captain: R W Guy)		
J Langmead & A Nash	2/1	1	v	R Claydon & A Hare		0
K Jones & J Webber		0	v	J Cook & A Allen	2/1	1
G Milne & P McMullen		0	v	G Wolstenholme & C Harries	2/1	1
S Amor & S Robertson		½	v	D Prosser & M Houghton		½
C Edwards & N Holman	2/1	1	v	G Krause & P Smith		0
		2½				2½
Jones		0	v	Claydon		0
Langmead		0	v	Wolstenholme	1/0	1
Nash		½	v	Cook		½
Robertson		0	v	Hare	2/1	1
Milne		0	v	Allen	2/1	1
Amor	2/1	1	v	Harries		0
McMullen		0	v	Prosser	5/4	1
Holman	5/4	1	v	Houghton		0
Edwards	4/2	1	v	Krause		0
Webber		0	v	Smith	1/0	1
		3½				6½
Grand Total		**6**				**9**

Broadstone
14th October 1989

(Captain: S C Davidson)				(Captain: R A Jowle)			
A Nash & N Holman		0	v	J Cook & J Payne	3/2	1	
S Amor & G Milne		0	v	J Bickerton & P Swinburne	1/0	1	
C Edwards & A Lawrence		0	v	G Wolstenholme & D Gibson	2/1	1	
D Powell & J Webber	3/2	1	v	C Ciesielski & M Welch		0	
P Clayton & J Nash	2/1	1	v	A Carman & C Harries		0	
		2				3	
Nash, A		0	v	Cook	2/0	1	
Webber		0	v	Payne	3/2	1	
Holman	2/1	1	v	Ciesielski		0	
Lawrence		0	v	Bickerton	3/2	1	
Clayton	2/1	1	v	Swinburne		0	
Amor		0	v	Wolstenholme	3/1	1	
Edwards	½		v	Carman		½	
Milne		0	v	Gibson	1/0	1	
Powell		0	v	Harries	4/3	1	
Nash, J	1/0	1	v	Welch		0	
		3½				6½	
Grand Total		**5½**				**9½**	

Burnham & Berrow
12th October 1991

(Captain: A J Ring)				(Captain: C R J Ibbotson)			
C Edwards & D Haines	6/5	1	v	P Streeter & M Welch		0	
S Crick & D Whittaker		0	v	C Watts & M McGuire	3/1	1	
I Veale & D Bradley		0	v	D Gibson & J Cayless	5/3	1	
D Powell & G Wolstenholme	3/2	1	v	D Probert & S Davis		0	
P McMullen & A Mutch		0	v	N Swaffield & A Robinson	3/2	1	
		2				3	
Edwards	1/0	1	v	Gibson		0	
Bradley		0	v	Streeter	2/0	1	
Wolstenholme	4/3	1	v	Watts		0	
Haines		0	v	McGuire	2/1	1	
Veale	5/3	1	v	Welch		0	
Crick		0	v	Probert	3/2	1	
McMullen	5/4	1	v	Swaffield		0	
Mutch	2/1	1	v	Cayless		0	
Powell		0	v	Davis	1/0	1	
Whittaker	2/1	1	v	Robinson		0	
		6				4	
Grand Total		**8**				**7**	

Kings Norton
13th October 1990

(Captain: J Nash)				(Captain: R A Jowle)			
S Amor & D Rigby		0	v	J Bickerton & J Payne	1/0	1	
C Edwards & D Haines	5/4	1	v	M Welch & N Stanton		0	
M Stanford & J Webber		0	v	D Beech & M Scothern	3/2	1	
A Lawrence & M Thompson	½		v	D Gibson & R Stevens		½	
D Bradley & R Simmons		0	v	P Sweetsur & L Westwood	2/1	1	
		1½				3½	
Amor	2/1	1	v	Bickerton		0	
Stanford		0	v	Payne	1/0	1	
Edwards	½		v	Stanton		½	
Webber		0	v	Beech	2/0	1	
Bradley		0	v	Welch	1/0	1	
Rigby		0	v	Scothern	4/3	1	
Lawrence		0	v	Gibson	5/4	1	
Haines		0	v	Stevens	3/2	1	
Thompson	2/0	1	v	Sweetsur		0	
Simmons		0	v	Westwood	2/1	1	
		2½				7½	
Grand Total		**4**				**11**	

Northants County
10th October 1992

(Captain: K A Clark)				(Captain: C R J Ibbotson)			
S Edgley & M Thompson		0	v	M McGuire & P Streeter	2/1	1	
G Wolstenholme & C Edwards	1/0	1	v	C Watts & D Probert		0	
P Trew & J Tomlinson	½		v	I Richardson & W Nicholson		½	
S Crick & M McEwan	4/2	1	v	M Welch & N Swaffield		0	
D Howell & G Harris	2/1	1	v	D Ross & D Gibson		0	
		3½				1½	
Edgley	3/2	1	v	M McGuire		0	
Edwards		0	v	Streeter	2/1	1	
Wolstenholme		0	v	Watts	3/2	1	
Thompson		0	v	Richardson	2/1	1	
Howell		0	v	Probert	5/4	1	
McEwan		0	v	Welch	7/5	1	
Harris	1/0	1	v	Nicholson		0	
Crick		0	v	Swaffield	1/0	1	
Trew		0	v	Gibson	1/0	1	
Tomlinson	1/0	1	v	Ross		0	
		3				7	
Grand Total		**6½**				**8½**	

Appendix
Members of the Dorset County Golfers' Association

Ashley Wood

Bailey, AC
Bell, ACH
Bishop, T
Bromby, G
Cherry, P
Clarkson, GR
Cornick, B
Crane, D
Cross, NW
Ellicott, R
Gamblen, DH
Glossop, EJ
Greenwood, MR
Hyde, R
Jeans, CR
Joyce, B
Jupp, WF
Lloyd, G
Nicholson, AP
Parsons-Fox, G
Rebbeck, HJ
Reid, F
Robbins, SA
Rogers, RF
Sangers, KJ
Saunders, AKE
Sharp, NS
Stocker, B
Swain, GB
Vincent, FW
Wagstaff, G
Walker, J
Watson, AJ
White, H
Whiting, BF

Bournemouth & Meyrick Park

Atyeo, D
Everley, G
Guy, L
Holmes, K
Hunt, R
Minardi, L
Owen, D
Payne, J
Reason, S
Thorn, L
Whitney, E

Bridport

Murrell, AF
Parry, TG

Broadstone

Abineri, PW
Allen, C
Allison-James, R
Boyle, MJD
Burcher, AC
Burke, L
Cobb, DJ
Coles, CE
Coles, J
Crawford, AM
Davison, TE
Durbin, K
Evershed, J
Gill, RA
Govett, EK
Grieves, J
Heywood, A
Higley, P
Howell, R
Hutchins, MD
Jones, AK
Jones, RE
Kenyon, H
Kirkman, AH
Lawford, R
Matthews, W
McGregor, R
Millward, D
Moore, A
Mundy, J
Nash, J
Phalp, K
Ridout, C
Roberts, G
Saxby, R
Scott, P
Smith, LW
Stewart, J
Stretton, G
Taylor, LW
Vale, R
Way, J
Welch, WJ
Williams, G
Yeoman, A

Bulbury Woods

Cocking, JJ
Holdsworthy, D
Pearson, A
Smith, D
Weston-Edwards, J

Came Down

Dixon, R
Finding, JW
Green, H
Morrison, AJ
Thornton, EC

Canford School

Cox, P
Holker, A

Chedington Court

Barrett, D
Fussell, S
Haws, AC
MacBean, A
Gudge, R
Jeeves, R
Meecham, G

Christchurch

Dodd, BG

Dudsbury

Hooper, GC
Kemp, A
O'Brien, P
Sedgbeer, BE
Sherwood, R
Spencer, E
Webb, TD

East Dorset

Allen, J
Chapman, SB
Cleall, SV
Goode, R
Hogan, GJC
Norton-Jones, EV
Soar, AA
Southgate, J
Stratford, A
Sullivan, JJ

Ferndown

Bowden, H
Croom, RC
Donnelly, R
Foster, F
Hales, MJ
McDougall, R
Niven, AE
Palin, RH
Wylie, JH

Highcliffe Castle

Crockford, N
Danks, C
Duncan, D
Dunn, DW
Edgley, N
Harding, D
Hillyer, DDW

Hope, RWA
Legg, JH
McCabe, DPT
Mills, AF
Phipps, GA
Redgwell, DA
Sargent, JA
Taylor, B
Taylor, JB
Turner, M
Viney, F

Isle of Purbeck

Barnes, P
Cadorath, AB
Griffiths, RV
Harrop, M
Hall, J
Mayo, KR
Penny, KWB
Pike, G
Reid, B
Saunders, KV
Stoddart, C
Suttle, M
Turner, MJ

Knighton Heath

Basset, R
Bonner, BP
Bowley, G
Brook, M
Byrom, HS
Corner, W
Cowan, D
Dale, D
Davey, LCH
Farnworth, A
Frazer, R
Gardner, R
Gardner, L
Gear, K
Glass, A

Godding, SW
Headland, P
Howlett, DS
Huxter, A
Jones, GT
Kent, J
Knight, JD
Lansley, FJ
Lehan, T
Lucas, RVJ
Madeley, J
Olivo, P
Polley, DCG
Powell, RB
Russell, S
Smith, KR
Tanswell, LK

Lyme Regis

Bain, KJ
Beason, SN
Benson, PH
Brown, MB
Girling, HC
Glossop, P
Grose, J
Hepworth, W
Hicks, K
Holland, E
Hull, AG
Jones, CG
Lawrence, AG
Leeming, H
Mahlich, RJ
McAuley, HF
Misslebrook, T
Nott-Bower, C
Olbrechts, E
Priest, SR
Potter, H
Reilly, P
Robson, DG
Salt, DCM
Scotting, H
Stewart, D
Ware, EE
Wilshaw, LA
Wood, HE

Moors Valley

Hamilton, JR
Holmes, DHA
Matthews, R
McCombie, A
Meharg, B
Meharg, D
Minkin, J
Stevens, T

Parkstone

Addis, P
Apicella, E
Bailey, JH Dr
Bateman, H
Bayne, DA
Brown, RK
Buck, GW
Calver, J
Crisp, DH
Crutcher, B
Davies, RE Capt
Dean, G W
Field, LS
Forman, W
Gibbs, M
Gibson, ES
Godwin, V
Greenfield, GT
Harman, R
Harris, RG
Hewitt, J
Hipkiss, RI
Holbert, PAR
Holding, CF
Holmes, DM
Hornby, D
Jackson, JW
Jackson, M
Kinson, B
Letchford, GC
Littlejohn, B
Longmore, K
Lunt, J
Marchant, L
Marsh, BH
Marshall, GH
O'Connor, P
Osmond, B

Peach, RG
Pickett, HB
Powell, J
Pownall, T
Robshaw, KV
Savill, L
Scollick, MNG
Scott, MR
Shakeshaft, R
Shaw, FK
Smith, DA
Stocker, T
Sugden, JG
Taylor, GK
Topp, E
Windebank, HO

Queens Park

Bowater, L
Britton, R
Ecell, A
Guppy, J
Harris, CR
Hockings, A
Jackson, J
Lister, J
McCall, R
Mitchell, R
Mullings, C
O'Niel, A
Parkinson, R
Poole, M
Pritchard, D
Ridout, SP
Stroud, I
Stubbington, J
Toole, MJ
Wood, R

Sherborne

Abel, KA
Chapman, F
Criddle, M Maj
Emery, AR
Gregory, DWJ
Heyes, JK
Hopkins, JR
Lawrence, RW
Pinder, S

Plumridge, PB
Porter, LS
Robson, IG
Rodway, J
Shelley, D
Sheppard, FV
Swift, RD
Williams, DJ
Woods, P

Wareham

Baker, WJ
Campbell, NB
Southgate, J
Tocock, SG

Weymouth

Dallow, D
Drummond, P
Garnett, AG
Gerring, JR
Green, RD
Hale, J
Peach, DE
Pratt, D
Robinson, C
Robinson, EB
White, RTH
Wilson, JC
Wilson, KJ

Yeovil

Ault, JD
Bailward, BT
Barker, K
Bennie, RNR
Chappell, TCA
Cole, RC
Corbett, B
Cornellus, B
Critchley, B
Cutts, JC
Darby, D
Eustace, DS
Hannam, C
Heal, A
Hebditch, J
Henshall, DE

Hird, RA
Holehouse, A
Knight, JFW
Lees, BH
Lewer, C
Lewis, K
Little, CM
Modica, J
Monsell, D
Morris, WE
Morton, J
Neilson, J
O'Rorke,
O'Shea, J
Oddy, RF
Olerenshaw, K
Osborne, J
Owen, LWT
Pym, HJ
Raymont, C
Raymont, PJ
Reeves, G
Ricketts, AFA
Riley, J
Searle, RE
Southcombe, PL
Southcombe, TA
Steer, R
Stokes, RM
Talbot-Weis, E
Talboys, GW
Thorne, RW
Watson, K
White,
Young, G